Playa del Carmen, Tulum & the Riviera Maya

Playa del Carmen, Tulum & the Riviera Maya

A Great Destination

Joshua Eden Hinsdale

The Countryman Press ✳ Woodstock, Vermont

THIRD EDITION

Explorer's Guide Playa del Carmen, Tulum & the Riviera Maya: A Great Destination

ISBN: 978-1-58157-132-5

Interior photographs by the author unless otherwise specified
Maps by Erin Greb Cartography, © The Countryman Press
Book design by Bodenweber Design
Composition by Eugenie S. Delaney

Published by The Countryman Press, P.O. Box 748, Woodstock, VT 05091

Distributed by W. W. Norton & Company, Inc., 500 Fifth Avenue, New York, NY 10110

Printed in the United States of America

10 9 8 7 6 5 4 3 2 1

This book is dedicated to my ever-supportive parents,
my beautiful wife, and our amazing
daughter, Maya—my favorite *exploradora*.

Explore with Us!

What's Where. At the start of the book you'll find an alphabetical listing of highlights, important information, and other details that you may want to reference quickly to navigate the book, the Riviera Maya, and its culture.

Geographic Orientation. Many of the cities and towns of the Yucatán Peninsula and the Riviera Maya are covered in this book, starting with Playa del Carmen, the conceptual and physical center of the Riviera Maya. Subsequent chapters cover the Riviera Maya to the south and to the north of Playa, followed by other destinations nearby that are not technically a part of the Riviera Maya, including Cancún, Cozumel, and the Costa Maya.

Many locations are found along Highway 307, which parallels the coastline as it traverses the region from Cancún to the north down to Tulum and beyond in the south. Whenever possible, addresses are given using Highway 307 as a primary reference point, which is especially useful for self-guided travelers who choose to explore the region on their own.

KEY TO SYMBOLS

✎ Child-friendly. The crayon symbol appears next to places or activities that accept and/or appeal to young children, or have a children's menu.

★ Don't miss this. The star symbol signifies a place or activity is highly recommended by the author, typically selected for its consistent, authentic, or general uniqueness of experience.

↭ Eco-friendly. This symbol indicates places that are environmentally proactive.

🐾 Pet-friendly. This symbol appears beside listings that welcome pets.

💍 Weddings. The wedding ring symbol shows establishments that are appropriate for weddings.

((ɪ)) Wi-Fi access. This symbol indicates establishments that are known to offer wireless Internet.

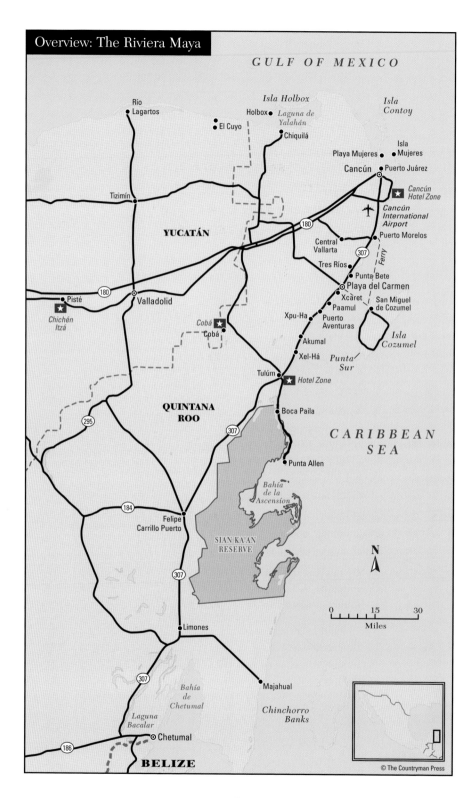

GULF OF MEXICO

Río Lagartos

Isla Holbox

Holbox ● Laguna de Yalahán

El Cuyo ●

Chiquilá ●

Isla Contoy

Isla Mujeres

Playa Mujeres ● ● Mujeres

Cancún ● Puerto Juárez

Tizimín ●

★ Cancún Hotel Zone

Cancún International Airport

YUCATÁN

180

Central Vallarta ●

Tres Ríos ●

Puerto Morelos

307

Ferry

● Punta Bete

◉ Playa del Carmen

Pisté ● 180 ◉ Valladolid

★ Chichén Itzá

Cobá ★ Cobá ●

Xpu-Ha ●

Xcàret ●

Paamul ●

Puerto Aventuras ●

San Miguel de Cozumel

Akumal ●

Xel-Há ●

Isla Cozumel

Punta Sur

Tulúm ● ★ Hotel Zone

QUINTANA ROO

295

307

Boca Paila ●

CARIBBEAN SEA

● Punta Allen

Bahía de la Ascensión

184

Felipe Carrillo Puerto ●

SIAN KA'AN RESERVE

N

307

0   15   30
Miles

Limones ●

307

Bahía de Chetumal

Majahual ●

Chinchorro Banks

Laguna Bacalar

186 ◉ Chetumal

BELIZE

© The Countryman Press

8

Contents

Acknowledgments

I AM FOREVER GRATEFUL for my friends, family, and total strangers who have directly or indirectly led to or assisted with this project:

My mother introduced me to *Jonathan Livingston Seagull*, Willie Nelson, the beach, and a sense of wonder and delight with life. She encouraged me to explore the world, took motorcycle riding lessons with me when I was 15, cried when I left for college, and always made coming home a warm and wonderful experience.

My father taught me to waterski, play baseball, and understand the stock market. He took me fishing, learned scuba so we could dive together, validated my wanderlust, and always led by example. He taught me that you can have an exciting life and still be responsible.

I met Andrea in Austin, Texas, and took her to Playa del Carmen hoping she'd fall in love with me (lucky for me, it worked). She travels with me when she can and understands that I still need to go when she can't. I carry her in my heart wherever I am. And when I return, she reminds me why there's no place like home. She is the most patient, most supportive, and most beautiful person I could ever know. Our daughter was born during a sultry summer in Austin, Texas, and was named Maya. We can't wait to teach her all of the wonderful things about the region and people that inspired her name.

Thanks also to my first dive buddies, Eric "Rico" Andrews, Keri Kennerly, Chris Glisan, Ellen Lock, and Amanda Miller; my colleague and friend George Hunter; my personal supporters Jeremy Reed, Sean Mitchell, Leslie Williams, Shawn Moran, Joy Taylor, Sam Shelby; my good-times friends Marshall York, Mike Leon, Sean Rasberry, and Derek Palisoul; our loving nanny Lesly Mendoza; Barry Diller; Jimmy Buffett; and everyone I've ever been to Mexico with or met while there. Special thanks to Henry Rankin, founder of Hollis Travel Labs, for his destination insight and market intelligence.

I am thankful for the kindness, support, and assistance of the hundreds of hoteliers, restaurant owners, tour operators, bartenders, taxi drivers, and others who I met and learned from during my research. Thanks to the hotel associations, tourism boards, and other official organizations that offered information and support. And thanks to the people of the Riviera Maya, who smiled at me as I walked the beaches and streets of their hometowns.

Foreword

WHEN I WAS ASKED to write a foreword to this guidebook, I thought about how I could spend 10 years traveling through Mexico, with each day bringing a sense of discovery, new faces, and plenty of surprises. I have been visiting Mexico for more than 30 years and love it so much that I make my home in Los Cabos, where I run the Cabo Wabo Cantina, hang out, drink tequila, and jam with friends. Whether I'm down there or across the country in Playa del Carmen and the Riviera Maya, it's always great to be in Mexico.

Many people have discovered the charms of Mexico during the past 30 years, but I find that some things never change. I can still get the thrill of being the only gringo in a backstreet cantina and find adventure and exploration around every corner. Often, a sunrise means my day is ending, not beginning. For me, Mexico is a magical and mystical place. There is a timelessness and sense of a deep-rooted folklore that is personified in the people.

Most of all, I love the white-sand beaches, the music, the food, the fiestas, and enjoying time with family and friends. It's a place where the warmth of the sun is equaled by the warmth of the people. My family and I try new food, meet new people, and generally kick back on the world's greatest beaches. Mexico inspires me. It might mean a new song, a new idea, or a renewed outlook on life. Whatever it does to you, Mexico will remind you to enjoy life.

See you on the beach!

Sammy Hagar

Introduction

MY PARENTS FIRST TRAVELED to the Riviera Maya in 1980, when it was known only as the not-so-catchy "area south of Cancún." They went to Xcaret when it cost 25 cents and the road was yet to be paved. They went to Xel-Ha and Garrafón, in Isla Mujeres, and marveled at the tropical fish and the deserted beaches. They ate lobster on the beach in Cancún and snorkeled the virgin reefs of Cozumel. When they came home, they showed me their pictures and talked of their adventures, and I knew I'd go there one day.

My first experience with the Caribbean was in Belize, when I was 16. I went diving at Turneffe Island and was blown away by the color of the water, the number of fish, and the relaxing island lifestyle. A year later, I went on a dive trip to Cozumel with a group of friends from school. I loved the food, the freedom, and the excitement. We took the ferry to the then-tiny town of Playa del Carmen and could hardly find a place that was open to eat lunch.

For each of the next 10 years, I went to Mexico every chance I could, eventually leading group trips, selling travel packages, and making friends around the country. In college, I spent a year at the University of Costa Rica, studying Spanish and traveling around the region every weekend. After graduating from the University of Texas, I went to work for a Mexico-based tourism developer and worked on the early stages of the creation of Playacar.

I moved to Cozumel, worked in a hotel, and traveled the region extensively. I later moved to Cancún, worked for the *Cancún News* (the English daily newspaper, now closed), and made frequent trips to Playa del Carmen. In 1993, I visited the construction site of one of the first all-inclusive hotels, in Xpu-Ha, for a photo shoot, but I could never have imagined the development that would follow up and down the coast.

Over the years, I have stayed active in the Riviera Maya community, splitting my frequent trips between Cancún, Cozumel, and Playa. As many others have, I've watched the area boom and grow, amazed with each trip at the new hotels, restaurants, and other attractions.

The region continues to draw me, almost magically, to its sandy beaches, taco bars, secret fishing holes, and buzzing nightspots. It is in my soul and has become a large part of who I am. I love being there, I love talking about it—and I love sharing it with other travelers.

LEFT: The hammocks at Xel-Ha are a perfect place for a nap.   Philip Gamon

What's Where in the Riviera Maya

AIRPORTS Most travelers will arrive in the Riviera Maya via the modern Cancún International Airport (CUN, www.cancun-airport.com). International flights also arrive at the smaller Cozumel International Airport (CZM) and transportation to the mainland is available via ferry. Charter and regional flights are also available at small airports in Playa del Carmen and on Isla Mujeres and Isla Holbox (see chapter 1).

ALL-INCLUSIVE At many hotels, everything a guest could require—including meals, alcohol, and entertainment—is included in the nightly rate. Exactly what is included, and what level of service is offered, can vary from hotel to hotel (see chapter 2).

BEACHES White sandy beaches reign supreme in the Riviera Maya. However, visitors will encounter the occasional rocky beach and many beaches are clearly nicer than others. In Mexico, all beaches are public property, although hotels and property owners along the beach are allowed to section off private areas and aren't required to provide beach access across their property.

BICYCLING Bike rentals are a popular recreation or transportation choice, particularly on smaller islands such as Isla Mujeres and Isla Holbox and within larger master-planned resorts. Many hotels offer courtesy bicycles for the use of their guests.

BOOKS Check out 11 great books—including tomes of history, mystery, madcap adventure, and flirty Spanish language—recommended to complement your trip, in chapter 10.

BOUTIQUE HOTELS The term *boutique* means many different things to many different people, and to Mexico hoteliers this is no different. However, in this book it generally refers to hotels that have a distinctive design or charm, quality service,

LEFT: Everyone has a favorite beach activity.

and fewer than 50 rooms, and are not affiliated with a large conglomerate. There are many different flavors of boutique accommodation, especially in Playa del Carmen and Isla Mujeres.

BUS SERVICE Regular transportation is available in the region on the local bus system. For $3–4 one way, travelers can ride on air-conditioned buses between Playa del Carmen, the Cancún airport, downtown Cancún, Tulum, and other area destinations (see chapter 1).

CAR RENTAL Travelers can rent cars at the airport or at tourist desks in Playa del Carmen, Cancún, Cozumel, and other destinations and resorts.

CARIBBEAN ISLANDS Three different island destinations located off the Yucatán Peninsula each sport a distinctive character and vibe. The more developed Cozumel and the enchanting Isla Mujeres can each be spotted from Playa del Carmen and Cancún, respectively, and both are accessible by ferry. The ferry to sleepy Isla Holbox lies three hours north of Cancún, prompting some visitors to opt for chartered air taxis.

CARIBBEAN SEA The striking turquoise waters of the Caribbean certainly sealed the region's fate when the Mexican government set about to create a new tourism destination in the early 1970s. Although Mexican and Mayan culture remain most dominant in the region, rivaled most closely by international influences, travelers can still find touches of the storied Eastern Caribbean waters throughout the Riviera Maya, particularly on Isla Mujeres and in Playa del Carmen.

CENOTES A rare geological feature of the Yucatán, a *cenote* (sen-NO-teh) is a freshwater sinkhole formed when the limestone ground caves in and fills with water from underground rivers. The U.S.-based National Speleological Society (www.caves.org/project/qrss) has an ongoing and well-advanced project to map the extensive network of freshwater caves (see chapter 5).

CHILDREN You don't have to leave the kids at home to have a fun vacation in the Riviera Maya. Many resorts have special facilities for kids, including playgrounds,

Keeping You on Track

Exploring is fun, but so is knowing where you are. The famous creators of the Cancun-map series of maps and travel information, Iowa couple Laura (a.k.a. "MapChick") and Perry, have explored the region for more than 30 years and likely know more about its back roads, secret beaches, and hidden attractions than does any nonlocal on Earth. They tag the area's top resorts, restaurants, beaches, and other highlights, but their true love is uncovering lesser-known attractions and off-the-beaten-path adventures. Their maps contain their unique take on the area and their personal recommendations and advice. These exhaustively researched and individually produced maps cover Cancún, Cozumel, Isla Mujeres, Playa del Carmen, and the Riviera Maya, and sell for $10 each (www.cancunmap.com).

This playground is in the middle of the town square in Playa del Carmen.

kid-friendly meals, activities programs, and complimentary child care. In-room babysitting can be arranged through hotel concierges, who maintain a list of recommended caretakers. Smaller hotels can often arrange for a housekeeper to look after the kids while the parents enjoy a tour or day trip. Nature parks, theme parks and zoos provide exciting day trip opportunities. At the beach, kids enjoy collecting shells, watching the pelicans dive for fish, and building sand castles. In most areas there is little wave action, so introducing kids to the ocean is a breeze. In 2005, a playground was added to the town square in Playa, complete with a sandy play area, jungle gym, monkey bars, slides, and a great ocean view.

CONSULATE OFFICES The United States, Canada, and the United Kingdom all have consular offices in the region. Each has an office in Cancún, and both the U.S. and Canada maintain offices in Playa del Carmen. There is also a U.S. office in Cozumel. Locations, phone numbers, and office hours can be found in chapter 10.

CORAL Even though coral remnants that washed ashore give much of the region's beaches that bright white and sometimes almost pink hue, coral itself is not to be touched. The rare piece that washes ashore will easily cut up a bare foot. More important, for those diving and snorkeling, coral is very fragile and simple contact can break off a piece or cause a chemical reaction that kills the organisms that took hundreds of years to form and are critical part of the earth's ecosystem. Learn more about coral protection and conservation from the World Wildlife Fund (WWF) at www.panda.org/corals.

CORAL REEF See Great Mayan Reef.

COSTA MAYA, OR THE MAYAN COAST The region known as Riviera Maya reaches its southern border in Tulum. The Mexican Caribbean coast that stretches from that point south to Belize is known as the Costa Maya. Quieter and slower than its neighbors to the north, it's noted for its many small, ecological themed hotels, large undeveloped areas, and protected preserves.

CUBAN CIGARS As of press time, it is against the law for Americans to spend money on Cuban goods and services. While this technically includes Cuban cigars purchased in Mexico, a lack of records for these exchanges makes it a pretty appealing dalliance for many travelers while abroad (see chapter 2). Remember that while what happens in Mexico stays in Mexico, bringing Cuban cigars back home to the States is another matter entirely.

CURRENCY The official currency of the Mexico is the peso. Although its value fluctuates daily against the U.S. dollar, there is rarely a notable difference in the rate during a visitor's trip. In tourist areas, prices are sometimes listed in American dollars and, because both currencies us the dollar sign ($), that sometimes breeds confusion. This book uses the dollar sign ($) to signify U.S. dollars and the word *pesos* when referring to Mexican pesos.

DIVING & SNORKELING The Mayan Riviera is one of the world's great destinations for saltwater and freshwater exploration. Check out chapter 7 for an in-depth discussion of dive sites, scuba certification schools, and recommended dive shops throughout the region.

DOLPHINS Travelers can sign up to swim with trained dolphins in a captive environment at Dolphin Discovery's centers (www.dolphindiscovery.com) in Puerto Aventuras, Cozumel, and Isla Mujeres. Other programs are also available from Delphinus (www.delphinusworld.com) at Xcaret and Xel-Ha parks and Cancún's Dreams Hotel and Dolphinaris (www.dolphinaris.com) at Wet'n Wild (see chapter 5).

Phantom Divers dive shop is one of Playa's most respected.

Some Things Are Cheaper South of the Border

Although the price of meals, drinks, and many everyday purchases are relatively close to what you'll find back home, some services are still a bargain south of the border. Here are a few ideas of how you can save some money while you're in the Riviera Maya:

Get new eyeglasses. Bring a written prescription or even a pair of well-calibrated glasses, and the technicians at area eyewear shops can match your prescription in a wide variety of frames and lenses for a fraction of what you'd pay at home.

Manicures and pedicures. Want acrylic nails or just need a fresh mani/pedi? Prices are half or less of what you'd pay back home, at salons catering to locals.

Watch repair. If you have an old watch that needs fixing and you've been putting it off, bring it on vacation. Drop it off one day and pick it up the next, and it'll be ticking like new. Watch shops in Playa are common a few blocks back from the beach, and their skilled craftsmen can fix almost anything.

Shoe repair. Shoes falling apart? Stop by a local shoe repair shop, and you can have new soles, heels, or other repairs done while you're away enjoying the ruins at Tulum. The price will be significantly less than back home, and the craftsmanship is top-rate.

Prescription medications. Local pharmacies will gladly fill prescriptions from U.S. doctors. Don't have a prescription? In many cases, one can be issued on the spot, for a limited charge.

DRUGSTORE

RAND NAME	MEXICAN NAME	GENERIC NAM
EC	CETRIZINA	VISERTRAL
JTEROC	VENTOLIN	SALBUTANOL
IN	CLARITOMICIN	MAXITRAL
EXA	SEROPRAM	CITALOPRAM
XICILLIN	GILMAXINA	AMOXILINA
VACID	LANZOPRAZOLE	RORIFRAN
LOSEC	OMEPRAZOLE	ALBOZ
NASE	FLIXONASE	FLTICASONE
RREX	RAPIVIR	VALACYCLOVIR
OQUIN	LEVOFLAXACINA	FLEVOX
AC	AZITROCIN	ZERTALIN
NTAC	RANITIDINA	ULSAVEN
OF	SIBUTRAMIA	YEDUC 15MG C/30
TOPRIM-D	SERTALINA	ALUPREX
GRA	TESTOSTERONE	TESTOPRIM-D C/3
TONIX	SILDENAFIL	VIAGRA
XERIL	PANTROPRAZOLE	CIPROTON
MA	CYCLOBENZAPRINE	BENCOPRIM
EMARIN	CARISOPRODOL	BLOCACID
TRA	ESTROGENOS	DNA-EC
STARA	TRIMETOPRIMA	SUXPRIM
RO	HIDROQUINONE	ELDOPAQUE
RADOL	CIPROFLOXACIN	GENOFLEX
NICAL	KETOROLAC	VEROLAX
NICAL	ORLISTAT	XENICAL
MISIL	TERBINAFINA	BINAFEX
OZAC	FLUEXETINE	FLOCET
ADURABULIN	NANDROLONE	DECA
STENON	TESTOSTERONE	SOSTENON
LIS	TEDALAFIL	CIALIS
ROPENT	CLEBUTEROL	OXI FLU
TIN-A	TRETINOINE	RETIN-A
NOVA	TRETINOINE	RETACNYL
LEGRA	FEXOFENADINE	ALLEGRA
ORIOL	TESTOSTERONE	ANDRIOL
RVAS	AMLODIPINO	AKEN
VADEX	TREMADOL	VELDROL
OPESHIA	TAMOXIFENO	FEMOXTAL
FLUCAN	FINASTERIDA	LUXFIL
XIFORT(VIAGRA)	FLUCONAZOL	ALFUMET
ITREX	IDUPROFENO	DOLPROFENO
TICORTEN	SILDENAFIL	MAXIFORT
	SUMATRIPTAN	NOGRAINE
		NOSIPREN

Helpful guide at the corner
farmacia

DRUG CARTELS Although Mexico's drug cartels undoubtedly have interests in Cancún and the Riviera Maya, as of press time, almost all drug-related violence in Mexico has occurred near the borders and not in resort areas. Check with the U.S. Department of State online at travel.state.gov for updates and, as always, don't go seeking out dark alleys in a foreign land.

DUTY FREE The notion of duty-free sales of alcohol, tobacco, and other taxable goods sometimes seems like a holdover from travel's more exotic heyday. But large shops selling duty-free goods can be found at the Cancún and Cozumel airports and many travelers continue to buy their allotment to take home. However, remember, if you're traveling to the United States and will have to transfer to a connecting flight, TSA officials will not allow you to bring a liquor bottle in your carry-on baggage when you enter the terminal for your domestic U.S. flight. So be prepared to transfer your purchase to your checked luggage after you pass through customs or say *adios* to your new bottle of tequila.

ECOLOGICAL There are a number of small "ecologically" themed hotels and bed-and-breakfasts in the Mayan Riviera, particularly on Isla Mujeres, Isla Holbox, and south of Tulum. Although this doesn't always mean they are "green" hotels or offer any particular efficiency, they typically feature a stronger connection to nature and often demonstrate a more conscientious behavior.

EMERGENCIES Bad things happen, even in paradise, so it's good to know where you can turn. For emergency police, firefighters, or ambulance assistance, call 066 (the equivalent of 911 in the United States) from any phone at no cost. You can also contact the Red Cross by dialing 065 from any phone. Other emergency phone numbers, along with information about area hospitals and medical facilities, can be found on the last pages of this book in chapter 10.

EUROPEAN PLAN (EP) The opposite of an All-Inclusive Plan, European Plan simply means at that hotel rates only include accommodations—food, drinks, and additional amenities or activities require an extra charge. This is how most hotels in the United States operate. See chapter 2 for a detailed comparison.

EVENTS Holidays, festivals, celebrations, and other special events can add an entirely new dimension to your vacation. For specifics, check out the event calendar in chapter 10.

EXPATRIATE It's probably safe to say that at least one out of five visitors to Playa del Carmen contemplates tearing up his return ticket home. Ex-pats are the ones who did, or who ultimately bought themselves a one-way ticket back.

FERRIES Overwater transportation to Cozumel and Isla Mujeres is available via modern ferries from Playa del Carmen and Cancún, respectively. Smaller ferries also provide service to Isla Holbox. For specifics, visit ferry operators Ultramar (www.granpuerto.com.mx) and Mexico Water Jets (www.mexicowaterjets.com.mx), and read the *Getting There* section for your respective island destination.

FIRE DANCERS Performing on the beach at the Blue Parrot (www.blueparrot .com/fireshow) and Fusion Hotel (www.fusionhotelmexico.com) in Playa del Carmen every evening, dancers twirl lit torches and lanterns through the night air, painting memorable patterns in the sky.

GAS STATIONS All gas stations are full-service and owned by the government's oil distribution company PEMEX, gas stations are plentiful along Highway 307 from Cancún to Tulum. Travelers heading south of Tulum or west across the peninsula should plan to fill up at every stop. Prices run a little higher than in most U.S. cities.

GAY & LESBIAN In recent years, the number of gay-friendly establishments in the region has grown. It is not uncommon to see gay couples and patrons in the international Playa del Carmen (some gay people call it "gay indifferent" rather than "gay friendly") or bohemian Isla Mujeres. Even Cancún has had a gay night-

PUERTO DE PLAYA DEL CARMEN

The ferry dock bustles throughout the day.

club for decades. Mexico itself has made headlines, legalizing gay marriage in Mexico City in 2009. Still, most of the country's residents remain very traditional and religious and it's always a good idea to exercise good judgment about public displays of affection when traveling in an unfamiliar area. For more gay-friendly options, visit www.purpleroofs.com.

GOLF The arrival of the Mayakoba Golf Classic in 2007 clearly signaled the region's arrival as a world-class destination for championship golf. Read up on the courses, and the big names who designed them, in chapter 8 and visit the Mexican Caribbean Golf Association online (www.cancungolf.org).

GREAT MAYAN REEF The largest coral reef in North America, second only to the Great Barrier Reef near Australia, is better known in scientific circles as the Mesoamerican Barrier Reef System. It begins off the coast of the Yucatán Peninsula near Isla Contoy and Isla Mujeres and extends south 197 miles past Belize, ending near the Bay Islands of Honduras. This living underwater environment is home to more than 600 species of fish nearly 100 varieties of coral. Learn more about the Mesoamerican Reef Alliance's preservation and protection efforts (www.icran.org/action-mar.html).

GRINGO In Playa, as throughout Mexico, Americans are usually referred to as *gringos*. Although it may sound a bit harsh to some Americans' ears (it does have a negative connotation in some other Latin American countries), it isn't at all meant as a derogatory in Mexico. So don't take offense. To the Mexicans, using the word

Americanos is confusing and a bit offensive to them, since all residents of North, Central, and South America could be considered "Americans." Also, because the full name of the republic of Mexico is Los Estados Unidos de Mexico, or the United States of Mexico, it's also not quite adequate to use the textbook translation of *estadounidense*, which is essentially "United Statesian," for citizens of the USA. Americans are sometimes referred to as *norteamericanos*, which means "North Americans," but that's not quite accurate, either, as it fails to distinguish between the United States and Canada, and the latter's citizens are known simply as *canadienses*. So, embrace your "inner gringo" and don't consider it a negative label. In this book, the word "American" is used to refer to residents of the United States.

HIGH SEASON As in much of Mexico and the Caribbean, the peak season lasts from early February until early May. The two weeks over Christmas and New Year's also are very busy, and most hotels charge their highest rates of the year during that time.

HONEYMOONS From intimate boutique hotels, quiet beaches, and relaxing spa treatments to bustling restaurant scenes, plush resorts, and adventurous excursions, the Riviera Maya offers honeymoon options suitable for almost every couple. Many venues, marked with a ♂ symbol, offer wedding planning services and they often also feature special packages for the newly married. But don't be afraid to custom design a unique honeymoon that suits your unique tastes, style, and budget.

HORSEBACK RIDING Always a popular activity, especially for couples and families, horseback riding options abound and there are many chances in the area to form that special bond with an equine friend. See chapter 5 for our recommendations.

HURRICANES With a season lasting from July through November, hurricanes have had untold impact on the Riviera Maya. Several storms, notably Hurricanes Emily and Wilma in 2005, caused enormous destruction to the beaches, buildings, and infrastructure. However, this damage has also led developers and the Mexican government to invest billions of dollars to improve and fortify the area. The greatest risk of storms typically occurs from late August through October, although this rule of thumb is unpredictable at best. Check the National Hurricane Center (www.nhc.noaa.gov) for recent activity and read about historical hurricanes in the area, in the special sections throughout this book.

IGUANAS If you don't see an iguana on your vacation, you probably didn't leave your room (or the nightclubs) very often. Given the close proximity of the jungle, the prevalence of this scaly reptile, and its general indifference to people, is legendary. Iguanas are commonplace anywhere there is significant vegetation. They're docile creatures, but look, don't touch. They can carry disease, and if you touch or harass them, you'll probably get hurt or into a lot of trouble.

JUNGLE Despite the beautiful white beaches and the significant development around Cancún, Playa del Carmen, and Tulum, much of the region remains as the natural Yucatán Jungle. Besides breeding iguanas, it's home to many species of flora and fauna, and at times can be unpredictable. The best way to experience it is as part of a tour or excursion (see chapter 5).

KITEBOARDING On what is essentially a surfboard with a sail, novices and experts alike navigate the smooth waters of the Mexican Caribbean on kiteboards. Lessons are available, most notably with the legendary Ikarus (see chapter 5), and kiteboard rentals and limited instruction are often included at larger all-inclusive resorts.

MAYAKOBA GOLF CLASSIC The only PGA Tour event in Mexico, the Mayakoba Golf Classic (www.mayakobagolfclassic.com) is named after its host resort. Televised across the United States since its 2007 debut, the tour is held on Mayakoba's El Camaleón course. Day passes start at $10, though a range of hospitality and accommodation packages are significantly more expensive.

MAYA The original residents of a significant part of subtropical Latin America, the Maya have left an indelible mark on the land. While the ruins of their former civilization are a large tourist draw, many of the local residents in the area are direct descendants of this people. Still known as Maya, many still keep aspects of the culture and the language alive today. Much as in the region itself, stories and details about the Maya can be found woven throughout this book. See chapters 2, 3, and especially 6 for details on their history and culture.

NIGHTLIFE Your options for nights on the town are primarily determined by your location. Playa has a robust nightlife with options for dance clubs, lounges, casual bars, and dancing on the beach. And Cancún has built much of its reputation on the grand scale of its nightclubs. Smaller towns usually present more limited options, but there's almost always a spot to grab a beer or another nightcap of your choice.

The beaches on Playa's main cove tend to clear out as the sun goes down.

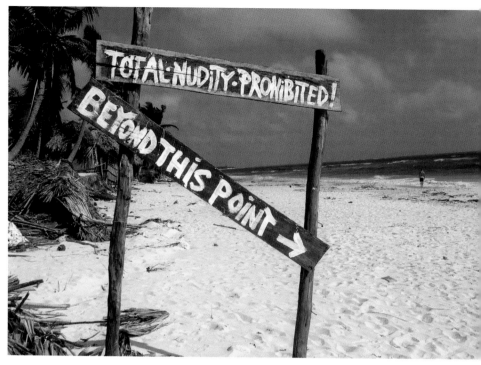

Although nudity is "officially" illegal, it's acceptable at some beaches in Tulum.

NUDE BEACHES Mexican law prohibits going nude (including topless for women) in public—and this includes beaches as well. But there are several locales where officials look the other way, or pretend they do. It's generally acceptable, and common, to see women sunbathing topless in areas of Playa del Carmen's beach, particularly at the beach clubs just north of Constituyentes Avenue. Several remote beach hotels cater to naturalists of varying extremes.

OCEAN PRESERVATION AND PROTECTION Although it may be hard to imagine serious threats to our oceans while sunning along the Caribbean sun or swimming in its pristine waters, scientists estimate that, in the last 50 years alone, half of the world's coral reefs have been destroyed and more than 70 percent of the oceans' fish populations have been consumed or slaughtered through commercial fishing operations. National Geographic Society explorer in residence and renowned marine scientist Dr. Sylvia A. Earle advocates that our actions from 2010 to 2020 will have profound impacts on the future health of the seas and the planet's ecosystems. Her frank, simple, and clear explanations of the damage, and what must be done to counter it, can be found in her 2009 book *The World Is Blue: How Our Fate and the Ocean's Are One*. It's fascinating and recommended reading for anyone moved by the beauty, wonder, and diversity of life along the Great Mayan Reef.

QUINTA Also known as avenida Quinta, or Fifth Avenue in English, this is the proper name of the main tourist thoroughfare in downtown Playa. All locals and many tourists refer to it by the name "Quinta." For purposes of clarity and consistency with other numeric street names, this book often lists it as "Fifth Avenue." However, if you want to speak like a local, or at least like a seasoned visitor, you'll want to say "Quinta."

QUINTANA ROO Named for a key figure in the Mexican War for Independence, Andrés Quintana Roo, who hailed from the Yucatán Peninsula, this Mexican state was officially formed in 1974. It contains the entirety of the country's Caribbean coastline, including Cancún, the Riviera Maya, and the Costa Maya.

PARKS Many destination-worthy parks are situated throughout the Riviera Maya, Cancún, and the Costa Maya. Options include seaside Mayan-themed adventures, water parks, crocodile zoos, and other showcases for local life. The best in the region are highlighted in chapter 5.

PESO See Currency.

PETS Although Mexico allows visitors to bring dogs and cats into the country temporarily, if accompanied by the required paperwork, it's rarely a good idea. Many hotels and resorts do not permit animals, and your pet will be at risk of catching diseases from local strays and other critters. Don't do it.

PLAYACAR The master-planned development of Playacar features many large, all-inclusive beach resorts, private homes, and a golf course, and lies immediately south of the paseo del Carmen shopping center and Playa's ferry dock. For travelers seeking all-inclusive comfort, with the option to easily wander into downtown Playa del Carmen, it can present a perfect destination choice. Learn more in chapter 1.

PLAYA DEL CARMEN The central destination that allowed the Riviera Maya to take root, "Playa" was once a sleepy fishing village with a ferry to Cozumel. It first caught on as a destination with European tourists who, along with divers from around the world, began frequenting the small hotels along the beach and prompting developers and entrepreneurs into larger and grander endeavors. It's expanded greatly and today is a full-fledged city. Despite its growth and popularity, downtown has retained elements of its fishing roots, blended with Mexican and international influences from Italy, Germany, the United States, and South America.

Fifth Avenue has gone from a sandy path to the most famous street in the Mexican Caribbean in 25 years.

Surf Before You Snorkel

Try these free online resources for more information about the Riviera Maya:

LocoGringo.com. This superb source for detailed aerial photos, virtual tours, and high-quality photos and descriptions of hotels, attractions, and beaches covers Playa del Carmen, the Riviera Maya, and surrounding areas. You can make reservations for hotels, condos, and villas as well as participate in its active message boards.

MayanHoliday.com. The author's blog and reservations site, regularly updated with news, travel tips and features related to travel in Playa del Carmen and the Riviera Maya.

InTheRoo.com. Lively discussion forums, index of special offers and comprehensive business directory for the Riviera Maya region.

RivieraMaya.com. The Riviera Maya tourism board's site has hotel and restaurant lists, plus attractions, travel stats, and tour info. Hotel reservations can be made online or by phone in the United States at 1-877-7-GO-MAYA (877-746-6292).

Playa.info or PlayadelCarmenInfo.com. This site offers active message boards, detailed hotel reviews from recent travelers, a live webcam, and real estate information.

PlayaMayaNews.com. A community site for people living in or visiting Playa del Carmen, it provides local movie schedules, classified listings, human-interest stories, health advice, culture, and community action. It makes an entertaining and interesting read whether you're actively planning a trip or just learning more about the area.

PlayadelCarmen.com. A commercial site devoted to area hotels, condos, photos, videos, maps, destination guides, and message boards.

SeePlaya.com. Fun site with insider information ranging from how to pick the right hotel to how to spot a fake Cuban cigar.

TripAdvisor.com. This site has user reviews, candid photos, price comparisons, message boards, and reservations information for hotels throughout the Riviera Maya. The site is not specific to the region, so you will need to search to find your specific hotel.

Travel.State.Gov. The U.S. State Department provides a wealth of travel information covering documentation requirements, health, safety, and overseas services.

RELIGION Catholicism is the primary religion in the Riviera Maya, though many of the ancient Mayan rituals are alive and well, oftentimes intermingling with traditional Catholic practices. Services are offered in various denominations, and the larger hotels maintain a list of current services and worship schedules. Tourists are welcome at all ceremonies, provided they dress and act appropriately and show respect for the local customs.

RIVIERA MAYA Stretching from Puerto Morelos to Tulum, and encompassing Playa del Carmen, this region has surpassed Cancún itself in the number of hotel rooms and visitors. However, unlike Cancún's high-rises, area's beloved low-rise development is spread out over a much greater and typically quieter area. English-speakers often refer to it as the Mayan Riviera, but this book has opted to use the local vernacular.

SIAN KA'AN BIOSPHERE RESERVE Located south of Tulum and covering 10 percent of the state of Quintana Roo, this federal land was set aside as a natural wilderness preserve (www.cesiak.org) in 1986. An official UNESCO World Heritage site (whc.unesco.org), it's home to more than 300 species of birds, 100 types of mammals, and a diversity of geographical features (see chapter 2).

SKY DIVING It's definitely an option off the shore of the former Mayan empire. See chapter 5 for details on recommended outfitters.

SNORKELING See Diving & Snorkeling.

SPANISH Mexico's official language remains dominant in the Riviera Maya, even amongst Maya. However many Mayan words continue to be used and augment the local lexicon. Tourists can probably get probably get by on English alone in Playa, Cancún, Isla Mujeres, and much of the Riviera Maya, but may want to consider enrolling in a local Spanish language schools or program (see chapter 10).

SPRING BREAK From late February through early April, with a crescendo in mid-March, American college students visit Mexico in full force. Although they're typically focused on Cancún, there's some spillover to Playa, Cozumel, and other Riviera Maya destinations.

SUSTAINABILITY Green tourism, development, and sustainable operations are definitely important in the Riviera Maya today. As in the rest of the world, what they mean in practice remains open for interpretation (see chapter 2).

THEME PARKS See Parks or chapter 5.

TIPS & GRATUITIES Outside of all-inclusive resorts or unless your tab specifically lists *servicio* after the tax, tips are expected for waiters (10 to 15 percent), and for massage therapists, tour guides, dive guides, and others providing an extended service ($10).

TOURS Numerous outfitters provide specialty tours throughout the region, and most can be booked at your hotels tourist or concierge desk. The best tours are highlighted in chapter 5 and local specialty tours are featured in their respective geographic chapters.

UNDERWATER SCULPTURE GARDEN Artist Jason deCaires Taylor began an ambitious project in 2009, creating MUSA (www.musacancun.com), an underwater garden of hundreds of sculptures of humans and common objects. Located near Isla Mujeres, 10 to 20 feet below the surface, MUSA (which stands for "Museo Subacuático de Arte" [Underwater Museum of Art]) is a beautiful and eerie accomplishment. Made from a material conducive to coral growth, the statues are designed to encourage new growth, while also drawing visitors away from fragile natural reefs (see chapter 5, www.underwatersculpture.com).

Learn about the cities of the Yucatán at this park in downtown Playa. Mike Stone

U.S. DEPARTMENT OF STATE As of press time, the U.S. Department of State (travel.state.gov) has issued no warnings to travelers visiting Mexico's tourism areas, including the state of Quintana Roo, home to Cancún, Playa, and the Mayan Riviera.

WATER PARKS, XCARET, XEL-HA & ZOOS See Parks or chapter 5.

WEDDINGS Countless opportunities for destination weddings, small and large, can be found throughout the Riviera Maya and many hotels and resorts (marked here by the ♂ symbol) have specialists on staff to help you plan. Learn more about getting married in Mexico in chapter 10.

YUCATÁN Geographically speaking, "Yucatán" can refer to the overall peninsula or easternmost quadrant of Mexico that juts into the Caribbean Sea, the jungle that engulfs much of that area, or the Mexican state that borders Quintana Roo to the northwest. The word also can be used to denote traditional, cultural geographical features long associated with this lush and storied region of Mexico.

BEFORE YOU GO

Travel should be easy, it should be carefree, and it should be comfortable. Unfortunately, that's not always the case. Getting around, having the proper paperwork, and making sense of unfamiliar rules and regulations can cause a fair amount of stress during any vacation, and travel to the Riviera Maya is no different.

An old adage that scuba divers use is, "Plan your dive and dive your plan." This concept should be applied to vacation travel as well. Taking some time before your trip to learn a bit about the region where you are traveling and to create a plan for how you're going to get around is essential to enjoying your vacation to the fullest. After all, wouldn't you rather use your vacation time relaxing on the beach rather than visiting the consulate, searching for maps, or asking everyone you see for help?

ARRIVAL BY AIR Most international visitors get to Playa del Carmen and the Riviera Maya by flying into the Cancún International Airport (CUN, www.cancun-airport.com), 45 miles north of Playa and 10 miles south of the resort city of Cancún.

Inaugurated in 1974, it's had regular renovations, leaving it in excellent condition. There are three terminals, and most visitors will arrive and depart at Terminal 3, which opened in 2007. It's quite modern and efficient, with Starbucks, Margaritaville Café, and other familiar conveniences.

CUSTOMS & IMMIGRATION All visitors must have a valid passport book to enter Mexico. Before your arrival on an international flight, you'll be required to fill out a tourist card (good for up to 90 days) and customs form. Usually handed out on the plane, they're available at the airport.

As you deboard, stay with your group as you're funneled to Immigration. The wait can last a few minutes to nearly an hour, depending on flight schedules. Have your passport and your forms ready, and then remember to save your copy of the tourist card, which the agent will return to you with your passport. You must have it when you depart. If lost, there's $40 fee and you can expect a bit of an interrogation at the airport when you leave. After you claim any bags, you'll proceed to the customs checkpoint. Hand your customs form to the agent standing next to the vertical traffic light mounted on a pole about chest high. You'll be asked to push the button. Green means "go," and red means your baggage will be opened and inspected.

AIRPORT TRANSPORTATION If your transportation's not prearranged through your vacation package, you'll find several options for getting to your hotel or wherever else you want to go.

Taxis Taxi service from the airport is heavily regulated; only specially licensed cabs are allowed to pick up passengers. As a result, fares from the airport are higher than for the return

Go Hog Wild in the Riviera Maya

For some travelers, taking a guided trip in a tour bus or even setting out on their own in a rental car is just too tame. For these intrepid travelers, renting a Harley-Davidson may be the best way to visit the ruins, discover hidden beaches, and make a style statement, all while getting a tan. Harley Adventures (Highway 307 at Constituyentes Avenue, 984-106-0500, www.harley adventures.com) offers 883 Sportsters, 1,200 Customs, and Softail Fat Boys for around $95, $145, and $195 per day. Riders are encouraged to exercise extreme caution while riding along busy sections of Highway 307 and any unpaved roads they encounter.

A single taxi awaits arrivals at the Cancún airport in 1970. Cancun History Center

trips to the airport. The official fare at press time from the airport to the Cancún hotel zone is $40, and a trip to Playa del Carmen will run you around $90 to $100 per vehicle.

Shuttle Buses Shuttle buses, called *colectivos*, are available for transportation to Playa del Carmen. You'll ride with other travelers, stopping at other hotels along the way, but it's a good way to save a few pesos. Fares to Playa del Carmen are $30 per person.

City Buses Public bus service ($8) runs between the Cancún airport and the main Playa del Carmen bus terminal (Quinta and Juárez), a short walk or

Bus Fare Samples

From Playa del Carmen to:

Cancún: 1 hour, $5

Tulum: 1 hour, $6

Cobá: 2½ hours, $6.50

Felipe Carillo Puerto: 3 hours, $10

Valladolid: 3 hours, $18

Chetumal: 4 hours, $22

Chichén Itzá: 4½ hours, $20

Mérida: 4½ hours, $22

taxi ride to most Playa hotels. Purchase tickets just after you clear customs and immigration and before you leave the airport. Look for the booths advertising ADO, the company offering the service. Once you have your ticket, you'll be directed to the departure location. Any local will point the way, but make sure you're getting on the right bus, and don't be talked into paying additional fares for different services.

Car Rental If you plan to do much local exploring and prefer a self-guided trip over planned excursions, renting a car may be your best option. And since the price of car rental for a day is about the same as taking a taxi from the Cancún airport to Playa del Carmen, it usually makes sense to pick up the car at the airport

A *colectivo* charges per person and makes multiple stops.

Fares from Cancún Airport to Area Destinations

	Colectivo/ Shuttle	Taxi (1–4 people)	Taxi (5–8 people)
Moon Palace	—	$50	$75
Cancún Hotel Zone	$15	$60	$100
Gran Puerto (Isla Mujeres ferry)	$20	$65	$105
Puerto Morelos	$25	$70	$95
Playa Mujeres	—	$80	$110
Mayan Palace	$25	$80	$110
Downtown Playa del Carmen	$30	$90	$125
Xcaret	$40	$120	$155
Paamul	$40	$120	$155
Puerto Aventuras	$40	$125	$155
Akumal	$50	$155	$190
Tulum	$50	$155	$190
Chiquila (Isla Holbox ferry)	—	$320	$390
Mérida	—	$415	$520
Chetumal	—	$440	$590

and drop it off on your way back. Alternatively, you can choose to get your car once you're at your hotel or drop it off early at one of your rental agency's offices in the Mayan Riviera.

When renting a car in Mexico, it's important to investigate your insurance options. You're required to carry at least liability, and it will be clearly marked on your rental contract. Collision and comprehensive add-ons are available and can add 50 to 100 percent to the car rental price. Verify in advance whether your existing car insurance or even credit card contract provides for rental car coverage, and ensure that the coverage extends to vehicles rented in Mexico. Many plans don't.

Playa Commuter Flights Mostly used by private aircraft, the small airfield in downtown Playa del Carmen, a few blocks behind the Playacar Palace hotel, also has charter flights available through Aerosaab (987-865-4225, www.aerosaab.com) to Cancún, Cozumel, Mérida, Isla Holbox, and nearby destinations.

The Cozumel Ferry

If you hit the schedule just right, getting to Playa del Carmen from Cozumel can take even less time than arriving through Cancún. The Cozumel International Airport (CZM) is smaller than Cancún's, with only two runways and a small terminal. As your plane slows to a stop on the runway, you'll think the wingtips are about to snip the treetops off the palm trees that line the strip, but it's a safe and modern facility, even if it lacks the pretensions of the more recently renovated Cancún airport.

The ferry boat to Cozumel takes less than 30 minutes.

Cozumel Ferry Schedule

Cozumel to Playa del Carmen	Playa del Carmen to Cozumel
5:00 AM	6:00 AM
7:00 AM	8:00 AM
8:00 AM	9:00 AM
9:00 AM	10:00 AM
10:00 AM	11:00 AM
noon	1:00 PM
2:00 PM	3:00 PM
4:00 PM	5:00 PM
5:00 PM	6:00 PM
6:00 PM	7:00 PM
8:00 PM	9:00 PM
10:00 PM	11:00 PM

The schedule can vary by day. Check the daily schedule at the ferry dock (www.granpuerto.com.mx, www.mexicowaterjets.com).

As in Cancún, taxi service at the Cozumel airport is regulated, and taxi fare or shuttle service must be paid for at a kiosk in the airport. Visitors with little luggage looking to save a few bucks can walk off the airport grounds and hail a taxi on the street. An official taxi will cost you $12 to the ferry landing, whereas a taxi hailed on the street will set you back only $5 or so. Either way, the ride is only 10 minutes and will take you through a quick tour of the town of San Miguel before letting you out at the base of the ferry landing (*muelle* in Spanish).

Ferry schedules are clearly posted (987-879-3112, www.mexicowaterjets .com.mx), and you'll have your option from a couple of different boats. Each boasts to be the newest and fastest, though any differences in the times are negligible. Seating more than 200, ferries have air-conditioning, snack bars, restrooms, and both indoor and outdoor seating. The ride takes from 30 to 45 minutes, depending on the boat and the water conditions. On windy days the ride can be a little rough, so it's recommended that you use the restroom prior to boarding or before departure, in case it's too rocky to safely move around. Fares range from $10 to $12 each way, depending on how many boats are available. Round-trip tickets are available and can save the hassle of standing in line again, though it's generally not much of an issue.

Upon arrival in Playa, you'll walk down a metal ramp onto the wide concrete pier. If you've checked bags, they'll be delivered to you on the dock, near the

Stay Out of Trouble

One good way to avoid run-ins with the local police is to not give them any good reasons to pull you over in the first place.

Never drink and drive—Nothing is more tempting to a local police offers than a rental jeep full of tourists with a cooler in the backseat and everyone holding Corona bottles as they drive down the road.

Wear your seatbelt—Just as in the United States, there is a mandatory seatbelt law in Mexico. The beat cops in Playa del Carmen sometimes stand on the street corner where it's easy to peer inside your car, so buckle up every time you get in the front seat of a car.

Pull over to use your mobile phone—Using a mobile phone or other similar gadget while driving is illegal in Mexico. It's also extremely dangerous when driving on unfamiliar roads, especially along Highway 307 and around downtown areas in Cancún, Playa del Carmen or Tulum.

ferry's bow. Tricycle taxis are available to help carry you and/or your bags to the street to catch a proper taxi or all the way to your hotel, if you're staying in the immediate downtown area.

ELECTRICITY Electrical power is the same as it is in the States: 110 volts AC. Outlets are the same size, and most U.S. plugs will work without any problem. Some hotels do not offer polarized plugs (where one prong is slightly larger than the other), so if your important electronic gadget has a polarized plug, grab an adapter at your local hardware or discount store. Adaptors are very inexpensive and could save the day if you have an uncooperative outlet at your hotel.

WHAT TO BRING The Mayan Riviera isn't considered a remote location. You're usually never more than 30 to 45 minutes from a grocery store, pharmacy, clothing boutique, electronics store, hair salon, or even hardware store, and modern supplies are readily available.

Packing for a trip to Playa and environs is all about comfort and bringing what you want to have with you to make your trip perfect. Unless you're planning on a serious camping trip to Sian Ka'an or a long-distance jungle hike, you should consider your packing to be an exercise in preparing for a luxury getaway or what suits your comfort. What you need to bring is largely determined by where you're staying and what you plan on doing.

STAYING SAFE Playa del Carmen is no longer a sleepy fishing village where everybody knows everybody and the doors are left unlocked. It is still a happy little town, though, where a lot of people do know one another and not all lock their doors. Petty theft is the main problem, and tourists are advised to watch their belongings, lock their hotel room, and not leave valuables unattended on the beach or elsewhere.

For the most part, Playa is quite safe. However, it's best to not be on remote

A quiet afternoon near Mamita's Beach   Ricardo Vagg

parts of the beach late at night, as incidents have been reported. Leave your jewels at home and, as when anywhere else, don't flash large amounts of cash or be too showy with expensive equipment or electronic gadgets. Use the hotel safe whenever possible and don't leave valuables in plain view in your hotel room or rental car. Report suspicious activity at your hotel to the front desk and be alert of your surroundings. Men should carry their wallet in their front pocket on crowded streets, and women should ensure their bags are fully closed and not swinging freely.

There have been reports of drug running, gang activity, and associated crime and violence in the area. If you go looking for trouble, you'll have a better chance of finding it. Visitors are strongly advised to keep their noses clean and to stay well away from any obvious trouble or precarious situations. Don't travel into the destitute neighborhoods, especially at night. Don't associate with questionable individuals, and stay away from problem areas.

The Tourist Police hut (Quinta at 10th Street) is manned nearly 24 hours a day and most officers are bilingual and can help with any problems. They patrol the beach and the main roads in town and are well respected by locals.

TIME ZONE The entire state of Quintana Roo is on Mexico Central Time, which is GMT –6 hours, the same as U.S. Central Time. Mexico honors daylight saving time on the same schedule as the United States, starting the second Sunday in March (clocks move forward by one hour) and ending the first Sunday in November.

Words and Phrases

English	Spanish	English	Spanish
Another one	Otra	Nice to meet you	Mucho gusto
ATM	Cajero automático	Orange juice	Jugo de naranja
Bathroom	Baño	Please	Por favór
Beach	Playa	Post office	El correo
Beef	Carne de res	Rain	Llúvia
Beer	Cerveza	Scuba diving	Buceo
Big	Grande	Shrimp	Camarón
Boat	Lancha	Shuttle bus	Colectivo
Bottled water	Agua en botella	Sick	Enfermo
Breakfast	Desayuno	Silly tourist	Turista loca
Bus	Autobús	Small	Pequeña
Car rental	Renta de autos	Sunscreen	Protector solar
Check/bill	La cuenta	Suntan lotion	Bronceadora
Chicken	Pollo	Swim	Nadar
Coffee with milk	Café con leche	Swimsuit	Traje de baño
Dinner	Cena	Tax	Impuestos
Downtown	El centro	Thank you	Graciás
Drunk	Borracho	Tip	Propina
Eat	Comer	Towel	Toalla
Fishing	La pesca	Waiter	Mesero
Goodbye	Adiós, hasta luego	Walk	Caminar
Good morning	Buenos días	Why	Porqué
Good night	Buenas noches	You're welcome	De nada
Happy	Felíz		
Hello	Hola		
How much	Cuánto		
Ice	Hielo		
I want	Yo deseo		
Lime	Limón		
Lobster	Langosta		
Luggage	Equipaje		
Lunch	Comida		
Money	Dinero		
Money exchange	Cámbio de dinero		
More	Más		
My name is	Me llamo		

TRY A LITTLE MAYAN

English	Mayan
Hello, what's up?	Ba'ax ka wa' alik?
What's going on?	Bix a bel?
I'm fine.	Ma'alob.
See you later.	Taak tu lakin.
I'm just looking.	Chen tin wilik.
How much is it?	Bahúux leti'?
Tastes good.	Ki'.
Hot pepper	Lik
Juice	K'aab
Where	Tu'ux
Plaza	K'íiwik
Thank you	Dios bo'otik
You're welcome	Mixba'al

It's beach weather all year long in the Riviera Maya. Brian E. Miller Photography/www.lomimonk.com

WEATHER

Month	High Temp.	Low Temp.	Ocean Temp.	Rainfall
January	80°F	66°F	75°F	3.75 inches
February	81°F	67°F	76°F	2.25 inches
March	83°F	70°F	77°F	1.75 inches
April	84°F	72°F	78°F	1.75 inches
May	87°F	76°F	80°F	4.75 inches
June	88°F	77°F	83°F	7.75 inches
July	89°F	77°F	85°F	4.25 inches
August	89°F	76°F	85°F	4.25 inches
September	88°F	75°F	84°F	9.00 inches
October	86°F	73°F	82°F	8.50 inches
November	83°F	71°F	81°F	3.75 inches
December	81°F	68°F	79°F	4.25 inches

History of the
Playa del Carmen Region

In the beginning all was invisible. The sky was motionless.
There was only water, the quiet ocean, the silence, the nights.
Then there came the word.
                    —From the *Popol Vuh*, sacred Mayan scriptures

PLAYA DEL CARMEN owes its growing popularity to the nearby resort town of Cancún, just 40 miles to the north, and Cozumel Island, just 12 miles to the east. The influence of these two towns has helped shape Playa since the days of the Maya.

Playa del Carmen is named for Our Lady of Mount Carmel, the patron saint of Cancún. She was named for a town in Italy, which was the first place where a chapel was built in her honor, in 1263, before her ascension into heaven.

The first recorded visitors to the beaches of what is now Playa del Carmen came during the Early Classic Period (A.D. 300–600) of the Mayan civilization. Then called Xaman-Ha (Waters of the North), Playa was a rest stop of sorts for travelers making their way from the great cities of the Mayan world to the island of Cozumel. These travelers readied their dugout canoes and prepared for the journey across the straits on the same shores that now house the restaurants, hotels, and nightspots of modern-day Playa del Carmen.

Cozumel, called Ah Cuzamil Petén (Island of the Swallows) by the Maya, was a sacred site and home to Ixchel, the goddess of fertility and wife of Itzamna, the god of the sun. Young women across the Mayan empire, from present-day Yucatán, Honduras, Belize, and beyond, journeyed to Cozumel on a sacred pilgrimage to pay homage to Ixchel and pray for fertility and healthy childbirth.

In return for the dozens of shrines and temples that the Mayans constructed, Ixchel is said to have gifted the people with the *cuzamil* (graceful swallow), which led the Maya to give the island its name. Many of the temples for Ixchel have survived, including San Gervasio, which can still be visited today.

LEFT: Maya-inspired sculptures adorn many resorts.   Philip Gamon

Growth

If you think the Riviera Maya's explosive growth came as a surprise to the Mexican government, think again. The growth plan was forecast in the mid-1970s by then-governor of Quintana Roo, Rojo Gómez. The following message was sent to President Luis Echeverría:

> *We have prepared an integral plan for the development of the coasts of Quintana Roo, whose beauty is unparalleled and which has many attractive sites. It has beautiful beaches, clear ocean water, wild jungles and hidden Mayan ruins, which have yet to be explored because of lack of access. We have located 100 km of coastline whose features promise a great future for tourism in the area.*

Meanwhile, on a sheltered sandbar known to the Mayans as Kankun (Nest of Snakes), the temples of El Rey were constructed as a ceremonial site and resting place for the society's nobles. The site is now adjacent to a golf course and across the highway from the Hilton Hotel, making it a popular destination for visitors to Cancún who want see Mayan ruins but are not able to get to the more major sites in the region, such as Tulum, Cobá, or Chichén Itzá.

Cancún did not have many other sacred sites because it was so narrow and did not have good access to the mainland, though the ocean breezes and proximity to various shallow lagoons did make it a nice place to live for the natives who fished along its shores and harvested food from the mangroves.

During the Postclassic Period (A.D. 1000–1500), the area around Playa del Carmen, Cancún, and Cozumel served as a major trade route and religious center, and the Mayan culture flourished and prospered. At its height, the walled city of Tulum contained splendors beyond belief, and the nearby town of Cobá was a spiritual center of the entire Mayan empire, with a population of nearly 50,000. Near the end of this period, the populations dwindled as the natives dispersed due to storms and wars and to seek gentler climates.

Juan de Grijalva, a Spanish explorer, passed close to Playa del Carmen in 1518 and then discovered Cozumel while en route to Cuba, several hundred miles to the east. He didn't stay for long, but word of his find traveled fast, and his countryman Hernán Cortéz returned the following year, bringing Catholicism and little appreciation for the Mayan way of life. Cortéz and his men demolished Mayan temples and built a Catholic church, and he also brought something else with him when he landed on Cozumel—smallpox. The disease spread quickly within the island's close-knit community, and the population was decimated, dropping from 40,000 to less than 200 within 50 years.

The first European settlement in the region was at Xel-Ha, just a few miles south of Playa del Carmen, which 200 hundred years, the Spanish traveled throughout the Playa del Carmen area and the Yucatán, spreading Catholicism and disease as they went. Many Maya resisted the new religion, and small communities retained their traditional ways and their sacred cultures. During the 1700s and 1800s, pirates set up shop on the nearly deserted shores of Cozumel, using it as a base for their marauding forays across the channel to Playa del Carmen and elsewhere around the region.

Meanwhile, trade continued in and around Playa del Carmen, given its location midway between the port city of Veracruz to the north and Honduras to the south. Local commodities, including salt and honey, were bartered for goods imported from other regions, giving the area a taste of the diversity, commerce, and—yes—tourism that would eventually secure its place in the Mexican economy.

John L. Stephens and Frederick Catherwood passed through the Riviera Maya in 1842 as part of their expedition to the Mayan ruins, documented in their excellent book, *Incidents of Travel in Yucatán.* In the book, Stephens writes about what they saw and the people they encountered, while Catherwood presents exacting drawings of the ruins. The book is incredibly precise and detailed, and it's still used by scholars, archaeologists, and Mayan enthusiasts today.

In 1848, the Mayans and various Spanish refugees began to resist the Spanish occupation more aggressively, leading to an uprising known as the War of the Castes. During the struggle, a large group of the oppressed set out from the Yucatán town of Valladolid and traveled across the peninsula, settling in Cozumel, which led to a regrowth of the island's population. Other natives took cover in the ruins of Tulum, which made a great fortress given its walled perimeter. The town of San Miguel de Cozumel was officially established in 1840, and several years later, U.S. president Abraham Lincoln pondered using the island as a place to send the freed American slaves and even went so far as talking to the Mexican government about purchasing it.

Due to the remote location and its dense, inhospitable jungle environment, Playa del Carmen and the surrounding area kept a low profile for the rest of the 1800s. In 1902, the region was finally granted status as a territory of the country of

Tulum was the most sacred site in the region for the ancient Mayans.

Riviera Maya Destination Marketing Office

Where Did My Bathing Suit Go?

If you continually misplace something on your trip, don't blame your traveling companion—it may be an *alux* (pronounced "aloosh") playing pranks.

Aluxo'ob are, according to Mayan superstition, mischievous elfin or childlike creatures that live in the tropical jungle and play tricks on those that don't believe in them or give them proper respect. Some stories claim that the *aluxo'ob* were originally clay or stone carvings placed in the Mayan religious temples that later came to life.

Many Maya and other locals claim to have had run-ins with *aluxo'ob*. They can cause the phone to ring at odd hours of the night, and when it's answered, no one is on the other end. They can move objects around the room and sometimes even steal bits of food. To curry the favor of the *aluxo'ob*, many people build them little houses or shrines on their property. Once appeased, the *aluxo'ob* become good-luck charms, helping to ensure a good harvest, bring about good fortune, and protect the believers from other dangers.

Many hotels in the Riviera Maya, even some large and well-established ones, have homes for the *aluxo'ob* on site, in hopes that appeasing them with a comfy dwelling will encourage them to be friendly, though they rarely talk about it. Ask your waiters and housekeepers, though, and chances are they'll know what you're talking about—and will probably have a story of their own to share.

Mexico, and it was named after Gen. Andrés Quintana Roo, of the Mexican army. That same year, on November 17, the town of Villa del Carmen was officially founded near the site of what is now Playa del Carmen's Leona Vicario Park. Charles Lindbergh stopped in Cozumel in 1928 in the storied *Spirit of St. Louis* plane. The island was used as a base by the U.S. Navy during World War II and was then abandoned again until the 1960s, when scuba adventurer and documentary film producer Jacques Cousteau visited the island with an underwater camera crew and began to show the world the beauties of the Great Mayan Reef (second in size only to Australia's Great Barrier Reef), which runs between Cozumel and Playa del Carmen for hundreds of miles.

Tourism visionary Fernando Barbachano purchased much of the land that currently makes up Playacar in 1966. The sale included nearly a mile of barren beachfront, stretching south from there the ferry dock now sits. The price tag was a now-paltry $13,600, but it was a serious risk at the time. He subdivided the land and sold it in small parcels, the first of which sold in 1977 for $15,550, proving just how masterful his idea really was. The single most important factor in the development of the region came in 1967, when the Bank of Mexico and the country's tourism development commission identified Cancún as the location for one of its mega-development projects (along with Ixtapa, Los Cabos, Loreto, and Huatulco). In the original government documents, the area was called "Kan Kun," which quickly morphed into the more Spanish "Can Cun," and then eventually shortened to just "Cancún."

Bridges were built, sewer lines were laid, and electrical poles sprang up. The first Cancún hotels, opened in the early 1970s, were the Palacio Maya, Playa Blanca, Cancún Caribe, Camino Real, and Club Med. In 1970, a wooden boat dock was built on the central beach in Playa del Carmen, and shortly thereafter, ferry service started to Cozumel. In 1974, Quintana Roo was granted Mexican statehood and the Cancún International Airport opened for business, with a bamboo and palm air-traffic control tower and a single taxi waiting for arriving planes. Two years later, the city's Pok-Ta-Pok golf course opened with 18 holes, many with views of the ocean and minor Mayan ruins. Over the next 10 years, Cancún grew from a coconut jungle visited only by traveling fishermen and a few *loco* gringos to a world-class tourist destination. The local population boomed as workers from across the country poured into Ciudad Cancún to find jobs and establish their families. The Playa del Carmen airstrip was laid in 1979 and the area's first hotel, the Balam Ha (where the Playacar Palace is now), opened the next year, and land along Fifth Avenue was given away to employees of the Calica mining company.

Cozumel experienced a growth spurt of its own as recreational scuba diving became more popular and affordable and more and more divers came to witness for themselves what they had been able to see only on the Jacques Cousteau television show.

Despite a few bumps along the way, including lack of airline support, the devaluation of the peso, and a series of hurricanes, Cancún and Cozumel continued to grow and prosper. Somehow, though, Playa del Carmen lagged behind, as the city to its north and the island to its east developed more quickly. As the

2012: The End of the World—or Just the Beginning?

The Mayan calendar ends at 11:11 AM on December 21, 2012 (the winter solstice), which coincides with an extremely close alignment of the path of the sun and the galactic equator (the Milky Way's midpoint). The Maya did not necessarily foretell the "end of the world," but they did say that on this date, the world as we know it will be complete, and a new "Golden Age" will begin. Mayan scripture reveals that the ancient peoples predicted that our society will have great advances in technology, that time and money will become meaningless, and that human beings will be upgraded from the center of the galaxy. The event is even cryp-tically captured in images carved into the walls of Mayan sacred temples.

Modern astronomy and archaeology researchers have recognized the amazing accuracy of the Mayan calendar and its ability to calculate and forecast the movement of the stars, and they have confirmed that the alignment will indeed happen as predicted. Whether it will have any great impact on life on Earth will soon be revealed.

Hollywood filmmakers presented their cataclysmic take on the subject with a movie released in 2009 called *2012*, starring John Cusack, Amanda Peet, and Woody Harrelson.

Next time you're in Playa, at least you'll have a good excuse to celebrate life, so wake up early to get the best beach chairs, order the surf and turf at dinner, and savor an extra top-shelf margarita.

Playa was a tiny outpost in the 1970s. The church in the center of this photo is still there, at the northwest corner of the town square. Cancun History Center

growth went on around it, Playa del Carmen was still known only as the ferry landing for boats traveling back and forth between Cozumel and the Quintana Roo mainland. A handful of fishermen lived in huts on the beach and a few optimistic entrepreneurs sold tacos and handicrafts to the hurrying travelers, but tourists and locals moved quickly through town on their way to the more established locales.

In its hippie heyday, Playa del Carmen's visitors would while away the day along the beaches south of town. The small cove now occupied by the Gran Porto Real hotel was close enough to the town square to be convenient but just out of sight of the ferry dock, making it the preferred place for those who liked to sunbathe au naturel. At night, tourists returned to the beach for the freewheeling and ultracasual nightlife under the stars, a refreshingly unpretentious antidote to the pulsating discotheques that were becoming so popular in nearby Cancún. During a full moon, locals and tourists alike congregated on the beach for a ceremonial "*lunata*" celebration, complete with bonfires, cold Coronas, and skinny-dipping—a tradition that must have made the Mayan gods smile (especially Ixchel, the goddess of fertility!).

But starting in the early 1980s, little by little, street by street, the tiny fishing village and ferry town began to grow. New shops, restaurants, and even a couple of hotels opened their doors, luring the passing visitors to stay a while. The first hotels were built of bamboo and palm fronds, with slatted wood doors—not to keep out thieves, but to prevent the wild pigs from entering and looking for food.

Disaster struck in September 1988 when Hurricane Gilbert slammed into Cozumel and the Riviera Maya with 170 mph winds, blowing the roofs off hotels, pulling trees out by their roots, smashing windows, and flooding the streets. Inside the storm, the barometric pressure was 26.23 inches, the lowest sea-level pressure ever recorded in the Western Hemisphere. The hurricane caused more than $80 million in damage in Cozumel alone, and it changed the face of the region for years.

In the early 1990s, Playa del Carmen became a regular stop for the cruise lines, exposing Playa to a new breed of revelers. Soon after, the outdated Cozumel ferry boats were replaced with sleek and modern jet-powered watercraft, which made the trip from the island faster and easier on the stomach and brought in even more visitors.

Guadalajara-based tourism giant Grupo Sidek purchased thousands of acres of land along the shoreline just south of the ferry landing, with designs to develop the area that had been dubbed "Playacar." First came the Continental Plaza (in 1992, now the Playacar Palace). Later that year, the Diamond Resort (now the Allegro Occidental) was inaugurated, marking the first opening of an all-inclusive resort in the Riviera Maya. A golf course opened in September 1994, and then hotel after hotel rose from the jungle, changing the face of the community forever.

On the other side of the ferry dock, development continued as well, but government-imposed density restrictions kept away large-scale hotel projects, and

Local Lingo

Cenote: A rare geological feature of the Yucatán, a *cenote* is a freshwater sink-hole formed when the limestone ground caves in and fills with water from underground rivers.

Colectivo: A sort of taxi-bus combination, a *colectivo* is a van or similar vehicle used for local transportation. It has semifixed routes and is cheaper than a taxi.

Costa Maya: The coastline south of the Riviera Maya (which officially ends at Tulum).

Federal: Used when referring to Highway 307, a federal highway.

Ha: Mayan for "water." You'll see it used everywhere.

Mole: A chocolate-based sauce made with dozens of herbs and spices, used in traditional Mexican cooking.

Muelle: Spanish for "dock," it's commonly used when referring to the ferry landing, which is also called the *embarcadero*.

Nopales: Sliced cactus from the nopal tree, it's used locally in breakfast juice and can be served grilled or sautéed with any meal of the day.

Palapa: Thatched palm used to make roofing in the Riviera Maya. The tight weave keeps out rain and has to be replaced every couple of years. The word is also used generically to refer to any structure that has a thatched-palm roof.

Pan dulce: Literally "sweet bread," it's used to describe a variety of delicious locally made breakfast pastries. For a quick start to your day, order a *café con pan dulce*.

Parada: Spanish for "bus stop."

Playa: Meaning "beach" in Spanish, this is the short name used locally when referring to Playa del Carmen.

Playacar: A name created in 1992 to refer to the tourist development located just south of First Street and the ferry dock.

Propina: Spanish for "tip." Make sure you check your bill to see if tip has already been added: *propina incluida*.

Quinta: Spanish for "fifth," it's the name used for Fifth Avenue, the main tourist strip in Playa del Carmen.

Riviera Maya: The name used to refer to the area from just south of Cancún to Tulum. The actual boundaries tend to change a little bit, depending on whom you talk to. The phrase was coined in the early 1990s and is sometimes said in English, "Mayan Riviera."

Tacos *al pastor*: Pork tacos cooked on a vertical spit, seared with licking flames and served with pineapple slices.

Tiempo compartido: Spanish for "time share." If a deal is too good to be true, such as a Jeep rental for $20 a day, chances are it's part of a *tiempo compartido* offer.

small, family-run inns dominated the landscape. From 1990 to 1997, the local population grew from 2,000 to 20,000, and 100 new families were moving to town each month, establishing Playa del Carmen as Mexico's fastest-growing city, a title it held for most of the first decades of the 21st century.

The main road paralleling the beach, avenida Quinta (Fifth Avenue), became the town's principal street and was lined with restaurants, shops, hotels, and other businesses catering to the tourist trade. Favored by European backpackers and U.S. and Canadian budget travelers, Playa del Carmen began to make a name for itself on the international travel scene. Known as the place where the hippie lifestyle was not only accepted but celebrated, "Playa," as the in crowd called it, had arrived.

In 1999, the area's mayor, Miguel Ramón Martín Azueta, worked to popularize the term "Riviera Maya" for the land between Cancún and Tulum, which had previously only been referred to as the Cancún-Tulum Corridor.

By the late 1990s, Quinta had extended more than a mile north of the ferry dock, and much of it was closed to vehicular traffic, creating a pedestrian-friendly walkway that developed a unique character unknown in other parts of the world. In the early 2000s, Quinta stretched past Constituyentes Boulevard (between 18th and 20th streets), and the area was dubbed "La Nueva Quinta," sometimes called "Little Italy," "Upper Playa," or simply "the New Playa." Italian-style cafés stood next to taco stands that stood next to gourmet steakhouses, creating a town with a truly eclectic and international flair. The beach north of Constituyentes also saw some changes. A second ferry dock was built, two large-scale resort hotels were constructed, and a couple of beach clubs sprang up, offering food and drink service, *palapa* and chair rentals, and towel service for the cruise passengers, day-trippers, and guests from hotels that aren't on the beach.

As the upscale all-inclusive hotels of Playacar introduced the town to more affluent travelers, the tone of the village continued to change. The thatched-roof bus station was rebuilt with electric displays and molded plastic seats. Across the

The old and the new mingle peacefully in Cozumel.

Looking for some ideas for your evening plans? Take a walk down Fifth Avenue for a wide selection of restaurants, bars, and shops. Riviera Maya Destination Marketing Office

street, McDonald's opened up, then a couple of Starbucks, and up and down the coast, more and more resorts were carved from the jungle. Renovations began on Quinta as work crews buried the utility lines and paved the gravel road with cobblestones, giving the road a bit of colonial inspiration to go along with its nouveau chic attitude.

Hurricanes Emily and Wilma, both devastating storms with deceivingly demure names, tested the region's will in the summer and fall of 2005 when they sliced similar paths across Cozumel, Cancún, and the Riviera Maya. Emily raged with sustained winds of 135 mph, shearing off rooftops, leveling trees and signs, shattering windows, rearranging beaches, and sending 60,000 tourists scrambling for shelter. Wilma completed the one-two punch by hammering the area three months later with 150 mph winds and a storm surge topping 11 feet in Cancún. Tourists were confined to shelters for days, and it took some nearly two weeks after the storm to finally get a flight back home. Hotels in Cancún were hit the hardest, though all along the Riviera Maya there was extensive flooding and wind damage. Some hotels closed for days, whereas others took weeks or even months to reopen.

The region bounced back, though, as the communities worked together to rebuild and restore the splendor of the area. In fact, the town's resilience through adversity seemed to prove its staying power, as the condo boom kicked into high gear in early 2007. One of Playa's original hotels, the Corto Maltes, turned to condos. The El Faro Hotel, site of the landmark lighthouse did the same. Up and down each block, workers could be seen converting hotels to condos and building new structures where there were none. The area north of Constituyentes saw an especially strong push, with new developments going up on nearly every block. Most complexes were small, with no more than 12 or 14 units, but others are much larger, threatening to change the face of the town.

In 2009, another challenge to the area arrived in the form of the H1N1 "swine flu" scare, which kept international tourists away, drove occupancy levels to rock-bottom levels and even causing many hotels to close, at least temporarily. Later in the year, though, the tourists returned.

A massive beach renovation effort pumped in thousands of tons of sand from the ocean seafloor, building up the beachfront and widening it in many areas,

15 "Old-School" Spots for Nostalgic Riviera Maya Regulars

1. Antigua Posada Barrio Latino hotel (Playa del Carmen)

2. Blue Parrot restaurant & bar (Playa del Carmen)

3. Casa Denis restaurant (Cozumel)

4. CasaSandra hotel (Isla Holbox)

5. Costa del Mar hotel (Playa del Carmen)

6. Don Emilione restaurant (Playa del Carmen)

7. Eclipse Hotel (Playa del Carmen)

8. El Cozumeleño hotel (Cozumel)

9. El Jardin el Jaguar restaurant (Playa del Carmen)

10. La Bamba Jarocha restaurant (Playa del Carmen)

11. La Habichuela restaurant patio (downtown Cancún)

12. La Rana Cansada hotel and La Ranita Bar (Playa del Carmen)

13. Ojo de Agua hotel and restaurant (Puerto Morelos)

14. Pension San Juan hotel (Playa del Carmen)

15. Playa Maya Hotel (Playa del Carmen)

which helped to reverse the effects of storm erosion and made the beaches wider and more beautiful than ever.

By the middle of 2010, the Riviera Maya had surpassed Cancún in the number of hotel rooms available and was celebrating its status as one of the top international tourist destinations in the world, with 35,000 hotel rooms and 6 million visitors a year—70 percent of whom are European. Expatriates from 46 countries around the globe call Playa del Carmen home, and the town seems to thrive on the notoriety.

And through it all, Playa has stayed true to its roots, somehow preserving its almost magical charm and exceptional character. It is still a place where travelers from around the world come together to lounge on the beach, toast the day with a cold beer, sip a hot cappuccino, and celebrate life. And in a town where backpackers from crowded hostels, newlyweds from fancy all-inclusives, and European trendsetters from chic new condos all cozy up to the same bars, it's easy to understand why Playa so easily works its way into your heart.

The ruins of Xaman-Ha can still be seen in modern-day Playa del Carmen. The main temple is along the beach just south of the Playacar Palace hotel and is now a popular spot for wedding ceremonies. Many other shrines dot the Playacar development, including the golf course. And though it may be hard to envision a time when the Maya carved their dugout canoes from local trees and plied the waters to Cozumel, today's visitors to Playa will undoubtedly feel a sense of the grand history, the sacred importance, and the incredible natural beauty that have lured visitors to its sandy shores for thousands of years.

As one longtime local resident puts it, "No one knows what makes Playa so special, but everyone seems to return."

Hurricanes of the Riviera Maya

1951, Hurricane Charlie: Made landfall in the Riviera Maya with 125 mph winds.

1955, Hurricane Janet: Walloped the tiny town of Xcalak and Chetumal.

1967, Hurricane Beulah: Came ashore as a category 2, causing widespread damage.

1980, Hurricane Allen: Weakened as it approached the region, sparing it from harm.

1988, Hurricane Gilbert: Smashed into Cozumel with 170 mph winds and a 15-foot storm surge, caused more than $80 million in damage on the island alone, stranded a 125-foot Cuban freighter (the *Portachernera*) on the beach in Cancún, and killed more than three hundred people after it crossed the Yucatán and hit northern Mexico.

1995, Hurricane Roxanne: Slammed into the Riviera Maya with 115 mph winds.

1998, Hurricane Mitch: This massive storm was expected to hit the area but curved away. An American tourist was killed in a boating accident near Cancún, related to the rough water.

2003, Hurricane Claudette: Skirted the area with tropical storm–speed winds before continuing on to Texas.

2004, Hurricane Ivan: Made a beeline for the Yucatán, causing heavy rains and high waves along the coast, before curving north and slamming Florida.

2005, Hurricane Emily: Struck Cozumel as a category 4 storm, then crossed the Riviera Maya near Puerto Aventuras, causing widespread damage, some severe, though the area quickly cleaned up and recovered.

2005, Hurricane Wilma: Just three months after Emily, Wilma became the most intense hurricane ever in the Atlantic Basin. The eye lingered over Cozumel and Cancún for nearly a day, causing severe damage to waterfront areas and flooding much of the region.

2007, Hurricane Dean: Made landfall in the middle of the night just north of Chetumal and Majahual, south of the Riviera Maya, as a Category 5 storm. Nearly 150,000 residents evacuated to shelters. Some small towns were cut off for days and about a third of the hotels in Tulum received at least moderate damage.

2008, Hurricane Dolly: Before it was a full-fledged category 1 hurricane, the weak tropical storm crossed directly over Cancún with no noteworthy damage.

2010, Hurricane Alex: Still a tropical storm when it crossed the Yucatán Peninsula, Alex did only minor damage before it entered the Gulf of Mexico, became a category 2 storm, and slammed into northeastern Mexico.

1

Playa del Carmen

PLAYA DEL CARMEN is in the geographic center of the Riviera Maya and the region's principal city. It's the seat of the municipal government and is home to the area's primary lodging, dining, nightlife, and shopping options.

Playa, as the locals call it, is the only town in the region whose development fills the land between Highway 307 and the beach. Within the past decade, it has even spilled onto the west side of the highway, an area that has seen development including major shopping centers and local housing.

No longer a sleepy fishing village, Playa has grown into a cosmopolitan beach resort, while somehow staying true to its roots, typified by its laid-back lifestyle, low-density development, international flavor, and casual come-as-you-are vibe. Visitors will find small local inns next to luxury villas, taco shacks next to steakhouses, and dusty cantinas next to stylish lounges. The mix of people and cultures, the variety of tourist offerings, and the welcoming spirit of the locals make it a unique travel destination, not just in Mexico, but in the entire world.

Playa is laid out on a perfect grid, so all *calles* lead to the beach, while all *avenidas* parallel it.

A WALKING TOUR OF PLAYA DEL CARMEN

Take a walk through some of the older parts of Playa del Carmen and glimpse samples of the town's Mayan past, its dynamic present, and its international-flavored future.

LEFT: Downtown Playa from 22nd to 12th streets.   Reina Roja Hotel

Playa del Carmen

C. 54 N.
C. 52 N.
C. 50 N.
C. 48 N.
AV. 46 N.

AV. 45 N.
AV. 40 N.

C. FLAMINGOS
C. GAVIOTAS
C. PELICANOS

Canibal Royale
Beach Club

AV. 5 N.
AV. 1 N.
C. 44 N.
C. 42 N.

C. 40 N.
C. 38 N.

AV. 35 N.
AV. 30 N.
AV. 25 N.
AV. 20 N.
AV. 15 N.
AV. 10 N.

Casa Ticul
Cueva del Chango

Arena Blanca
Pueblito
Escondido

Mahékal
Beach Resort

307

C. 34 N.
C. 32 N.
C. 30 N.
C. 28 N.
C. 26 N.
C. 24 N.
C. 22 N.
C. 20 N.

EuroBike Rentals

Banana Hotel
Quinta Palmera
Farolito
Vagabunda
Yaxche Maya Cuisine
Reina Roja

Hotel Las Palapas

Mamita's Beach Club
Kool Beach Club

Royal
Resort
Dock

AV. CONSTITUYENTES

C. 16 N.
Ikarus Kiteboarding

Hotel Gran
Porto Real

C. 16 N.
C. 14 N.
C. 12 N.

Spa Itzá
Bus
Station

C. CORAZÓN
C. 14 N.

Secret Ruin

Blue Parrot Suites
Coco Maya Beach Club

Coco Bongo
Mosquito Blue Hotel

Blue Parrot Beach Club

Hotel Deseo
Hotel Basico
C. 10 N.

Mandala Bar
Calle 12 Party Zone

The Abyss Dive Shop

307
C. 8 N.
C. 6 N.
C. 4 N.
C. 2 N.

Government Offices
Wal-Mart
Hostel Playa

Plaza 28 de
Julio Park

Mambo Cafe

Barrio
Latino

Ajua
Maya

Plaza Pelicano Movie Theater
Tank-Ha Dive Center

Pension
San Juan

Yan-Tem
Sacbe

Lighthouse

Playa Maya
Fusion Hotel

CARIBBEAN
SEA

Pedestrian Walkway

0   1/8   1/4
Miles

Gas
Station
AV. JUARÉZ

Police/
Post Office

Bus Station

Chapel

Alux Cave
C. 1 S.
C. 3 S.
C. 7 S.

Playa Mart

Town Square

Gazebo

Carlos 'n
Charlie's

Señor Frog's

Playacar Palace

Ferry (To Cozumel)

AV. MUNICIPALIZADA
PASEO COBA
307

Xaman-Ha
Ruins

Aviary
Xaman Ha

© The Countryman Press

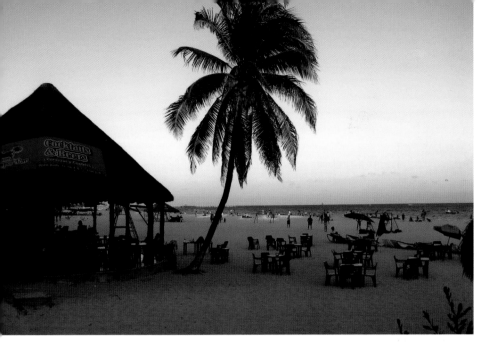

The town square in Playa del Carmen borders the beachfront.

600 Years of Arrivals & Departures

Start at the very center of the Riviera Maya—the gazebo in the town square where avenida Quinta (Fifth Avenue) meets Juarez Avenue. Stand in the center of the gazebo and gaze out at the bustling plaza, with its park benches, flowering plants, and shade trees (notice the painted white trunks). Walk toward the water and consider buying a cup of fresh fruit (cantaloupe, watermelon, mandarins, mangoes, cucumbers, and coconuts), topped with chile and lime for $1.50. If you're already thirsty for a cold beer or frosty margarita, the La Palapa bar at the beachfront is a good place to watch the action on the beach while sitting in the shade. Head south from the bar and you'll see a low-rise cement building on your right, serving as military barracks and topped with radio antennas. The soldiers at the entrance are armed with machine guns and are usually willing to pose for a picture.

It's all smiles in the Riviera Maya. Penny Atkinson

Keep going south to the ferry dock, which was first built in 1969–70 and has regular departures for Cozumel Island, located 11 miles offshore. Peek inside the Sr. Frog's Bar and check out the VW bus turned into a DJ booth and the swinging barstools modeled after lifeguard throw buoys. Turn right and head uphill toward the Carlos'n Charlie's restaurant. Cut left a half-block up, at an arched passageway between two shops and walk toward the Playacar Palace hotel. This was the first "large" hotel in town and was called the Continental Plaza when it opened. You'll see a small Mayan shrine on a little ridge to your right, but keep walking parallel to the creek and a block past the hotel to where the road takes a sharp left toward the beach and you'll see an even bigger one.

This is the Xaman-Ha (Waters from the North) structure, an important ceremonial shrine discovered in 1528 by Francisco de Montejo (the same Montejo whose name was given to a local beer from Mérida that's sold

A small Mayan shrine is tucked away in this alley off Fifth Avenue.

around town). Maya women would pray here before heading across the straits to Cozumel in their dugout canoes to worship Ixchel, the goddess of fertility. A placard at its base tells more of the story. Follow the trail around the ruin and cut back toward the tennis courts, heading back north on Coral Negro Street through a quiet residential area with million-dollar homes straddling the wet-weather creek. Go past the guard post and peek over the rail to your left to see a cave that has been carved into the creek bed. Access was blocked off in the late '90s, but it's still interesting to look down and ponder what sort of ancient Mayan rituals may have taken place there 600 years ago. Curve to the left and follow the short street to the next intersection, where you'll see a local sports bar with a Spanish fountain at the corner. Turn left here and then take an immediate right on the first street and head west on a short road that dead-ends into the fence at the head of the runway of the Playa del Carmen Airport, built in 1979.

Turn right here and you'll be heading north on 15th Avenue, flanked by an elementary school on your right. The first intersection is Juarez Avenue, where there's a tourist information office directly across from where you're standing, if you're interested in picking up some brochures on tours and other attractions. Turn right onto Juarez and head back in the direction of the beach. This is a hectic street with mopeds and taxis buzzing by, plus buses arriving and departing at the ADO bus terminal that will be on your left, which is the former site of the town's original tortilla factory.

Keep going straight and you'll arrive at the tiny Playa del Carmen chapel, which was erected in 1964 and underwent major renovations in 2007 to add the water bridge, rear glass wall, and resurfacing of the exterior whitewash. Respectful visitors are welcome to step inside the church and enjoy the ocean view behind the altar and a calming respite from the bustle of the town square. No padded kneelers are present, as worshippers simply kneel on the floor. No photography is allowed and donations placed in the receptacle by the door are appreciated to help with regular upkeep.

This may be a good time to stop at the Playa Mart shop, located at the same intersection as the bus station, for a bottle of water, quick snack, or maybe an enormous velvet sombrero and a bottle of mescal with a worm at the bottom. Next, you'll want to head north on Quinta, the main pedestrian thoroughfare through the heart of the tourist zone. On your right, you'll see a religious shrine of another kind—the local McDonald's. Take note, though, even this American hamburger joint has a thatched-palm roof, as if that somehow helps it blend in. An ATM is on this same block, if you're feeling low on cash. Stay on Quinta for two blocks, enjoying the rush of locals mixed with guests of nearby hotels, day-trippers from the all-inclusive resorts along the coast, and cruise ship escapees stretching their legs. Chances are good you'll be offered fake Cuban cigars, drink specials, a date with someone's sister, or a prescription for Valium, if you hang around very long. You might also see flute-toting musicians, a parrot "driving" a remote-controlled car, or a tiny colorful monkey on someone's shoulder—all willing to pose for a picture for a few pesos.

Playa del Carmen's original church is in the town square.

Even the McDonald's has a thatched roof in Playa.

Sneaking Around

The second intersection is Fourth Street, and you'll want to turn right here, heading downhill toward the beach. On your left, you'll pass a convenience store and an old painted sign for the Yan-Tem Beach Club. The facility is mostly defunct now but has avoided the condo rush because it hides a large freshwater *cenote,* making it nearly impossible to build around. Enter through one of the corridors leading behind the convenience store, or even go straight into the Yan-Tem entrance to catch a glimpse of the *cenote,* currently occupied by a family of resident turtles and used as an aqua playground for the families living on the property.

Backtrack a bit up Fourth Street and go past Quinta this time. On this block, you'll discover a castlelike structure that was built as the town's first indoor shopping mall in the early 2000s, though it was so ill conceived, with no parking and a mazelike interior, that it only lasted a few months before closing down. On the left is the Ajua Maya cantina, a popular restaurant featuring nightly live music and playful Maya waiters who entertain you during your meal. Be sure to shout "Aaahooo-waaa" as you walk by, and if you're hungry, take a lunch break here and show them this book for a free round of tropical drinks. Keep heading uphill on Fourth Street to 20th Avenue and turn right. A small shop on your left sells taxi driver uniforms, Playa del Carmen firefighter ballcaps, school uniforms, and other apparel and accessories that aren't meant as tourist items, but that really do make for fun souvenirs.

Most people never realize this lagoon even exists.

The Mexican flag flies proudly over the municipal building in downtown Playa del Carmen. Brian E. Miller Photography/www.lomimonk.com

Keep going another block to the city hall municipal building. Turn into the main structure on your left and enter the courtyard to view a nice fountain backed by a huge colorful mural depicting life through the years in Playa del Carmen. The park across the street has a walkway with goalpost-like arches bearing the names of various towns within the Playa del Carmen municipal district, plus upright rocks displaying the state song and others showing how to count to 20 in the Mayan language. Depending on the day, there may be a free show going on at the amphitheater on the northeast corner of the park. Head back toward the beach on 10th Street and look for the Hotel Básico on your right. This hotel has garnered tons of media attention for its avant-garde design and daring use of materials, including cement walls infused with Caribbean sand, tire tread floors, latex window coverings, and twin rooftop swimming pools made from petroleum tanks.

Pass through the lobby with an "it's okay, I know what I'm doing" nod to the handsome desk attendants and take the industrial-style elevator to the top floor. Here you'll be graced with an awe-inspiring view of the ocean, the lighthouse, and Fifth Avenue. Order a cocktail (I recommend the pear martini or the signature Básico cocktail) and linger for a bit in one of the swanky poolside-sundeck cabanas while enjoying the view. On your way back through the lobby, check out the selection of art and history books for sale, then turn right on 10th and head toward the lighthouse that crowns the beachfront condo complex.

Walk out on the beach and look beyond the waves and you can see the hotels that make up Cozumel's northern hotel zone. Walk to your left on the beach and you'll find the Blue Parrot Beach Club, where you'll see topless sunbathers of every shape and size and maybe catch a glimpse of the fire dancers rehearsing for their nightly show, which takes place each night after the beach club becomes a nightclub. Cut up through the complex next to the dance floor, past the reception area, and out to the street.

Playa's Past & Present

You're now at the eastern end of the 12th Street Party Strip, as I like to call it, though locals haven't progressed from calling it simply *la doce*. Head uphill past Ba Ba Club, La Mezcalinna, Los Danzantes, Kartabar, Di Vino, and the other patio lounges that make up Playa's trendiest district. Turn right back onto Quinta and head north for a couple of blocks. Look for a sign on your left for calle Corazón. This angled alley is worth a short loop to look at the shops and sit for a while in one of the hand-carved wooden chairs.

When you get back on Quinta, look across the road for a statue of a Maya god, with feathered head-dress, which marks a small passage-way that leads to a nearly forgotten Mayan ruin, about the size of a Volkswagen Beetle. It sits behind a chain-link fence, marked with a signpost from the National Insti-tute of Archaeology, but is other-wise nondescript, with no placard explaining the history, or other fan-fare. Still, though, it's fun to see and try to envision how the Maya may have used it. Perhaps it had something to do with the gulley that you can see if you follow the hallway to the right of the ruin, past some of the town's least-trafficked storefronts.

Keep heading north on Quinta and you'll approach a tree on your right, heavily adorned with glass orbs and rings of lights, first put there when the UltraFemme and UltraJewels shops opened in late 2007. It's especially nice to see at

This statue on Constituyentes honors the Olmec, who lived in the region even before the Maya.

night, when it provides a warm glow visible from blocks away. The big intersection ahead is Constituyentes Avenue, marked with a large Olmec head (the predeces-sors of the Maya) statue in the center of the traffic circle. Across the street is Aca Los Tacos, which serves good tacos and great margaritas. Take a picture with the giant cow, which is Playa's version of Kip's Big Boy. The structures to the north of here didn't exist 10 years ago and now constitute the area known as the "New Playa," "Little Italy," or the "International District," depending on whom you talk to.

If you're not tired yet, keep walking north on Quinta. The primary tourist dis-trict continues for another 30 blocks or so, with dozens of restaurants, bars, and shops ripe for exploring. Turn right anywhere along this stretch and you're only two blocks from the beach. This is where Mamita's Beach Club and other popular wave-watching spots can be found.

After all that walking, I think it's time for a Corona. Or a margarita, or a piña colada . . .

Checking In

Best places to stay in and around Playa del Carmen

For some travelers, selecting a hotel is part of the fun of a visit to Playa del Carmen. There are more than 400 hotels offering some 35,000 rooms in the Riviera Maya, many of them in the greater Playa area. Within a 2-mile radius, visitors can see more than 90 hotels, many of which, while not necessarily large, would be perfectly suitable for most needs. (Many of the area's hotels—about 75 percent—have 30 or fewer rooms.) Although many people choose to book a hotel prior to arriving, most of the year it's completely possible to show up without a reservation and take a stroll around town to look at different properties and current prices before making a final decision. Most hotel operators will happily give travelers a quick tour of their property and rooms, and sometimes will be willing to negotiate a discounted price.

Accommodations range from student hostels and inns with very few amenities that cater to budget travelers to large self-contained resorts with first-class facilities and services. "Concept hotels" such as Hotel Básico and Reina Roja, offering trendy accommodations (and typically nightlife) in uniquely designed surroundings, have become an integral part of the local hospitality landscape.

Many hotels offer a wide range of room choices, with simple beach cabanas, modern hotel rooms, and luxury villas within the same resort. The most important considerations are location (on the beach, on Quinta, or in town), budget, and desired atmosphere (romantic, singles, quiet, traditional). The selections in this chapter are organized into three different budget categories—budget, midrange, and luxury—and within each category there are a wide range of choices to please a wide range of tastes.

BUDGET HOTELS

Generally located a few blocks from the beach, between the town square and 30th Street, these properties are considered to be clean and safe but don't have many of the amenities that many travelers are accustomed to. Most don't have swimming pools, beautiful views, or on-site restaurants, and the rooms may not have in-room bathrooms, air-conditioning, or balconies. Prices range from $15 for a bed in a hostel dorm room to $65 for a well-kept room in a family-run inn with

There are dozens of budget hotels within a short walking distance of the bus station.

ceiling fan, purified water, and in-room safe. These hotels are popular with budget travelers, students, and short-term visitors who just need a place to stay for a couple of days while traveling through.

The 16-room Italian-owned ★ Antigua Posada Barrio Latino (Fourth Street between 10th and 15th avenues, 984-873-2384, www.posada barriolatino.com) is a popular base for Europeans, student travelers, and those who could stay at one of the more luxurious properties around town but choose the smaller inn for its local charm, traditional character, and fami-ly-like service. Just 1½ blocks from Quinta, the hotel provides quick access to the town's restaurants and nightlife. Rooms are secure and clean, with pri-vate bathrooms and ceiling fans. Many have air-conditioning. The owners can book most of the same tours that the larger tour agencies can, but they return their sales commission to their guests, resulting in a nice discount.

With less than 20 rooms, a com-mon terrace, and a rooftop sundeck, the three-story Banana Hotel (Quinta at 32nd Street, 984-803-0201, www .hotelbanana.net) has the feel of a large and friendly home. Set in the middle of the action, it's a few blocks from Kool and Mamita's beach clubs. The young and outgoing staff can make local rec-ommendations and plan day trips.

There's always something going on at Siesta Fiesta (Quinta between Eighth and 10th streets, 984-803-1166, www.siestafiestahotel.com), a hot spot in the middle of Playa's busy pedestrian walkway, which can be a good or bad thing. A restaurant and bar in the cozy courtyard features several hours of live music each night and a large-screen TV for live sporting events and recorded concerts. Vacation camaraderie is espe-cially strong here, making it a great spot to meet and socialize with other travelers.

The friendly, family-run, 12-room ★ Pension San Juan (Quinta between Sixth and Eighth streets, 984-873-0647, www.pensionsanjuan.com) is located right on Quinta. There is an incredibly charming outdoor kitchen for guest use on a terrace overlooking Quinta, which gives you the sense that you're in your own private café.

The small, 16-room, Hotel Alux (14th Street between 10th and 15th avenues, 984-803-2482, www.hotel alux.com) features contemporary Mexican design and hacienda-inspired furnishings—a good choice for visitors who don't mind being a couple of blocks removed from the action.

A longtime favorite for budget travelers, the 36-room Hotel Vista Caribe (Quinta at Sixth Street, 984-873-0349, www.hotelvistacaribe.com)

The Pension San Juan is a budget-minded hotel on Fifth Avenue.

25 Popular Spots for Student Travelers

1. 100% Natural restaurant (Cancún & Playa del Carmen)

2. Antigua Posada Barrio Latino hotel (Playa del Carmen)

3. Babe's Noodle House restaurant (Playa del Carmen)

4. Banana Hotel (Playa del Carmen)

5. Blue Parrot bar (Playa del Carmen)

6. Cabañas Copal clothing-optional hotel (Tulum)

7. Casa Tequila-La Tequilaria Shop & Bar (Playa del Carmen)

8. Coco Maya Beach Club (Playa del Carmen)

9. Colores Mexicanos Hostel (Playa del Carmen)

10. El Farolito restaurant (Playa del Carmen)

11. El Fogon restaurant (Playa del Carmen)

12. El Oasis restaurant (Playa del Carmen)

13. Hostel Playa (Playa del Carmen)

14. Hotel Bucaneros (Isla Mujeres)

15. Java Joe's coffee shop (Playa del Carmen)

16. La Zebra Beachfront Cabanas & Cantina (Tulum)

17. Litros bar (Playa del Carmen)

18. Marsan grocery store (Playa del Carmen)

19. Mezcalinna bar (Playa del Carmen)

20. Pizza Pazza restaurant (Playa del Carmen)

21. Screamink Tattoos (Playa del Carmen)

22. Señor Frog's bar (Playa del Carmen)

23. The Weary Traveler hostel (Tulum)

24. Urban Hostel (Playa del Carmen)

25. Vagabunda restaurant (Playa del Carmen)

has a great location on Quinta only a block from the beach and boasts a small swimming pool and flower garden.

The family-owned 29-room Maya Bric/Tank-Ha Hotel (Quinta between Eighth and 10th streets, 984-873-0011 or 984-873-0302, www.mayabric.com or www.tankha.com) is a good spot to meet other divers if you need a dive buddy. It has two names and Web sites, but is really the same place. Maya Bric is the original name of the hotel, and Tank-Ha is the on-site dive shop and the name used when marketing the hotel to divers. There is a shaded pool for basic dive instruction and

divers can book their trips on-site.

With its stucco walls, palapa roof, green grass, and stone walkways, La Ziranda (Fourth Street between 15th and 20th avenues, 984-873-3933, www .hotellaziranda.com) charms from the moment you see it. Each of the 16 rooms opens onto a grassy courtyard. No credit cards.

One of Playa's original hotels, the 14-room Posada Las Iguanas (Constituyentes at 1st Street, www.posadalas iguanas.com) still retains its small-town charm. The relaxing pool is located amid a tropical garden filled with flowering plants.

Ocean Safety

Many beaches along the Riviera Maya use a colored flag system to alert swimmers of the ocean's condition:

Black: No swimming allowed. Used to denote swift current, dangerous tides, lightning, or other serious problems. Seldom seen and should be taken very seriously.

Red: Caution urged. Dangerous conditions possible. Used to mark crashing waves, presence of rocks, or other potential hazards. Common at high tide or on windy days. Good swimmers can still enter the water but should be careful.

Yellow: Stay alert. No known issues, but swimmers should stay aware. Most common flag flown in the area. Used on all but the calmest of days. Competent swimmers should not be dissuaded from enjoying the water.

Green: Ideal conditions. Safest swimming possible. Seen only on the best of days.

Student, single, and extreme budget travelers also have some great local spots to choose from. Located about half a mile from the beach and directly across from the Walmart, the inexpensive Hostel Playa (25th Avenue at 8th Street, 984-803-3277, www.hostelplaya.com) is a good alternative for students and budget travelers who want a safe spot without frills. Rooms feature a natural wood motif and have mosquito netting, orthopedic mattresses, and clean bedding. Guests can use a fully equipped kitchen and a common living room with sofas, TV, and DVD player. At night, the central lounge area takes on an almost magical atmosphere, conjuring visions of a granola-traveler's version of the Hogwarts dining room, as small groups gather around tables drinking beer, digging through guidebooks, and sharing tales from the road. Cash only.

Topped with a *palapa* and filled with budget travelers from around the globe, student favorite Urban Hostel (10th Avenue between Fourth and Sixth streets, www.urbanhostel.com.mx) has bunkrooms, private rooms, communal bathrooms, basic kitchen and laundry facilities, and a lounge area with TV, and a computer with free Internet access.

Affordable and safe, Colores Mexicanos Hostel (15th Avenue between 2nd Street and Juarez Avenue, 984-873-3701) is a great spot to meet other travelers. It offers private rooms and four-person dormitories a few blocks from the beach and the downtown bus station.

MIDRANGE HOTELS

Located on or near Quinta, or even on the beach, these hotels are sufficient for most travelers. Many have swimming pools, restaurants, bars, and other amenities. They generally have air-conditioning, and all have private bathrooms. Prices range from $60 for a standard hotel off the beach to $120 for a property with a premier location (on Quinta or the beach), air-conditioning, and upgraded amenities. They are popular with travelers who want to stay somewhere comfortable with a local feel, without spending too much money.

The 29-room ★ Fusion Hotel (Sixth Street at the beach, 984-873-0374 or 1-800-224-6250 from the U.S., www.fusionhotelmexico.com) has a great beachfront location, just a block from the most bustling part of Quinta. The rooms are oriented around a central courtyard and are reminiscent of a Spanish villa, with winding staircases and meandering sidewalks. The beach club features a nightly fire show.

Open in 1984, ★ La Rana Cansada (10th Street between Quinta and 10th avenues, 984-873-0389, www.rana cansada.com) is one of Playa's oldest and most beloved hotels. Loyal guests return year after year for the consistently comfortable colonial-style

accommodations, central location, true beachtown ambience, and friendly service from the Swedish hosts and Maya staff. Just a couple blocks from the beach and a half-block from Quinta, the hotel has 15 simple, individually designed rooms (upgrades with air-conditioning are available), a community kitchen, and a lounge area.

One of the original beach hotels in Playa, the modest 38-room colonial-style Costa del Mar (First Avenue between 10th and 12th streets, 984-873-0850, www.hotelcostadelmar.com) has kept up with the times but retained its simple and relaxing nature. The beachfront El Pirata serves draft beer and snacks at a wooden bar with swinging bar stools. Directly adjacent to the Blue Parrot bar (see Drinks & Dancing), guests have ready access to the nighttime revelry. Rooms near the beach can be a bit loud at night, so

The beach at the Fusion Hotel has drinks and snacks during the day and a fire dancer show each evening.

choose one near the street if you want to go to bed before the clubs close.

The artsy 18-room Eclipse Hotel (First Avenue between 12th and 14th streets, 984-873-0629, www .hoteleclipse.com) has themed rooms, including the two-story Robinson Crusoe Suite, the De Luxe Suite, and the Caribbean Palapa Suite. Each eclectic and casually rustic room features original décor and artwork, a unique floor plan, wooden furnishings, and other extras, including some with air-conditioning. The courtyard has some large palm trees, hammocks, and gardens. It is a favorite of traveling artists, young couples, backpackers, and others who enjoy character and charm in their accommodations. The German owner speaks several languages, has been in the area for years, and is happy to dispense excursion-planning advice.

With shaded hammocks set amidst a lagoonlike sunken garden and waterfall, ★ Luna Blue Hotel & Gardens (26th Street between Quinta and 10th avenues, 984-873-0990, www.lunablue hotel.com) evokes a lost-in-time quality not always easy to find in a modern resort destination. Formerly known as the Zanzibar, it was completely renovated in late 2005, partly with the help of Hurricane Wilma and partly with the help of the ambitious new owners from San Francisco, who have worked to constantly update and refine the hotel, both inside and out.

Even though it's right on Quinta, the similarly named Hotel Lunata (Quinta between Sixth and Eighth streets, 984-873-0884, www.lunata .com) also seems somewhat secluded, given its narrow entrance through a private hall, adding an air of privacy and sophistication not found in other downtown hotels. The décor is contemporary hacienda style, designed by architect Angel Isles, with archways, earth tones and blues, river stones, dark woods, iron, and tile. The hotel has the feeling of an old-style guesthouse, with only 10 rooms, each with its distinct charm.

The relaxed 28-unit Blue Beach Hotel (on the beach between 12th and 14th streets, 984-873-1204, www.blue beachhotel.com) features a range of room styles and prices. Although the beach is a bit rocky, and the shallows have many fishing boats with their anchors stretched to the beach, it offers convenient access to the downtown beaches and entertainment.

Hotel Quinto Sol (Quinta at 28th Street, 984-873-3292, www.hotelquinto sol.com) is a Mediterranean/Mexican hacienda-style hotel in the heart of Quinta's international section. The midsize hotel has much of the same style and class as some of the area's more expensive hotels, yet its prices are more moderate.

Located above a busy restaurant and bar, the 14 rooms and penthouse suite at ★ Posada Freud (Quinta between Eighth and 10th streets, 984-873-0601, www.posadafreud.com) define *funky chic.* Request a room with air-conditioning.

Slightly reminiscent of Melrose Place, the 18-room condo-style Adelia Maria Suites (First Avenue between 24th and 26th streets, 984-879-3393) has a courtyard pool and friendly, social atmosphere.

LUXURY HOTELS

The best of the best, these hotels and resorts cater to international travelers accustomed to the finer things. Most big hotels have multiple swimming pools, restaurants, bars, fitness rooms, business centers, and concierge service. The smaller concept hotels are lighter on on-site amenities, but high on style and status. All generally have efficient air-conditioning, satellite TV, spacious rooms, well-designed bathrooms, guest balconies, and on-site restaurants, and many also have room service, Internet access, and other amenities associated with a first-class hotel. Room rates range from $125 per night for a highly rated tourist-class hotel up to more than $500 per night for a room at a top-of-the-line, all-inclusive resort.

Constructed on the former site of Playa's original nudist beach, the family-friendly, all-inclusive, 287-room ♂ ★ Gran Porto Real Playa del Carmen (Constituyentes Avenue at the beach, 984-873-4000, www.realresorts.com) was the first large-scale hotel built on the town's main tourist strip rather than Playacar. It has Italian and Mediterranean décor and overlooks a waveless cove at the southern end of Playa's central beach. There are five restaurants, four bars, a nice pool, a car rental desk, a day spa, and a kids' club. Guest favorites include the 24-Hour Room that's always stocked with snacks, drinks, and even bottles of booze; and the thatched-roof beach bar, with rope-swing barstools, and a view of the entire main bay. This is also one of the very few hotels with a view of the sunset over the ocean. Perfect for guests that like the full range of services offered by a large-scale resort but want to be in the middle of the Playa del Carmen bustle rather than tucked away in Playacar or further out in the Riviera Maya.

Its sister property across the street, the adults-only ★ ♂ THE ROYAL Resort Playa del Carmen (Constituyentes between First Avenue and the beach, 984-877-2900, www.realresorts.com) is even more upscale. With 418 rooms and a grandiose porti-

co reminiscent of Cancún or even Las Vegas, it is by far the largest hotel on the Playa del Carmen side of town. A large concrete dock stretches out from the beach in front of the hotel, but the sand itself is great, the water is calm, and it's one of the better beaches in the area. In fact, it's the site of many weddings, which make for a fun distraction for the sun-worshippers that always inhabit the waterfront area. It has six restaurants, four bars, a massive pool, an ultraluxe day spa, a temazcal sweat lodge, and a full fitness center. Next door is Mamita's Beach Club, a popular day-tripping site for cruise passengers and trendy beach-goers.

Located in the newly bustling northern part of Quinta, the independently owned, adults-only ★ Casa Ticul Hotel (Quinta between 38th and 40th streets. 984-267-3501, www.casaticul .com) opened in early 2008. Although named after an old Yucatán city south of Mérida known for clay pottery and leather shoes, the environs here are decidedly more contemporary. A cozy lobby feels like a stylish home in 1930s Europe and the quaint courtyard, small pool, and sundeck look especially charming after the sun goes down. Thoroughly modern, the 20 rooms feature dark wood furnishings, luxury bedding with pillow-top mattresses, and nice bathrooms with rain showers. A great stretch of beach is 2½ blocks away.

SOMETIMES IT SEEMS that all the small Playa hotels aspire to belong to the new guard of concept hotels, but there are some noteworthy standouts.

Built around a central pool and swanky bar, ★ Hotel Deseo (Quinta and 12th Street, 984-879-3620, www .hoteldeseo.com) offers 15 very minimalist, but very cool, rooms. Think Miami Beach meets Beverly Hills meets Riviera Maya. The walls are

Hit the Beach

Playa, plage, spiaggia, beach: However you say it, and in whatever language, the white powdery beaches of the Riviera Maya are undeniably—and justifiably—the region's main draw. Although not quite as flourlike as the shoreline in Cancún, the crushed-shell beaches in and around Playa del Carmen are world renowned for their softness, white color, and cleanliness.

The moon rises.

All ocean beaches in Mexico are considered federal property and are open to the public. No hotel, land owner, beach bar, or other entity may legally restrict access to the beach. That being said, it is common for hotels to cordon off an area for the exclusive use of their guests, and this is generally accepted as it seems to do more good than harm for the most number of people. All-inclusive hotels, for instance, may serve food and drinks on the beach, and it is helpful to their servers if their guests are slightly removed from other beach-goers. Some beach bars set up a perimeter around their beachfront tables and do not allow minors to enter and can even have a cover charge, but the area cannot extend all the way to the water line, so nonpatrons can still freely pass. In some spots, resorts have set up a roped-in area where their guests can use beach chairs and beach umbrellas without being hassled by passing vendors or other nonguests.

Amazing beaches abound in the Riviera Maya. Riviera Maya Destination Marketing Office

Licensed vendors can set up chairs and shaded *palapas* and can legally charge for their use. The general rule is, unless you're staying at the hotel that owns the facilities, you are not allowed to use them. Still, though, many tourists successfully beach-hop and visit a number of different beaches and rarely have problems using any lounge chair they happen by. Sometimes ordering a drink can earn you access to a good beach spot, and having a beach towel that matches the color of the ones the hotel provides helps, too.

Many of the main beaches, including the beach just north of the ferry dock in Playa and along the shallow cove of Akumal, are secured by federal lifeguards, who are well equipped and well trained to handle most emergencies. The nature parks, including Xcaret, Xel-Ha, and Tres Rios (see chapter 5), have private guards on duty to keep an eye on bathers and assist with any problems. With the lack of undertow, little poisonous marine life, clear water, and well-marked swimming areas, accidents are relatively uncommon, though, and the beaches are considered quite safe.

Some areas, though, do require a bit more caution. Keep an eye out for submerged rocks, shallow reefs, and off-course WaveRunners. Be careful also to avoid the black spiny sea urchins, floating debris, and diving into shallow water. If you're exploring remote areas, it's a good idea to stay in a group and not wander off alone. It's also important to keep in mind that although the Riviera Maya is generally safe and most of the people are friendly and welcoming, every town has its bad apples, and you don't want to encounter them. Even though the beaches are government property, locals may not take too kindly to tourists wandering too far from the beaten path and encroaching on their home territory. Be careful not to enter private property that is adjacent to the beach and be respectful of locals who have claimed a beach area for themselves.

Petty theft can be a problem anywhere, including on the beach. Keep a watchful eye on your belongings if you stray from them or, better yet, take turns playing in the waves and leave someone on the beach to watch your things. And don't assume that just because you're on a remote spot and can't see anyone that no one can see you. Stories abound of snorkelers who come back to their beach blankets after a stint on the reef only to find their bags pilfered. Although some may choose to deny that there could be crime in paradise and instead blame the pesky and ever-curious white-faced monkeys, the thieves' penchant for cash,

A lifeguard stand on Playa's main beach shines in the moonlight.

MP3 players, and digital cameras leads me to believe the culprits are looking for more than bananas.

The city police in Playa del Carmen sometimes patrol the popular beaches of town on ATVs. They are mainly looking for rowdy drunks and local drug users, so the average tourist, even a Corona-guzzling one, is almost never bothered. In some areas, generally remote beaches, the Mexican navy performs foot patrols, presumably checking for drug runners and drop-off sites. Be respectful, and they will pass by with just a friendly wave.

Playa del Carmen's most popular beach zone is just north of Constituyentes Avenue and THE ROYAL Playa del Carmen hotel (18th Street) all the way to 40th Street. This includes the KOOL, Mamita's, and Canibal Royale beach clubs.

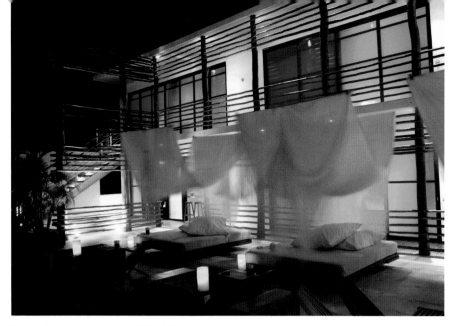

The posh outdoor lounge at Hotel Deseo   Grupo Habita

crisp white, and lounge music is piped in from the hotel bar. On the nightstand, you'll find incense, earplugs, and condoms. The beds are amazingly comfortable, and the rooms have stage lighting, so you can create your own shadowbox show, if you're so inclined. It's a good place to meet other travelers, and it's always a plus when there's a happening bar right outside your door. Best bet for the young and single crowd.

The same owners operate Hotel Básico (Quinta at 10th Street, 984-879-4448, www.hotelbasico.com), a 14-room, three-story hotel just down the road. The beige façade owes its unusual color to the Caribbean sand mixed in with concrete to form its solid walls. Designed by a well-known avant-garde firm in Mexico City called Omelet (its founder says their design style takes "huevos"), the theme is rooted in 1950s Mexico and Latin America, when oil production and construction boomed and beach vacations were a sign of prosperity. The building shines with the creative use of tile from Mérida, glass, rubber, and latex. Rooms have high beds with built-in minibar and lighting system, exposed plumbing, corner rain shower, and colored neon accent light. The patio level features a Veracruz-style seafood restaurant, and the visually striking rooftop terrace features canopy sunbeds, a trendy bar, a projection movie screen, ocean views, hammocks, and two smallish plunge pools modeled after holding tanks commonly found at Mexican oil fields. Rooms that overlook the street can get a bit loud, so consider this when choosing yours.

Although Mosquito Blue (Quinta between 12th and 14th streets, 984-873-1245, www.mosquitoblue.com) carries a Quinta address, it fronts 12th Street, somewhat concealing its entrance. Composed of a mix of Mexican and Mediterranean architecture, it oozes a hip and cool style that you'll notice as soon as you enter the lobby. The 45 rooms in the two-story building face the interior courtyard. Amenities

Local Lingo—Out on the Town

2 x 1: Look for this sign at the entrance to a bar, and you'll know that their two-for-one happy hour has begun!

Anejo con coca: *Anejo* is a golden blend of aged rum, and it goes great with Coke, making it a bit of an upgrade from a standard rum and Coke. To order one in a loud bar, grasp your chin and move your hand downward, as if stroking a beard. Then, with the same hand, hold your pinkie under your nose for a moment, then wipe it away, as if you're snorting a powdered Colombian export from under your fingernail.

Barra libre: Some bars offer *barra libre* nights, where your cover charge includes open bar, or basically all you care to drink. This normally includes bottled water, so it's a good chance to hydrate as well.

Cantinero: Spanish for "bartender."

Chela/chelada/michelada/chamochela: *Chela* is used colloquially to mean "beer." A *chelada* is a beer served in a glass of fresh lime juice and salt. For a real local treat, try a *michelada*—a *chelada* plus Worcestershire sauce, Tabasco sauce, and tomato juice. A recent twist, a *chamochela,* adds a tamarind-like fruit called a chamoy to the traditional *michelada.*

Consumo minimo: Translating from Spanish into "minimum consumption," it's a common policy at popular bars and clubs, where instead of a cover charge, your entry fee includes drink coupons equivalent in value to the amount you pay to get in. Such a policy keeps out patrons who just want to socialize and dance but not buy anything.

Cuba libre: "One revolution is still necessary: the one that will not end with the rule of its leader," wrote Cuban spiritualist José Martí, describing his desire for a free Cuba, which in Spanish is *Cuba libre.* It's also the name used locally for a rum and Coke, served with a wedge of lime. In the Riviera Maya, bartenders will still understand if you just order a "Cuba."

Desechable: Remember, no bottles on the street, so if you want your drink to go, ask for it in a *desechable,* and it will come in a Styrofoam cup. Many bars also have a stack of disposable cups at the exit, so if you've got one for the road, leave your glass behind.

En las rocas: Spanish for "on the rocks." Try your margarita *en las rocas* and earn a bit of respect from your *cantinero.*

Frog's/Carlos: Abbreviated versions of Señor Frog's and Carlos'n Charlie's, it's how the locals refer to the popular drinking establishments.

Lager: Used when ordering a Dos Equis (XX) beer in the green bottle, as opposed to the XX Amber, which is the dark beer in the tinted bottle. You can also hold your index fingers together to form an *X* in front of you, then pump your hands twice, indicating *dos equis,* or "two Xs." To order two or more Dos Equis, first flash the number of drinks you want with your fingers, then proceed to make the *X* sign.

Nohoch: The Mayan word for "big." Order your favorite cocktail *nohoch,* and it'll be served in a tall glass.

Hotel Básico is an award-winning "concept hotel." Grupo Habita

include a library, a lounge area, a pool, and an on-site restaurant specializing in Italian cuisine and imported wines. It's a great choice for couples and singles seeking to impress new friends.

Meanwhile, the boutique beachfront ★ Mosquito Beach Hotel (on the beach between 12th and 14th streets, 984-873-1245, www.mosquito beachhotel.com) sets itself apart from its sister property with an on-site Mayan spa, sleek furnishings, premium bedding, and an exclusive style that exudes a sense of privilege and superiority, right down to the trendy red and black lounge chairs along the hotel beach.

One of Playa's tallest buildings, the literally over-the-top Hotel Reina Roja (20th Street between Quinta and 10th avenues, 984-877-3800, www.reinaroja hotel.com), glows red from the outside and approaching visitors will spot it a block away. Mexican-owned, the hotel evokes Amsterdam's red-light district with bondage mannequins on display and its crimson glow that's replicated in

the guestrooms. A party hotel for party people, it features a large bar, popular with the locals, and a massive rooftop bar with city views and a swimming pool. Five themed rooms—including the "After Hours Room" with DJ booth, disco lights, dance floor, and outdoor smoking area—are available for the extra indulgent. This isn't a

Mannequins at play at the Reina Roja bar.

exactly a cozy place, but it's very high in gimmick value, making it good for wooing a date or looking like you're in-the-know.

Guests traverse a wooden bridge from Quinta to reach the calmer lobby of the upscale ★ Blue Parrot Fifth Avenue (Quinta between 10th and 12th streets, 984-879-4781 or 1-800-435-0668 from the U.S., www.blue parrot.com), the most recent extension of the local Blue Parrot brand. Eighteen spacious, Asian-inspired rooms are complemented by a Thai-influenced restaurant and bar, adorned with ornate *palapas* and perched above a decorative pool. The scene is much more serene and sophisticated than at Blue Parrot's beachfront location, where guests have privileges at the Blue Parrot beach club.

The 22 units at the affiliated Blue Parrot Suites (First Avenue at 14th Street, 984-873-0083, www.blueparrot .com) have Bahamas-like contemporary rattan décor with modern amenities and name-brand furnishings. A bit removed from the rest of the beach-front Blue Parrot complex, it is quite calm and relaxing. There is a small pool, and the beach is only a block away. Check in at the Blue Parrot bar on 12th Street 1½ blocks away.

Playa Palms (the beach between 12th and Fourth streets, 984-803-3908, www.playapalms.com) was known as the Blue Parrot until 2007 and this essentially remains the hotel at the Blue Parrot bar. As such, it offers the quintessential Playa del Carmen experience. It's more of a tropical community center than a hotel. Housed in a condo-style complex a block away from the reception and bar area, the 39 luxury rooms are spacious studios and suites with contemporary/tropical décor. A few have oceanfront views, but most are set back a bit from the beach, looking across at other units, with a partial ocean view to one side. There is a narrow pool between the buildings and a welcomingly shady courtyard. There is also a small group of rustic beachfront bungalows just north of the beach bar.

With 25 rooms, the Aventura Mexicana (22nd Street at 10th Avenue, 984-873-1876, www.aventuramexicana .com) boutique hotel is large enough to have a nice pool, two outdoor Jacuzzis, and gourmet restaurant, but still small enough to benefit from personal serv-ice, a tranquil atmosphere, and a dose of class. The décor is reminiscent of a Mexican hacienda, but with many modern upgrades. It has multiple sun-decks where sunbathing in various states of undress tends to occur and is particularly popular with gay travelers.

Built above a restaurant in Playa's

The Playa Palms hotel is on the beach and just a block from Fifth Avenue.

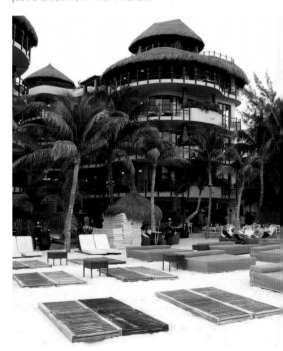

It May Be Paradise, but It's Still the Jungle

Even though Playa del Carmen and the Riviera Maya are exotic and wonderful beach vacation destinations, they're still relatively undeveloped and are in close proximity to the jungle. Set your expectations accordingly.

You should also remember that there are hassles and frustrations inherent to any travel situation. You're on vacation to have fun and celebrate life, so try not to let little challenges you encounter bother you.

If a chicken walks into your beachfront restaurant and pecks at your crumbs, don't get mad—take a picture. If a gecko streaks across the wall of your hotel room, don't call the front desk—give him a name and consider him your pet. If your shower runs out of hot water, don't complain to the concierge—it's good for your sunburn. And most important, if you find yourself at odds with your travel partner, it's time to hit the nearest bar, order a margarita, feel the warm breeze, and remember why you came here in the first place.

happening international district, the upscale, Argentinean-owned executive-style ★ Quinta Palmera Boutique Hotel (Quinta at 30th Street, 984-803-5007, www.quintapalmera.com) has only six rooms. It's great for guests seeking an urban loft–like lifestyle over the scrubby beach ambience common to many local inns.

Also offering minimalist rooms, a swanky lobby, and channeling the spirit of Fashion Week, In Fashion Hotel Boutique (North 12th Street between Quinta and 10th avenues, 984-879-4740, www.infashionhotel.com) was designed to please the critical tastes of traveling divas, trendsetters, and other fashionistas. Across from Coco Bongo, the hotel has a swimming pool on the second level and overlooks the nightly street party on Zona Doce. Original paintings, sculpture, and photography are featured throughout this venue that's part Mexico City, part New York.

Another recent arrival to Playa's stylish boutique hotel scene, the up-scale Hotel El Punto (Quinta and 8th Street, 984-803-0288, www.hotelel punto.com) uses deep reds, dark wood,

and natural stone to offset its elegant, understated style. A rooftop bar and tapas restaurant overlooks the ocean.

OTHER AREA HOTELS celebrate the local, relaxed character of traditional Playa or the region in general. One of Playa's original hotels, ☞ ★ Las Pala-pas (34th Street at the beach, 984-873-0616, www.laspalapas.com) is still one of its most revered. It's a bit north of the main strip, so the beach is a touch more secluded, with no rocks, making it a great place to play in the water. Amenities include a shady pool, Mayan-inspired lawn art, and an inter-pretive walking trail through the jun-gle. The hotel's 75 rooms are housed in spacious individual cabanas near the beach or in two-story villalike build-ings around a pair of grassy courtyards. The beachfront rooms don't have air-conditioning, but most of the rest do.

Appearing a bit Mediterranean, with cool blues and whites, the Playa Maya Hotel (on the beach between Sixth and Eighth streets, 984-803-2022, www.playa-maya.com) can only be reached by the beach, making it

The second-story pool at the In Fashion Hotel.   In Fashion Hotel

one of the few places in town where you get to feel the sand each time you come and go. Family owned, the hotel has 20 rooms, giving it an intimate and relaxed feeling absent at some of Playa's more-trendy options. A small pool makes for a nice dip, though the beachfront is the main attraction. It's one of the best in the area with sandy water access, generally calm waves, and plenty of bikini-clad (or not) people-watching. A casual seaside restaurant serves up delicious coconut shrimp, fish ceviche, and other seafood and Mexican dishes.

This eight-villa collection of Blue Pearl Suites (1st Avenue between 10th and 12th streets, 1-888-898-9922 from the U.S., www.thebluepearl.com.mx) feels more like a private apartment complex than a hotel. Located just a half-block from Zona Doce, it somehow retains its privacy and serenity. The owners, a charming couple from Mexico City, moved to Playa to live out a stress-free life focusing on conservation, recycling, and natural living. All units feature local handcrafts, natural fibers, and hammocks.

Beachfront Mahékal Beach Resort (38th Street and Quinta, 800-836-8942 or 1-877-235-4452 from the U.S., www.mahekalplaya.com) is laid out like an old Mayan village, with low-rise, thatched-roof cabanas housing most of the rooms. One of the original hotels built in the area, it retains its local charm while keeping the facilities up-to-date. It is one of the last hotels on the northern edge of town, offering a remote sense of privacy.

★ Villas Sacbe (First Avenue between 12th and 14th streets, 984-879-3918, www.villasacbe.com) offers privately owned one- and two-bedroom condos, each with its own unique and trendy décor. The complex has a narrow, meandering pool and Jacuzzi, and it's a great place to stay in luxury and still be close to the Zona Doce.

5 Welcoming Hotels for Gay & Lesbian Travelers

Although gay travelers are generally welcomed throughout the region, these spots make a particular effort to attract and engage gay travelers. For more gay-friendly options, visit www.purpleroofs.com.

1. Aventura Mexicana hotel (Playa del Carmen) Gay men from around the world often mix with straight couples and European travelers at this 48-room hotel with a rooftop Jacuzzi and sundeck.

2. Hotel Secreto (Isla Mujeres) Same sex couples fit right in at this stylish, private island boutique.

3. In Fashion Boutique Hotel (Playa del Carmen) Aspiring to be all things fashionable, this new hotel highlights art, fashion, and minimalist style, and markets itself to the *Project Runway* set.

4. Le Rêve Hotel & Spa (Punta Bete) This small upscale resort caters to couples and encourages gay groups to rent out the entire hotel for private parties, dedication ceremonies, and celebrations.

5. Mosquito Beach Hotel (Playa del Carmen) This stylish beachfront boutique is popular choice for gay travelers.

Many of the guests at the Playa Maya Hotel visit each year. Playa Maya Hotel

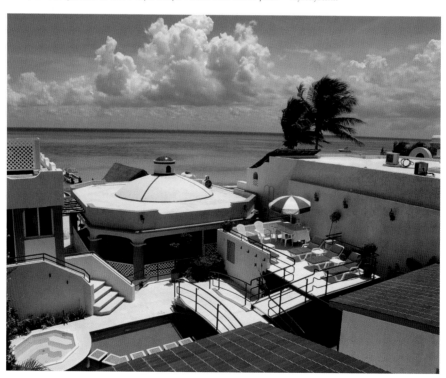

Although located on a fairly busy intersection blocks from Playa's busy International District, solitude and relaxation await just inside ✿ Arena Blanca's (38th Street between Quinta and 10th avenues) locked gates and stone walls. A small table seems to float like an island in the center of the swimming pool, visible from each of the 11 rooms in the three-story, classic Spanish building. Units, with domed brick Catalan ceilings, premium linens, tile floors, and marble countertops, are individually owned. Make reservations on such Web sites as VRBO.com, HomeAway.com, or the locally operated www.PlayaisFun.com.

Asian design influences abound at the ★ Aldea Thai Resort (28th Street and the beach, 984-803-1400, ext. 403 or 1-866-473-4421 from the U.S., www .aldeathairesort.com), including ornamental statues set throughout the grounds. Thatched roofs, dark stone tiles, exposed natural wood beams, and sleek accents ensure a modern and upscale tropical environment.

On a corner, just a block off Quinta and around the corner from the calle Corazón district, the 45-room La Tortuga (10th Avenue and 14th Street, 984-873-1484, www.hotellatortuga .com) offers stylish rooms and a private and upscale ambience.

Local Flavors

Taste of the town—restaurants, cafés, bars, bistros, etc.

Playa del Carmen offers an incredibly wide variety of cuisine types and dining establishments. From hole-in-the-wall taco shacks offering complete meals for less than $3 and traditional Mexican steakhouses serving fine cuts of Angus beef and live lobster to stylish lounge-style restaurants serving Mediterranean and international cuisine, Playa is sure to please.

Breakfasts are normally inexpensive, with many restaurants posting their specials on a chalkboard out front. Choices include traditional Mexican dishes such as *pan dulce* (sweet pastry), huevos rancheros (ranch-style eggs) and *huevos mexicanos* (Mexican-style eggs), and there are also American favorites such as pancakes, omelets, and steak and eggs, and European classics such as bagels and lox, croissants, and crêpes.

Lunch is generally quite casual, with many travelers choosing to eat fresh seafood, sandwiches, or burgers on the beach or next to their hotel pool. Most restaurants in town are open for lunch, too, with happy-hour specials starting early and plenty of seats available at the sidewalk restaurants along Quinta.

Once the sun goes down and the stars come out, the lights of the restaurants, bars, and shops of Playa's main street start to twinkle, and candlelight glows from many eateries. The town begins to feel a bit like an international bazaar, with the restaurants competing for your business, hawking their specials, offering free drinks with a meal purchase, and tempting diners with live music, wafting smells, and attractive hostesses.

Choosing where to eat is sometimes half the fun, with many visitors making several laps along the entire 2-mile-long street, checking out the night's offerings and taking in the scene. Many restaurants put together sample entrées and place them on display next to their menus, showing you

Not sure what to eat? Walk down Fifth Avenue for some ideas. Ricardo Vagg

the exact size of their plump steaks, lobster tails, giant shrimp, or fish fillets. Each block has several options to choose from and one famous block, on Quinta between 28th and 30th streets, there are 12 restaurants, including seven intimate eateries in a row, each three tables wide and two or three rows deep, ranging from a Mediterranean restaurant offering lamb and hookah pipes to an Asian noodle house to an Argentinean steakhouse.

If you're not sure what you're in the mood for or if you have a group of travelers with varied tastes, you're in luck, as many of the restaurants have extensive menus, spanning the range from tacos to pasta, from fish to steak, and from pizza to burgers.

Restaurants in this book are labeled *inexpensive, moderate,* or *expensive.* The average meal price at an inexpensive restaurant is less than $7 per person. Moderate restaurant

meal prices range from $7 to $20. Expensive restaurants offer meals starting at $21 and higher.

All of the locations in the *Budget Dining* section are ultracasual eateries catering to locals, students, and other budget travelers. They're good places to sample the local fare and use your Spanish. They typically don't accept credit cards and may have restrooms that aren't up to the cleanliness standards expected by some travelers. They're still regulated by the health department and serve only purified ice and water.

BUDGET DINING

One of Playa's original taco restaurants, hole-in-the-wall ★ Las Arracheras (First Avenue South between 15th and 20th avenues) is still one of the best, selling fantastic grilled meats for a price that makes you want to go back

Peso-Pinching Activities

Traveling on a budget? Try these free and fun activities:

- Take free salsa lessons Tuesday and Thursday at 7 PM at La Bodeguita del Medio (see Dining).
- Walk along the interpretive nature trail at the back of the parking lot of the Las Palapas hotel (see Luxury Hotels).
- Visit the Xaman Ha ruins in Playacar, just south of the Playacar Palace hotel (see chapter 2).
- Head to the beach and build a sandcastle in the shape of the great pyramid at Chichén Itzá.
- Get up early to watch the sun rise over the Caribbean. Some people like it even more than watching a sunset.
- Take advantage of the free appetizer/drink coupons offered by many restaurants along Quinta in Playa del Carmen.
- Stroll the park across from the municipal building and learn to count in Mayan from the educational displays.
- Grab your snorkel and take a dip in Manatee *cenote,* across from Blue Sky Resort in Tankah (see chapter 2).
- Watch the fire dancers perform their nightly show on the beach of the Blue Parrot bar (see Drinks & Dancing) at 11 PM.
- Join the locals for a street party in Cozumel, complete with live music, each Sunday evening in the town square.
- Snorkel the protected cove at Akumal Bay and see moray eels, stingrays, and barracuda lurking in the shallows.

Don't forget to bargain at souvenir shops.

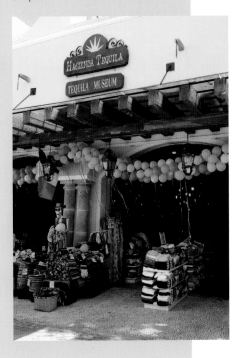

every night. Sit at plastic tables and sip a cold drink while you pile your sliced meats high on corn tortillas, add spicy salsas, and enjoy the taste and atmosphere of the "real Mexico"—only a five-minute walk from the start of the main tourist district.

The casual Argentinean-owned

★ Tango Taco (10th Street between 10th and 15th avenues) serves up Argentinean meats, Mexican tacos, and amazing prices (huge grilled steaks go for about $10) just a block off Quinta. Closed Mondays.

★ El Fogon (30th Avenue between Fourth and Sixth streets, in front of Harmon Hall) serves a mixed-grill plate (*parrillada mixta*) big enough to serve three people. Try the fried nopal cactus.

A favorite with locals and ex-pats, the palapa-shaded ★ Vagabunda (Quinta between 24th and 26th streets) serves traditional American and Mexican breakfasts, crêpes, omelets, pastas, and cappuccino.

After their shifts, you may spy your bartender or waiter at the 24-hour, cheap and tasty El Fogoncito (30th Avenue between 28th and 30th streets). Top dishes include tacos *al pastor* (cut right from the fire) and fried meat sandwiches served on a toasted bun, called *tortas de carne.*

You can also eat seafood with the locals at Coctelería el Paisano Veracruz (avenida Juárez, just west of Highway 307), specializing in shrimp cocktail but also serving fried fish, ceviche, and other dishes. It's located away from the tourist zone, and you're likely to be the only traveler there. Most of the waiters don't speak English, but don't let that keep you away. Chances are you'll be able to communicate enough to order or someone at the restaurant can help translate.

El Faisán y El Venado (Highway 307, just north of avenida Juárez) is a popular local spot for tacos, quesadillas, and seafood. At midday workers fill the plastic tables and order from the *comida corrida* menu, which offers hearty meals prepared and served quickly.

Just like the busy taco stands near where the locals live, the popular Aca Los Tacos (Constituyentes at Quinta) serves fresh, hot tacos *al pastor* (cut right from the fire), beef tacos, and cheese tacos. Tables along the patio overlook the traffic circle near THE ROYAL Resort. Open 11 AM–1 AM daily.

Killer Taco (First Avenue between 10th and 12th streets) a good place for

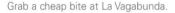

Grab a cheap bite at La Vagabunda.

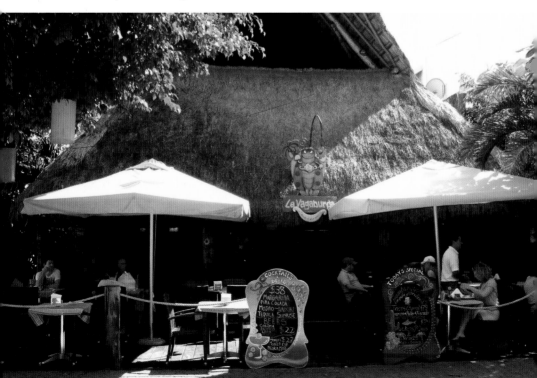

Dine for Less than $15/Day

Get a cup of fresh fruit (with salt and lime) for $1 at the town square.

Breakfast—Tequila Barrel: Huevos rancheros served with refried beans, toast, and coffee ($5).

Lunch—Cart next to the town square bus station: Plump chicken tamales steamed in banana leaves ($1.50/each).

Dinner—Vagabunda: A value-conscious restaurant in the heart of New Playa. Fresh tacos with tangy salsa. ($4.50).

Drinks—Pick up a quart of beer from a grocery or convenience store and sit on the seawall in the town square, watching the world go by.

---

cheap tacos on the way to or from 12th Street. The menu is written on a chalkboard and features beef tacos, quesadillas, burritos, and even pork tacos *al pastor,* cut right from the spit. Everything on the menu is $5 or less. They don't sell alcoholic drinks, but feel free to stop next door and get a beer to go. Cash only. Open late.

If you're tired of tacos, slices start at $1.50 at Pizza Pazza (Quinta at 14th Street; 10th Avenue between Eighth and 10th streets), and drink combos are available. Open late, they're a favorite for satisfying after-party munchies.

MEXICAN & MAYAN

With a great mix of authentic food, entertaining waiters, good service, and a great location, ★ Ajua Maya Lobster & Steak House (Fourth Street between Quinta and 10th avenues, 984-873-2523 or 818-581-4075 from the U.S., www.ajuamaya.com) has become very popular with repeat

guests. The owners are on-site most of the time and are great at remembering the names of customers they may see only once or twice each year. Food ranges from traditional Mayan dishes to lobster, fish, Black Angus beef, flambés, Caesar salads, pasta, fish tacos, and Mexican favorites. Upstairs, ★ ♂ Hacienda Maya (www.hacienda maya.com) offers upscale dining on a palapa-covered balcony. Here, the owners of Ajua Maya serve 19th-century French-influenced Mayan and Mexican cuisine, with dishes featuring Angus beef, venison, Cornish game hens, breast of duck, and prawns. The candlelit restaurant is a great spot for a romantic date and both restaurants are great spots for rehearsal dinners, wedding receptions, and special-event meals.

Feeling more like a private party at a stately hacienda in rural Mexico than a beachtown restaurant, ★ La Adela (Quinta between Sixth and Eighth streets) offers some of Playa's best Mexican food and a warm and

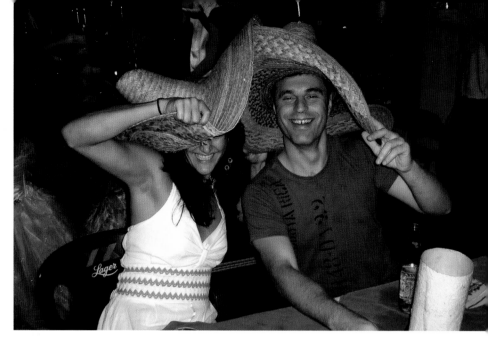

You'll say "Ajuuuuuaaaa!!!" when you go to Ajua Maya cantina.

inviting atmosphere that makes diners want to linger and soak it all in. Upscale Mexican cuisine, mole enchiladas, and seafood top the menu. Diners are drawn to the combination of traditional and whimsical décor, but it's the food that brings them back for a second time. Seating is available indoors or outside on the pedestrian walkway.

Occupying a prime corner at the northern edge of the paseo del Carmen Mall, Carlos'n Charlie's (10th Avenue at First Street, 984-803-3953, www.carlosandcharlies.com) could be called the anchor tenant of the entire shopping plaza. This Mexico standard offers consistently good Mexican food, seafood, and pasta, though the main draws are the lively atmosphere, unique décor, and friendly waiters.

⭐ La Cueva del Chango (38th Street between Quinta and the beach, 984-804-9190), or the "Monkey Cave," is an eclectic spot that manages to be rustic, funky, and romantic all at the same time—perfect for a special occasion or just a night out. The menu features several cuts of steak, fish, shrimp, fajitas, and other Mexican specialties. The candlelit tables are in a junglelike setting, making it very soothing and exotic.

With its Spanish-tiled roof and strolling mariachi bands, ⭐ La Parrilla (Quinta at Eighth Street. 984-873-0687) puts diners in the mood for good Mexican meals, and it delivers. The best dishes include beef fajitas, grilled shrimp, and *chiles rellenos,* and there are also fresh salads and vegetarian dishes. Save room for the flambé desserts and flaming coffees, prepared tableside. Open noon–1 AM daily.

Offering seating along the sidewalk, in a spacious red interior or on a second-story terrace overlooking Quinta, ⭐ Yaxche (Quinta at 22nd Street, 984-873-2502, www.mayacuisine.com) is one of Playa's most respected restaurants. It serves authentic Mayan cuisine, including fish, chicken, and turkey, all cooked with native methods using traditional spices. "Yaxche" is the Mayan name for *la ceiba,* a green-leafed tree believed to bring good luck. Try the Mayan Kiss after-dinner drink, made with Xtabentún and Kahlúa.

Across 16th Street from Natural Spa and above a liquor store, ★ Los Aluxes (Quinta at 16th Street) offers a quiet place to enjoy a good meal while still being near the hustle of Quinta. It has good happy-hour drink specials, and at night several tiki torches illuminate the alfresco dining area, giving the place an exotic and romantic vibe. The menu features classic Mexican specialties, plus seafood and steaks.

Occupying a prime piece of real estate on 12th Street, the lively contemporary Mexican restaurant Las Dioses (12th Street between First Avenue and the beach) has a somewhat traditional menu but an ambience and look that are far from plain. Tables are

spaced apart to allow diners a good view of the parade of revelers passing by on their way to the beach clubs for a night of partying. It's a good place to try sipping a smoky shot of mescal.

A sports bar and Mexican cantina, Pez Vela (Quinta at Second Street, 984-873-0999) has several settings in one spot: There is a bar with swinging bar stools, a central dining area with plastic tables, a few sidewalk tables, and some TV-front tables, perfect for watching live sports games, which seem to always be on. The menu, which includes tacos, grilled shrimp, and burgers, is inexpensive and good for the price. For the best deal, order beer by the bucket (five bottles).

Part of the Don Emilione hotel near the bus station, Don Emilione (Quinta at Second Street, 984-873-2073, www.donemilione.com) offers tables along the sidewalk, plus an air-conditioned dining room. Popular

Authentic Mayan food with an upscale style at Yaxche

Mayan Cuisine

Contributed by Destination Riviera Maya *magazine*

Traditional Mayan cuisine integrates the delights of land and ocean: the beans, vegetables, and fruits cultivated, mixed with the products of fishing and hunting as part of the customs of a centuries-old society. Corn, chocolate, honey, and turkey not only are the main ingredients of delicious meals and beverages but also are an integral part of Mayan religious rituals, where chocolate became known as the "drink from the gods." Numerous spices such as peppercorn, coriander, achiote (similar to paprika), and cinnamon are used to make *recados*, special seasoning pastes that enliven chicken, fish, or beef dishes. Some traditional Mayan dishes include the following:

Cochinita pibil: The word *pibil* means "to roast in a hole," and luckily, modern cooks have devised a method that requires no shovel. The dish is typically made with pork and marinated with red *recado* and bitter orange. It is wrapped in banana leaves with onions and steamed or roasted, and then served with onions marinated in vinaigrette.

If you like it spicy, ask for salsa habanero. Brian E. Miller Photography/www.lomimonk.com

Poc chuc: Char-grilled pork marinated in sour orange with black beans, purple onion, tomato, and Mayan spices.

Papadzules: Tortillas stuffed with hard-boiled eggs and covered in a pumpkin seed and tomato sauce.

Frijol con puerco: Pork and black bean stew served with chopped radish, onion, tomato, and pieces of lime, eaten with a corn tortilla.

Relleno negro: Turkey, ground beef, and hard-boiled eggs in a blackened chile sauce.

Tikinxic: A whole fish marinated in achiote and sour orange with tomato, white onion, and green pepper slices, then wrapped and grilled in a banana leaf.

Panuchos: A fried tortilla filled with refried beans, pieces of turkey or chicken, lettuce, tomato, onion, and avocado.

dishes include soup, pasta, lobster tacos, calamari, steak, shrimp, and vegetarian dishes. After your meal, order a flaming Mayan coffee and homemade cheesecake.

With its red, black, and white color scheme, El Jardín del Jaguar (Quinta at Eighth Street, 984-873-0650) seems to be stuck in the 1970s, except for the fact that most of Playa didn't exist then.

Don't sit; swing at the bar at Pez Vela.

Serving seafood, steaks, and Mexican food, the restaurant is great for people-watching.

One of the few air-conditioned restaurants on Quinta, Frida's (Quinta between 12th Street and calle Corazón) offers a Mexican menu amid décor intended to honor to Frida Kahlo. There are also patio tables for those who would rather people-watch than cool off.

Other popular stops include El Farolito (Quinta between 28th and 30th streets), an urban taqueria serving tacos, cold beer and margaritas to a mixed crowd of locals and tourists, and Origenes Cocina & Bar (Quinta at 38th Street), which uses traditional spices to prepare its contemporary Mexican cuisine. El Templo (Eighth Street between Quinta and 10th avenues) serves typical Mexican dishes on a large second-story terrace on a busy side street, an ideal spot for relaxing and sipping a cold beer.

ITALIAN

Beloved in Playa, ★ Ristorante Da Bruno (Quinta at 12th Street, 984-873-0048) is known for both its authentic Italian menu and its premium people-watching perch in the heart of Quinta. The owners and chefs are Italian, he pasta is made in-house, and the food tastes fresh and hearty. Top dishes include gnocchi, pizza, ravioli, antipasti, prosciutto, mahi-mahi, lobster, and, of course, tiramisu.

At La Fe Restaurante (Quinta

Fast Food in Paradise

Face it: After a few days of beer drinking, taco eating, and sensory overload, it's nice to be in the familiar confines of a McDonald's, Starbucks, or another American chain.

Although all chains offer the same fare you know back home, the McDonald's outlet across from the bus station is worth a peek. It may be one of the company's few franchises to sport a *palapa* roof.

Burger King
South side of the town square, by the ferry dock

Johnny Rocket's
Paseo del Carmen Mall

McDonald's
Paseo del Carmen Mall
Quinta at Second Street
Highway 307 by Chedraui

On the ferry dock, across from Señor Frog's (take-out only)

Starbucks
Quinta at 10th Street
Quinta at 28th Street

Subway
Constituyentes at 10th Avenue
Paseo del Carmen Mall

between 26th and 28th streets) you'll think you've been transported to an Italian beach town and stumbled upon a friendly neighborhood restaurant where everybody knows one another. Tables line the sidewalk and covered terrace and are filled each evening with local and visiting Italians, sipping imported wines, munching on fresh bread and feasting on pizza, pasta, and seafood dishes. The boisterous late-night crowd spills well into the blocked-off road, turning the bar scene into a bit of a street party, with techno music booming and gelato, cappuccino, wine, and tequila each being enjoyed in abundance. Italian and French voices are much more common than English or Spanish, but everyone is welcome to join in the fun.

Serving three meals a day, the sidewalk café ★ Il Baretto (Quinta at 26th Street) is also somewhat of a headquarters for the Italians residing in Quinta's international neighborhood. More than just ex-pats appreciate Il

Baretto's pasta, pizza, seafood, and beef menu items, though. The restaurant also serves imported coffee drinks, espresso, and cappuccino and is known for sumptuous desserts.

Another local favorite, the tiny sidewalk Romagna Mia (Cozumel Avenue [First Avenue] between 30th and 32nd streets) near Mamita's Beach, serves traditional Italian cuisine, including pasta carbonara, *strozzapretti,* gnocchi, and lasagne. Try the ham and cheese *piadinas*—an easy dish to share.

The Café de la Luna (Fourth Street at 15th Avenue) is an authentic spot for great pastas, pizza, lasagne, cold beer, and a decent wine selection amid pleasant outdoor seating.

Long a destination restaurant in Cozumel, Cancún, and Isla Mujeres, Rolandi's (paseo del Carmen Mall, 984-803-4121) outpost in Playa offers a casual ambience with an upscale flair. Wood-oven pizzas highlight the menu, along with pastas and desserts.

INTERNATIONAL

An elegant bar and eatery, ★ The Glass Bar (Quinta at 12th Street, www.divino.com.mx) has cushioned chairs, linen tablecloths, and personable waiters. The menu features Italian and Mediterranean food, pasta, fish, steak, and an extensive wine list, featuring selections from Mexico, the Mediterranean, and beyond. Outdoor seating is slightly less exclusive but still very upscale and comfortable, offering a great view of the goings-on along Quinta. Credit cards accepted.

Known for its gourmet Argentinean cuisine and large wine list, ★ Ula Gula (Quinta at 10th Street, 984-879-3727, www.ula-gula.com) features white linen tablecloths, candlelit tables, and a sultry but casual terraced dining room over Quinta. It is a favorite of trendy locals, American ex-pats, and visiting diners from around the world who value luxury. Downstairs from the restaurant, there's a tiny lounge on the street corner decorated in white and tan. It has a trendy vibe, with an interior decorated with candles, and a nice, romantic view of Quinta.

A French-owned gourmet restaurant and wine bar, ★ Byblos (14th Street between Quinta and 10th avenues, 984-803-1790) is one of the few other spots in town where you can enjoy a delicious dinner in an air-conditioned dining room with white linen tablecloths and exceptionally high service levels. Menu highlights include carpaccio, foie gras, pasta, risotto, grilled fish, flambéed lobster, veal chops, rabbit, New Zealand beef and lamb, duck, apple tarts, and crêpes flambéed with Grand Marnier.

At the front of Blue Parrot Fifth Avenue, the inspired "jungle-chic" ★ Playasia (Quinta between 10th and 12th streets, 984-879-4781, www.blue parrot.com) showcases a scenic waterfall, and Ewok-esque treehouse seating over a jewel-tone pool. Crystal chandeliers, glowing orbs from Morocco, and candles set a decidedly romantic tone to the entire space. The menu ranges from traditional sushi favorites to Japanese, Thai, and Vietnamese specialty dishes. The two Bangkok-inspired bars play chill-out music and are a great place to hang out, even if you're not having dinner.

You've heard of cave diving, but ★ Alux (avenida Juárez between 65th and 70th avenues, just west of Highway 307, 984-803-0703) offers cave dining. Housed deep within a natural cave, formed thousands of years ago, and featuring live music nightly, it makes for a romantic spot for dinner or a drink. The food is not the best, but the novelty of the experience more than makes up for it. Local promoters occasionally host all-night rave parties here, which can get extremely crowded and are best avoided if you're prone to claustrophobia.

Cool colors, flowing tapestries, dim lamplight, and flickering candles highlight the décor at the Mediterranean-style ★ Kartabar (12th Street at First Avenue, 984-873-2228, www.kartabar .com). The menu features Lebanese and Mediterranean cuisine and seafood, including beef carpaccio, Provincial Mussels (baked with Parmesan, garlic, olive oil, bread, olives, and parsley), calamari, falafel, stuffed grape leaves, tabbouleh, shrimp stew, lobster ravioli, and mahi-mahi. It's also a great spot for an after-dinner drink or for a romantic tête-à-tête. The scene is somewhat social, but folks tend to keep to their groups more than not. Things really get going around midnight, when the dinner crowd yields to the late-night lounge scene, steeped in style and exclusivity.

Kartabar is one of several trendy lounges on 12th Street.

Much more casual and lively, ★ Karen's Seafood, Steak House and Pizzas (Quinta between Second and Fourth streets) has nightly live music and one of Playa's most all-encompassing menus. Crowds tend to linger in the fun and joyful atmosphere, so getting there early for a good table is recommended.

Maktub Caffe (Quinta between 28th and 30th streets) is known for its authentic Arabic menu, including couscous, hummus, pitas, gyros, and grape-leaf rolls. An indoor hookah bar has six low tables surrounded by pillows for lounging and smoking.

A swanky lounge/restaurant with indoor seating, candlelit tables, comfy sofas, and sidewalk tables facing Quinta, Di Vino (Quinta at 12th Street, 984-803-1270, www.divino.com.mx) offers upscale selections such as grilled fish, steak, and lobster. As the night goes on, diners swap out for drinkers, and the lounge scene begins. The swank factor multiplies and the indoor couches become the favored seats,

making an ideal spot for candlelit canoodling. Food is served until late at night, but you'll see more swizzle sticks than butter knives as the night goes on. It's also a great spot to woo a date or show your feelings for your special someone. Credit cards accepted.

Boasting an "eat, drink, lounge" concept, the fusion restaurant Amaris (paseo del Carmen Mall, 984-803-4050) features décor and cuisine from Asia, Central America, and the Mediterranean. It has a marble bar, plasma TV, and indoor/outdoor seating. Best bet is the chicken satay—grilled chicken strips with peanut sauce.

Popular with local hotel executives, the casual Chicago Don Jose's (Sixth Street between Quinta and 10th avenues) has an unusual menu for Playa (featuring BBQ ribs, imported certified Angus steak, lamb, lobster, and grilled shrimp), proving a welcome taste of home for many travelers.

Spanish-style tapas and cocktails are served with ocean views at La Azotea Bar & Tapas (8th Street and

Nightlights of Playa del Carmen

Each night, many points of light blink into existence up and down Fifth Avenue, in hotels and along the beach. They give Playa a new overlay, setting the stage for romance, laughter and interpersonal adventure.

Jellyfish Lamps: Carved from gourds and melons, these showstopper lanterns adorn shops, restaurants and hotels, collectively giving Playa a distinctive sense of place. Made by hand, they feature illustrations, shapes, or other carvings. Multicolored glass is often inset into carved pockets, allowing vivid hues to jump out. The strings of shells and hanging from many of the lamps earned them their name.

Catholic Votive Candles: These tall candles—usually displaying important religious figures such as Jesus Christ, the Virgin Mary, or other key sainted figures—are traditionally lit in prayers, as devotions, and in remembrance of departed family.

Christmas Lights: Good old-fashioned twinkle lights make for festive restaurant décor year-round. You might spot them in plants and trees or adorning restaurant arches. Bring a string from home to hang in your hotel room to create instant, magical mood lighting.

Wall Sconces & Tin Lamps: Often spied in courtyards, restaurants, lobbies, and condos, these artistic clay, metal, and wooden shades make popular design accents. Bright lights tucked inside shine through small intricate holes and patterns in the shade itself, creating brilliant points of light amid an ambient, low-lit setting.

Moroccan Lanterns: Similar to the sconces and lamps, these more elaborate hanging lanterns feature more ornate and precise patterns, as well as colored glass panes. They tend to show up as signature décor elements, particularly in bars and restaurants seeking to evoke an exotic flavor.

Restaurant Table Candles: Short, stubby red table candles, and local homemade varieties, give you firelight to call your very own while dining in many of the city's sidewalk restaurants.

Many shops on Fifth Avenue feature colored lamps.

Torches: Typically perched above the fray, on the beach or along private hotel paths, these flames add a further flare of excitement to your evenings.

Fire Lanterns: Featured in the infamous fire dancing shows, these lanterns are literally set aflame and swung at the end of chains. During their performances, dancers paint vivid, overlapping circular patterns in the air and around themselves.

Quinta, 984-803-0288, www.hotelel punto.com) atop Hotel El Punto. By day, the restaurant serves snacks and cocktails to folks who stop by and look out over the Caribbean Sea. At night, stylish patrons lounge amidst the deep red lighting, nosh on tapas, and enjoy being seen.

El Zocalos (Eighth Street between Quinta and 10th avenues) interior may have a strong Mexican theme, but the menu is international fusion. The food—including *chiles rellenos* (stuffed peppers), Caesar salads, steak, and pasta—is good, and the waiters are professional and accommodating.

Le Bistro (Second Street between Quinta and 10th avenues), serves seafood and vegetarian options in a in a more casual setting accompanied by live music. Set just off the main plaza, it's a good spot to wait for the Cozumel ferry.

The upscale La Caprichoza (Quinta between 12th and 14th streets, 984-801-8034) offers fish, lobster, steaks, pasta, and fresh salads. Located upstairs, the restaurant's soothing, welcoming atmosphere (including live music most nights) makes you want to take a break from Quinta and stay a while.

Guests at the nearby Los Tulipanes (Quinta at 14th Street, 984-873-1255) stay after dinner for the loungelike atmosphere and soothing décor. Candlelit tables, soft music, and icy margaritas beckon passersby to stop in and stay for a while. The menu features steak, fish, and pasta selections, plus a house specialty, Molcajete Azteca, which combines chicken, beef, octopus, and baby onions.

Promising "fresh food from the sun," sharp and modern Sol Food (Quinta between 20th and 22nd streets) serves dishes from Italy and the Mediterranean (rather than the soul food famous in the southern United States), including cold salads, baked linguine, and grilled shrimp.

In the center of the new section of Quinta, the Spanish-themed Tintos y Tapas (Quinta between 28th and 30th streets) sidewalk café and bar serves a delicious paella several times per week, plus other regional specialties, and features a respectable wine list.

The two-level Sur Pizzeria, Grill & Wine Bar (Quinta at calle Corazón, between 12th and 14th streets, 984-803-3285) offers fan-cooled dining overlooking Quinta. The décor is slick and mod, with indirect lighting, soothing lounge music, and a strong Mediterranean vibe. The affordable menu includes pizza, grilled steaks, fish, chicken, and steamed shrimp.

Despite its name, Wine & Cigars Bar (Quinta at 14th Street) serves meals below a canopy of trees and has live music, a swing bar, and a handful of candlelit tables spilling out to the curb, making it one of the more relaxing spots along this busy strip. Guests are encouraged to linger and light a cigar after their meal.

Upscale French bistro La Route des Vins (Quinta at 38th Street, www .laroutedesvins.com.mx) offers traditional French cuisine, include beef and seafood, dishes in a warm atmosphere. Chocolate fondues are available for dessert. A lounge welcomes those preferring to just sample the wine selection.

Nearby, the Guatemalan chefs at Cocina 38 (Quinta at 38th) create international dishes with fresh Mexican ingredients. The quiet and casually upscale restaurant offers a nice wine selection and is a good choice for dates. At the same intersection, Como Como (Quinta near 38th Street, www.como como.mx) offers rich Mediterranean flavors that keep ex-pats and international locals coming back.

A Sunset Facing East?

Because the Riviera Maya faces east, it is not known as a good place to witness a tropical sunset. If your beach vacation just won't be complete without watching the golden orb disappear into the horizon, there's still hope. Try these five tips for catching a sunset in the Riviera Maya.

1. Take a champagne sunset cruise aboard the Fat Cat 41-foot catamaran in Xaac Cove near Puerto Aventuras and watch the sun sink into the Caribbean (www .fatcatsail.com).

2. Walk to the point at the north end of Playa del Carmen Cove, in back of the Gran Porto Real hotel, and watch the sun go down next to the lighthouse.

3. Climb to the top floor of the paseo del Carmen mall and enjoy a rare sunset over downtown Playa and the jungle beyond.

4. Take a day trip to Isla Cozumel and stay for sunset, then take a late ferry back to the mainland. Since the town's main beaches and town square face west, the sun sets over the ocean, just like in the postcards.

5. For the ultimate unobstructed sunset view, schedule a sundown skydive and look down, not up, at the setting sun (see chapter 5).

The beach behind the Gran Porto Real is one of the only spots in town to see the sun set over the water.

ASIAN & SUSHI

With two locations, ★ Babe's Noodle House (Quinta between 28th and 30th streets; 10th Street between Quinta and 10th avenues) offers inexpensive and well-portioned Asian and Thai dishes for lunch and dinner. They serve chicken, beef, pork, vegetarian dishes, coconut rice, spring rolls, and egg rolls.

Located on the beach side of the El Jardín del Jaguar hotel, the tiny ★ Kabuki (Eighth Street between

Quinta and the beach, 984-803-5816) is one of the best sushi spots in town. Delivery available.

Sushi Itto (paseo del Carmen Mall; 10th Street at First Avenue, 984-803-4127) offers fresh sushi, plus a variety of cooked rice and noodle dishes, at its two locations. The shrimp and rice is especially good. Delivery available.

STEAK

The beautiful, luxurious and dark-hued ★ John Gray's Place (Quinta at calle Corazón, between 12th and 14th streets, 984-803-3689, www.johngray restaurants.com), popular with ex-pats and regulars, has a first-floor bar and lounge area and an upper-level dining room with cozy tables, candles, and a subdued, modern, and upscale atmosphere. The menu is international, with great steak and seafood.

★ Pancho Villa (Fourth Street between 10th and 15th avenues), a casual patio restaurant at the Hotel Plaza, offers surprisingly good steaks and seafood, considering its unassuming setting and budget-friendly menu. Close to the beach, it's perfect for a quick bite between sunning sessions.

SEAFOOD

A delicious meal at the ★ Hotel Básico Seafood Restaurant (Quinta at 10th Street, 984-879-4448, www.hotelbasico .com) provides the perfect opportunity to experience this unique concept hotel. Run by a staff from a small town outside of Veracruz, the restaurant serves authentic Mexican Gulf Coast seafood in a style they call *maiz mariscos,* which means "corn and seafood" (though it sounds better in Spanish). The patio has a timeless quality, with 1950s-style concrete floors,

lights twinkling in the trees, candles and lanterns around the tables, a market kiosk housing the food-prep area, and seating along a balcony overlooking the street. Menu favorites include shrimp empanadas, seafood cocktails, ceviche, stuffed blue crabs (*jaibas rellenas*), fried whole fish, grilled octopus, and lobster. It's a good spot to sample some traditional Mexican desserts, such as *cocada con helado* (coconut ice cream), flan, and *budin de elote* (corn pudding). To make things more authentic, order your beer as a *michelada* or *chamochela* and savor the local flavors. Depending on the night, there are dance classes, tortilla-making demonstrations, or a marimba band.

Located next to the Playa town square, gourmet ★ La Casa del Agua (Quinta at Second Street, 984-803-0232) features European and Latin fusion cuisine, including fresh fish, shrimp, and shellfish, plus Angus beef and a few traditional Mexican dishes. Water features decorate the dining room, and candlelit tables are covered in white linen, giving it a contemporary, romantic feel.

One of Playa's older restaurants, the two-story ★ Blue Lobster (Quinta at 12th Street, 984-803-2651) opened in 1991 and specializes in live lobster and seafood (including a daily $14.95 lobster special), plus such unusual dishes as octopus puffs, fish with curry and anisette, and coconut shrimp. Key lime pie is popular and there's live music in the evenings.

Across from the Santanera nightclub, the inexpensive ★ El Oasis (12th Street between Quinta and 10th avenues, 984-803-2676) has shrimp tacos, fish tacos, and other seafood and Mexican dishes. The dining room is large and softly lit, and the décor is decidedly Mexican. It is always lively with a pre-party crowd.

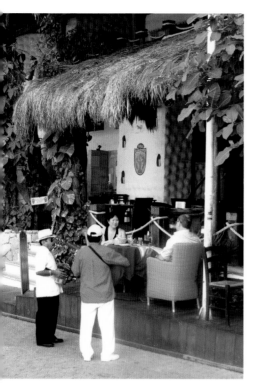

A sidewalk serenade at Blue Lobster restaurant

Join the locals at the vibrant ★ La Bamba Jarocha (30th Avenue between 36th and 38th streets, 984-803-0965), a bit off the main tourist trail. It's safe and friendly, and the waiters will be happy to help you order. Favorites include fried or grilled fish, seafood cocktails, fresh oysters, and paella. A traditional baked rice dish called *arroz tumbada* is served on Sunday only.

Big Lobster (Quinta between Fourth and Sixth streets, 984-873-2026) offers two-for-one beers, whole fish, fajitas, surf and turf, and, of course, lobster. Friendly waiters provide a bit of entertainment during your meal.

Local favorite Las Brisas (Fourth Street between Quinta and 10th avenues) specializes in shrimp cocktail and ceviche, and also serves fried fish and grilled shrimp. Seating is in an open, covered dining room, allowing the breeze to flow through.

Another spot popular with expats in the know, Los Aguas Chiles (Quinta at 38th) offers great seafood with delicious sauces and drink specials.

CAFÉS & LIGHT FARE

Facing the Olmec statue and fountain at a busy intersection, the ★ Ah Cacao (Constituyentes at Quinta, 984-803-5748, www.ahcacao.com) makes all sorts of chocolate delicacies, including hot/cold drinks, to-die-for brownies, ice cream, cookies, and old-fashioned chocolate bars. It also has gourmet coffees from around Mexico. Stop by and ask for a sample.

Open for breakfast, lunch, and dinner, ✐ ★ 100% Natural (Quinta between Eighth and 10th streets, 984-873-2242, www.100natural.com.mx) is one chain restaurant that feels completely local. There are several different eating areas, from the sidewalk and tables next to a waterfall to covered tables with ceiling fans upstairs. The menu has omelets, enchiladas, sandwiches, seafood, steak, and other dishes. The fresh fruit juices and smoothies are delicious and good for what ails you. Special concoctions exist for lowering cholesterol, boosting energy, curing hangovers, improving memory, and others. The prices are good, and the food is always fresh and delicious.

Complete with espresso bar and sidewalk tables with seemingly permanent smoking patrons, the very European ★ Café Sasta (Quinta between Eighth and 10th streets) has good coffees, pastries, and snacks.

Casual café Hot Baking Company (10th Street between Quinta and 10th avenues; calle Corazón at 14th Street,

100% Natural restaurant has fresh fruit smoothies and healthy meals.

984-806-0781) serves tea, coffee, fresh-squeezed juice, eggs, omelets, muffins, bagels, banana bread, carrot cake, cookies, pastries, and sandwiches.

Whimsically named kiosk Caffeina (Quinta between 20th and 22nd streets) serves Illy brand coffee, sandwiches, pastries, cookies, and other goodies. It's in the new stretch of Quinta, surrounded by boutique shops and restaurants.

A good spot for espresso, cappuccino, and iced mochachino, Java Joe's (10th Street between Quinta and 10th avenues, 984-876-2694) also serves bagels, cakes, pastries, sandwiches, and boxed lunches perfect for a day trip.

With its location close to the town square, natural-foods café Sabor (Quinta between Second and Fourth streets) is popular with locals and folks waiting for a bus or ferry. The menu offers homemade *pan dulce* (sweet pastry), sandwiches, juice, and coffee.

Tutto Dolce (20th Avenue at 10th Street, 984-803-4936) offers a nice air-conditioned respite from a hot day and a good spot for fresh breakfasts and lunches, including empanadas, quiche, pizza, lasagne, fresh fruits, and coffee.

Located in the Los Itzaes Hotel, the small El Espacio (10th Avenue between Sixth and Eighth streets) serves coffee, pastries, and sandwiches. The staff can prepare a meal to go for the beach or a car trip.

Hungry . . . but Don't Want to Go Out?

Delivery Express offers restaurant food delivery to hotels, condos, and other locations throughout Playa del Carmen. The service works with many local restaurants, including Hot Baking Company, Il Baretto, Maktub, Kabuki, 100% Natural, and El Oasis. There's a 15 percent service fee, and tips are not included. Delivery is available 11–9. For more information, call 984-803-5986.

Bars & Nightlife

When the sun goes down, the action on Quinta heats up. Tourists hit the town with their sun-kissed skin and newly purchased tropical outfits to enjoy the evening breeze, have dinner, gaze at the twinkling lights, and then, quite frequently, have a few drinks. Fortunately, there are plenty of options for nightlife on and around Quinta and the beach. Whether you're looking for a casual beach bar, live tropical music, TV sports, or a cosmopolitan discotheque, you'll find what you're looking for in Playa. There are clubs and bars all along Quinta and at various spots along the beach. Many travelers will take a few laps around town to see what's going on before settling on a place to go. As the night goes on, the crowd thins a bit, becomes less populated with Americans, and funnels to the after-hours clubs, some of which continue serving drinks until sunup.

The most popular area for nightlife is 12th Street, where bars and clubs line both sides of the road all the way from 10th Avenue to the beach. An eclectic crowd assembles from midnight to 2 AM at the tiny hole-in-the-wall bar between the main entry to Santanera and the pizza shack next door. They serve beer in giant Styrofoam cups and have only a couple of tables, with the crowds spilling over into the street for a nightly impromptu street party.

DRINKS & DANCING

Look for the brightly lit Vegas-style sign facing 12th Street and you'll find ★ Santanera (12th Street between Quinta and 10th avenues, 984-803-2856, www.lasantanera.com), which is frequented by the cool kids from Mexico City and around the world. But don't worry, even this place has an unpretentious and down-

The Riviera Maya deftly combines culture, cuisine, recreation, and really big margaritas into one fun resort destination.

to-earth atmosphere and a patio bar. Club décor seems to pay equal homage to Mexican professional wrestling and the Catholic church. Downstairs, it's like a traditional nightclub, a bit reminiscent of the House of Blues, but without a stage. Upstairs, a large palapa roof contains the crowd of dancing, socializing, and margarita-drinking patrons. DJs spin the latest tunes, including American pop, Mexican rock, tropical music, and a bit of funk. The crowd is a good mix of locals and visitors, gay and straight. Opens at 8 PM, but it doesn't start hopping until at least midnight. Last call is 4 AM.

The opening of ★ Coco Bongo Playa del Carmen (12th Street between Quinta and 10th avenues, 998-883-5061, www.cocobongo.com .mx) in 2008 marked Playa's unofficial departure from its hippie heyday and

Mucha Ropa, Mucha Ropa!

The equivalent to the English "take it off, take it off," *mucha ropa, mucha ropa* is just as clichéd and out of fashion. In the Riviera Maya, the main gentleman's clubs are in Playa del Carmen, along Highway 307. They are generally considered safe for tourists, though as anywhere, it's best to keep your wits and not do anything that you think could get you in trouble. That being said, the law allows for quite a bit, and you're sure to find your choice of willing participants—for a price.

One such club is **Baby's Hot** (Highway 307 at Sixth Street). A small hangout for locals, it doesn't see many gringos and can seem a bit rough around the edges to many foreigners. Cover charge is posted at $25, but they're flexible if they think you'll spend some money once you're inside, especially if you threaten to go down the road to visit their competitors instead. A few blocks south is **Marlin Men's Club** (Highway 307 and avenida Juárez). It's the most stylish of the nonmembership clubs, featuring a pool table, laser light show, massages, escort girls, show girls, table dances, private dances, and multiple stages. Its cover charge is negotiable. Farther down Highway 307, across from the southernmost entrance to Playacar, is **Chilly Willy's,** a palapa-roofed sister club to the longtime nudie institution in Cancún. Cover charge is posted at $20, and the club seems to open only certain times of the year.

Each club offers table dances in a private curtained room for $15–20, payable directly to your dancer of choice, waiter, or floor manager (who is eager to assist with your selection). More intimate encounters can be arranged for an additional fee (around $200 for the complete package), and each club has private rooms for rent by the hour.

Drinks are relatively inexpensive, though if a dancer asks you to buy her a drink, the fee is significantly higher—up to $15 for a single cocktail—so unless you're ready to drop a lot of money, you're probably best off saving your pesos for a dance, as it's roughly the same price. Cash is the preferred payment method, so bring some bills and stay aware of your surroundings.

All taxis know these clubs well and will often recommend one to you since they get a kickback for dropping people off there. Negotiate your price in advance (it shouldn't be more than a few dollars from any Playa del Carmen or Playacar hotel), and if you want to try to get in without paying a cover, ask to be dropped off a block or two away so you're not obligated to your taxi driver in any way. No need to have your cabbie wait for you; there are plenty waiting outside when it's time to leave.

Be smart. Be safe. Have fun.

ushered in a new era of mass international tourism that continues to reshape this once sleepy fishing town. Although smaller than its sister club up the coast in Cancún, it's still Playa's largest, most modern, and most extravagant nightspot. In fact, is should be viewed more as a tourist attraction that you must experience than as simply a nightclub. Live performances, including lip-synching celebrity look-alikes, flair bartenders, DJs, dancers, and—most notably—high-flying acrobats keep the

One last Corona before catching the plane home

audience entertained all night long, making it feel like New Year's Eve every night of the year. Smoke machines, a video wall, laser light show, balloon drops, confetti explosions, and compressed air blasts help ensure that there's always something pumping energy into the crowd. Cover charge is $60 and includes open bar with domestic beer and liquor drinks. Open nightly from 10:30 PM to 5 AM.

Coco Bongo is by far Playa del Carmen's largest nightclub.

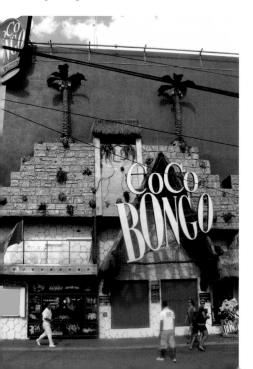

The king of *palapa* bars in Playa, ★ Blue Parrot (12th Street at the beach, 984-206-3350 or 1-800-435-0668 from the U.S., www.blueparrot .com) is a sort of community center, with a hotel, popular lounge chair–laden beachfront, lively meals, and flowing beers. At night, it's one of the best parties in town. The main oval-shaped bar is about 100 feet long and is ringed with swinging bar stools, plus several tables and chairs leading all the way to the water's edge. Food is served until 6 PM, and around 11 PM, local fire dancers perform, flinging sparks and ash dangerously close to the thatched roof, not to mention the entranced crowd, made up of Americans, Canadians, locals, and people from around the world. The show is amazing, though, with attractive young performers showing off their skill and daring. An open

Top 10 Songs to Load on Your iPod

The right song can help secure a memory, make good times even better, and share an experience with friends. Try some of these to capture the spirit of the Riviera Maya:

1. "Margaritaville" by Jimmy Buffett. Said to have been written on a flight from Cozumel to Houston, it's a song about a mythical island at the bottom of a Cuervo bottle.

2. "Mexico" by James Taylor. This is a classic tale of an extended vacation: "The sun's so hot, I forgot to go home."

3. "Stays in Mexico" by Toby Keith. A countrified reminder to keep your vacation exploits to yourself.

4. "Mexico" by Nash Girls. Young women having fun at the beach.

5. "Married in Mexico" by Mark Wills. A south-of-the-border romance complete with beachfront nuptials.

6. "I Got Mexico" by Eddy Raven. Sometimes, that's all you need.

7. "Blame It on Mexico" by George Strait. "Too much guitar music, tequila, salt, and lime." I know I've used this excuse before.

8. "Ten Rounds with Jose Cuervo" by Tracy Byrd. Crazy things can happen with tequila, especially after 10 rounds.

9. "Mail Myself to Mexico" by Buddy Jewell. Vacation fantasies go postal.

10. "One Step Closer to Cancún" by Elmer Thudd. Inspirational song about an upcoming vacation.

bar is available or visitors can just pay an entrance fee starting around $10. A covered lounge area offers romantic cushioned seating areas on top of the sandy beach and a stage, where a DJ spins throbbing electronic beats sure to set the mood for a fun night.

Popular with day-trippers, cruise passengers, Mexico first-timers, and vacationers at hotels in the adjacent Playacar development, ♂ ★ Señor Frog's (Plaza Marina, at the ferry dock, 984-873-0930, www.senorfrogs.com) is always a good bet for good cover bands, reggae music, audience-participation gags, goofy contests, and a bit of risqué fun. It is built out over the sand and has a great view of the Palace Resort beach and the ferry dock. There is live music nightly and DJ dancing until the wee hours, and there are many audience-participation opportunities, including sexy body contests, drinking contests, and sing-alongs. The menu features Mexican standards, plus pasta, seafood, and burgers.

With live salsa music every night, ★ Mambo Café (Sixth Street between Quinta and 10th avenues, 984-803-2656, www.mambocafe.com.mx) has developed quite a following with the local crowd. Tourists are more than welcome to join in the fun, but some dancers take their moves very seriously, so try to keep up or at

With nearly 100 beaches to explore, the Riviera Maya is a wonderland for adventurous travelers. Gary Walten/logogringo.com

least stay out of the way. There's a $5 cover charge, depending on the day of the week and the band. An all-you-can-drink open bar is available. On Wednesdays, ladies may drink for free 10 PM–midnight.

La Bodeguita del Medio (Quinta between 36th and 38th streets, 984-803-3950, www.labodeguitadelmedio .com.mx) is a Cuban-themed restaurant during the day and evening, but its crowd gets more rowdy and the music gets louder as the night goes on. Live salsa music is featured most nights. For a break from the crowd, seek respite on the back patio overlooking a steep, rocky arroyo and ask for a marker to add your name to the wall of fame. Originally founded in Cuba in 1942, it boasts a slightly kitschy décor with Cuban art, flags, and paraphernalia. There are daily drink specials and free salsa lessons Tuesdays and Thursdays at 7 PM.

Beach club by day and nightclub by night, Coco Maya Beach Club (14th Street at the beach, Playa del Carmen) is an alternative to the sometimes over-hyped scene at the Blue Parrot next door. No fire dancers here; just hip DJ music, a handful of couches arranged around the dance floor, and a few additional sitting areas set up in the sand. At the main bar, drinkers vie for the bartender's attention while a movie projector plays old Mexican classics on a wall nearby.

With its rainbow flag and suggestive name, Playa 69 (Quinta between Fourth and Sixth streets, 984-879-3217, www.rivieramayagay.com) is far from subtle about being Playa's dedicated gay bar. There's live and recorded male entertainment, and it's a great spot to meet gay and free-spirited locals, ex-pats, and travelers from around the world. Starting around midnight, the scene lasts until about 4 AM.

TRENDY LOUNGES

During the day, ★ Mandala Bar (12 Street at First Avenue) may look as if it closed down a month ago, but at 10 PM, the red leather couches are pulled from storage and set up along the street and the music starts to pump, making this one of the hipper places to linger over cocktails. The bar is popular with revelers from around the world with a vibe that's more Miami Beach chic than it is Playa casual. The centerpiece is a large dance floor that fills up as the night goes on. The sexy crowd is far less pretentious than one would guess by appearance alone. Cover fee is charged most nights, though a little finagling can usually get you in for free.

At the ★ Deseo Bar (Quinta between 10th and 12th streets, 984-879-3620, www.hoteldeseo.com) you can indulge in ultra-hip lounging in an atmosphere as

A rustic beach near Tulum

10 Tips for Enjoying Your Trip

1. Rent a car. Being mobile and free gives you a whole new perspective on a destination. You won't need it the whole time, but get one for a few days and explore the coast on your own. Pack a cooler, beach towel, map (freebies are available at the airport and most hotels), and mask/snorkel, and hit the road. Make sure to hit Tulum, hidden beaches, and lost-in-time villages.

2. Learn a little Spanish. A little goes a long way, and it helps you feel like you belong. It's also a nice gesture to make to your Mexican hosts, who will appreciate the effort and are usually happy to take some time to teach you new words. For bonus points, learn a little Mayan. Even saying "hello" or "thank you" in the native language is a sure way to get smiles from the locals, many of whom speak it fluently.

3. Take care of yourself. Don't get dehydrated or sunburned. Drinking plenty of purified water will keep your energy level up and can prevent serious illness. Don't be stingy with the sunscreen, either: A trip-ruining sunburn can happen in less than an hour if you're not used to the sun and you don't protect yourself. And while you're at it, put on insect repellent before heading out at night. While others are scratching their ankles, you'll be enjoying your margarita.

4. Order the whole fish. Native to the region, this dish has been a favorite for hundreds of years. The fish is scaled and gutted but left whole, and it is then lightly fried and usually served with tomatoes and onions. It's a good dish to share, with each diner forking off the pieces he or she wants. Even the skin is crispy and tasty, full of healthy fish oils.

5. Request a mariachi song. Sure, you can hear them playing at the table across the way, but there's nothing like being surrounded by the band as they play at your very own table. It makes for great photos, also, so request a song, try to sing along, and take some fun pictures. Tip $3–5 per song.

6. Check out the late-night scene. Sitting at a rope-swing bar stool and dancing under the stars is a longtime Playa tradition, and it's alive and well at the Blue Parrot (see Drinks & Dancing). The party going at around 11 PM, when the fire dancers put on their show, followed by DJ music and dancing on the beach or in the chic palapa-covered lounge room.

Into a more relaxing scene? Linger over a glass of wine at the Glass Bar (see International Dining), savor mojitos at Diablito, or practice your lounging skills at Kartabar (see Trendy Lounges). Not tired yet? Head to Santanera (see Drinks & Dancing) and learn to dance like a local.

7. Stroll along the beach. Leave your sandals behind and take a long walk on the powdery white-sand beach. If you're staying in Playacar, head south toward Xcaret and follow the beach until a rocky point bars your way, and you'll find a secluded and picturesque spot to rest before heading home. If you're staying near Quinta, head north past Mamita's Beach Club all the way to the Reef Club hotel and the deserted beach beyond (Playa Chun-Zumbul).

8. Visit a *cenote*: These freshwater sinkholes, unique geographical features, are a lot of fun. The refreshingly cool water feels great after a day in the sun, and the virtually unlimited visibility makes you feel like you're floating in space. Hidden Worlds (see chapter 5) is the most expensive, but it's also the best.

9. Snorkel or scuba dive on the Great Mayan Reef. Take the plunge for a chance to see colorful corals, tasty-looking lobsters, stern-looking barracuda, slippery eels, majestic turtles, and hundreds of tropical fish.

10. Get up early. Although the sun sets over Quintana Roo mainland, it rises over the Caribbean. Combined with the solitude and quiet of the early-morning hours, watching the sunrise is a spiritual and calming way to

There are many postcard-worthy sites throughout the Riviera Maya.
Gary Walten/logogringo.com

start your day. Next, head to your favorite café for a cup of coffee and some *pan dulce* (sweet pastry) as you watch the shops open up and the tourists start their rounds.

nontraditionally Mexican as the $8 martinis they serve. You'll feel cool as soon as you crest the top stair that leads to the bar from Quinta. It's a lot like being in L.A. or Miami when you're at Deseo, but without the attitude. The glimmer of the pool, the glowing lights from the rooms ringing the deck, and the projection TV on the wall next door set a surreal stage for some serious lounging. Most of the patrons are hipsters from Mexico City, and they all seem to know one another, but find your spot at the bar, at a poolside bed, or at one of the lounge chairs near the hotel rooms, and you'll fit right in.

Across the street from the entrance to the Blue Parrot, ★ Ba Ba Club & Lounge (12th Street at First Avenue, 984-745-0584, www.omplaya.com) gets busier as it gets later. The décor foretells what may happen if Martha Stewart were to make over a pirate ship, with dark wood furnishings, flowing red sails, candles, and well-maintained fixtures. Formerly known as the OM Lounge Bar (and still affiliated with the OM in Tulum), the expanded club features a dance floor and private harem tables. International DJs spin lounge and chill-out music while patrons dance on the tables, conspire at dark tables, and enjoy watching the busy street scene. Open 5 PM–4 AM daily but if you (and your friend) don't want to go home, you may be able to snag one of Ba Ba's hotel rooms above the bar.

To visit the Básico Terrace Bar (Quinta at 10th Street, 984-879-4448, www .hotelbasico.com), enter the Básico lobby on 10th Street and take the elevator to the top floor. If you're there in the daytime, you'll be treated to a breathtaking view of the ocean, and at night you can see the twinkling lights of Quinta. There are several seating areas, hammocks, canopied sunbeds, and unique aboveground pools.

A favorite among the Mexico City crowd, the loud and flashy Los Danzantes (12th Street at First Avenue, 984-873-1159, www.losdanzantes.com) next door opens up to the street and serves dinner and late night revelry with cocktails, mescal, and 90 different wines.

See and be seen at this swanky open-air Diablito Cha Cha Cha (12th Street at 1st Avenue, www.diablitochachacha.com) while you sip mojitos, Cuba Libres, daiquiris, and other tropical drinks. The lights are dim, but the people-watching is still second to none as the well-heeled, international set grooves to African and Latin rhythms while showing off their trendy vacation duds.

CASUAL DRINKS

Primarily a local hangout, ★ Litros (First Avenue between 10th and 12th streets) offers 33-ounce beers for $3 and equally large mixed drinks for $7. It's a good spot to sit on the sidewalk and watch the crowd gather for the Blue Parrot. The small indoor area has funky lighting and Mexican rock music. Can't finish your drink? It's okay to get it to go, as long as it's in Styrofoam.

Visitors looking for a shady spot to sip a cold drink can discover what the guests of the La Rana Cansada hotel already know. ★ La Ranita Bar (10th Street between Quinta and 10th avenues, 984-873-0389, www.ranacansada.com) will find themselves at home at this traditional rustic Mexican setting that says "beachtown cantina." Patrons can sit at the bar, in the lounge area, or out in the courtyard, surrounded by flowering tropical plants.

A good spot to watch a live sporting event on TV, ★ La Taberna (Fifth Street

Requesting a Mariachi Song

The strolling mariachis you see in the restaurants, walking down Quinta, or some-times even on the beach work for tips. The typical price per song is $3–5, but ask ahead to be sure. Duos can cost less, and larger groups cost more. Not sure which song to request? Here are a few longtime favorites to choose from:

"El Son de la Negra": This raucous song is often the first song played when the mariachis make their grand entrance; it's also a lively, uplifting song to play any-time the room needs a lift.

"La Bamba": Everybody knows the words—at least some of them. This is an uplifting song of hope and can really get the crowd going.

"La Cucaracha": The sad tale of a bad day for a cockroach. It's a funny and entertaining song that's easy to sing along with. Kids love it, too.

"Las Golondrinas": A sad song known to bring grown men to tears. It tells the tale of the swallows flying on and is often played when someone is gone or going away.

"Las Mananitas": This is the song played for birthdays and celebrations. Request it for a friend who is celebrating something special.

"Maria Isabel": An easy song to sing along to, it tells the story of lovers on the beach. It has a happy tropical sound that you'll remember for a long time and is especially popular in Cozumel.

A good time to request "Vamos a la Playa," another local favorite.

between Quinta and 10th avenues, 984-803-0447) has a wall of computer worksta-tions, with Internet access going for $1.50 an hour. There are dartboards, pool tables, and multiple TVs, and also cold air-conditioning, so it's a good spot to go after a long day at the beach, when you just can't bring yourself to sit at a patio bar. They serve good tacos, burgers, grilled chicken, nachos, steak, quesadillas, and seafood cocktails.

The American-dominated happy-hour favorite ★ Beer Bucket (10th Street between Quinta and 10th avenues) offers loud pop and rock music, beer specials, mixed drinks, and a come-as-you-are attitude. Seating is on the ground floor or on an upper deck overlooking the street. While not a great choice to impress a date, it's a fun place to party with friends and make some new ones. As the night goes on, the scene gets a little crazier, making for a fun night on the town. They play U.S. sports on TV for the playoffs and other key games.

The Tequila Barrel (Quinta between 10th and 12th streets, 984-873-1061, www.tequilabarrel.com) is a Playa classic. A dark wood bar gives a traditional hacienda feeling to the interior, while a large-screen TV near the back plays sports and news. When nothing good is on TV, there is live music. Sidewalk tables spill out onto Quinta, making this a great spot to sip a cocktail and watch the parade of people walk by. The bartenders are friendly and welcoming, and the bar stocks more than 85 types of tequila, plus a huge selection of imported cognacs, whiskeys, and Scotches. The kitchen serves up traditional Mexican and American breakfasts, plus burgers, wings, fajitas, and other bar foods. The bar's Web site has a live webcam and archives photos taken at the bar each night.

Help Support the Playa del Carmen Fire Department

The local fire department, Bomberos de la Riviera Maya, frequently sets up a kiosk in the Playa del Carmen town square near the ferry dock. They sell hats and T-shirts with the department logo to raise funds to buy updated equipment for the rescue squad. The department's various fire-houses welcome guests who want to take pictures and are eager to exchange patches with other fire departments around the world. Make donations and purchase souvenir merchandise online at www.bomberosdelariviera maya.org.

The Tequila Barrel has sidewalk tables and a back room with sports betting.

Dancing on the Sand: Top Spots to Have Sand between Your Toes and a Drink in Your Hand

Blue Parrot, 12th Street at the beach. Get there early to reserve a coveted water-front table. If you fall out of your chair, you'll land on powder-white sand. Dancers spill out from the wooden dance floor all the way to the water line.

Fusion Beach Bar & Grill, Sixth Street at the beach. This relaxed beach bar offers a festive but laid-back alternative to the Blue Parrot down the beach. Most nights, fire dancers perform on the beach at 10:30 on weeknights and midnight on weekends.

Mamita's Beach Club, 28th Street at the beach. Who says you can't go dancing during the day? The folks at Mamita's prove that getting your groove on by sunlight can be just as fun as by moonlight. The party gets going in the early afternoon and peaks just before sundown, then quickly dwindles. Arrive early to claim a coveted beach bed.

Señor Frog's, Plaza Marina, at the ferry dock. Built above the beach at the base of the ferry dock, this resort-town stalwart packs in a primarily American clientele in search of good Mexican food, pop music, and sometimes love. Dancing patrons can get their drinks to go and boogie on the beach below.

The courtyard bar and restaurant Siesta Fiesta (Quinta between Eighth and 10th streets, 984-803-1166, www.siestafiestahotel.com) is a popular meeting spot where travelers congregate to watch live sporting events on the big-screen TV and listen to live music (several bands per night). After the live music, the staff puts live sports or recorded concerts on the TV, and the party keeps going. There are tables near the stage, several bar stools, and sidewalk tables for those seeking a bit more peace and quiet. Vacation camaraderie is especially strong here, making it a great spot to meet other travelers. Food is available all day long. There is also a quaint hotel offering comfortable and affordable accommodations.

Giving a little taste of the jungle to the sidewalk bar scene, Living Garden Bar (Quinta between 14th and 16th streets) opened in 2007 and quickly developed a loyal following. Some tables front Fifth Avenue but others are set back in a tree-covered setting, surrounded by tropical plants, dappled lighting and jungle décor. It's a nice place to chill out for a while and grab a snack. The temperature seems to drop about 10 degrees as soon as you step inside.

New Orleans–themed Bourbon Street (Quinta between Sixth and Eighth streets, 984-803-3022) has live music, projection TV, beer specials, and a crowd of ex-pats and regulars who always make for good conversation. You'll hear much more English than Spanish here, making it a nice respite when you need a taste of home. The music and crowd tend to be a bit more mature than other places along this stretch.

Despite the American name, 2 Dollar Drinks (10th Avenue between Sixth and Eighth streets, 984-803-3895) is popular mostly with locals who come for the cheap drinks (beer is $1, mixed drinks are $2), the soccer games on TV, and the camaraderie of friends. Tourists are welcome, though, so feel free to give it a try and maybe make a local friend.

The hole-in-the-wall Karaoke Bar (Sixth Street between Quinta and 10th avenues) is a fun spot to have a few beers and do something you wouldn't do back home—sing in front of a crowd of strangers! The song list features popular hits in English and Spanish.

Mezcalinna Bar (12th Street between the beach and First Avenue) offers cheap drinks if you don't want to pay cover for a club. Enjoy your drink in the crowded bar or get it to go and join the street party.

Watch sports games and music videos on a projection-screen TV at George & Dragon Pub (Quinta between Constituyentes & 18th Street) while sipping actual draught Guinness beer, one of the very few places to do so in the Riviera Maya.

BEACH CLUBS

The bustling ★ Mamita's Beach Club (28th Street at the beach, 984-803-2867, www.mamitasbeachclub.com) attracts a trendy crowd that gathers every afternoon to soak up the sun and sip cold beers and frosty margaritas. It's usually packed with day-trippers, cruise passengers, and sun worshippers staying in Playa, but not on the beach. There's a small pool and several cabana-style beach beds, available on a first-come, first-served basis. A DJ spins lounge and pop music suitable for bar-top dancing, while other patrons join in a game of group soccer-ball juggling. Mamita's rents lounge chairs and umbrellas and offers beachside drink and meal service, with fish, shrimp, tacos, and other Mexican specialties topping the menu.

Channeling 1950s Brazil, ★ Canibal Royale (48th Street at the beach, www .canibalroyal.com) offers a trendy tri-level spot to sit by the beach, swim in the pool, and imbibe. Guests must buy food and drinks to use the facilities, but the

Lounging at the Canibal Royale beach club.

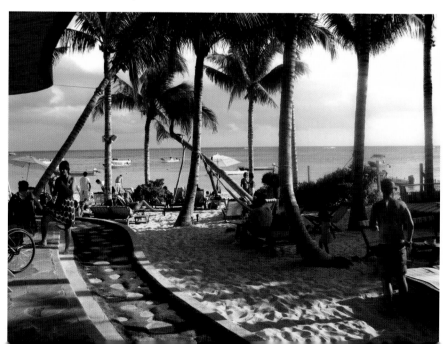

Common Beers of the Riviera Maya

Bohemia: Served in a dark bottle with gold foil on the neck, Bohemia is a bit more expensive than other beers. With a robust taste, it's a bit of a status symbol.

Bohemia Dark: Introduced to the Riviera Maya in 2008, this darker cousin of Bohemia offers a richer head and creamier, almost stout-like finish.

Corona: Although it's brewed in Mexico, it seems to be more common in the States. Not all bars carry it, so if you're normally a Corona drinker, it may be time to expand your horizons. Normally served with a slice of lime.

Dos Equis: Advertised on billboards throughout the region, Dos Equis (XX) comes in lager (green bottle) and amber (tinted bottle). The lager is much more common and goes better with lime.

Leon Negra: Somewhat of a microbrew, this dark and flavorful beer is locally brewed in Mérida, the capital of the state of Yucatán. Sometimes hard to find.

Modelo Especial: Sold by the bottle or in single cans in the convenience stores, this light-bodied lager is favored by many locals and goes nicely in a beach cooler.

Montejo: Crafted at the same Mérida brewery as Leon Negra, this beer adds a touch of class to your bar visit, when it's available.

Negra Modelo: A dark beer sometimes sold at a slightly higher price than others, it's normally served in a glass and goes great with steak.

Noche Buena: From the makers of Bohemia, this dark seasonal brew is only available in the winter holiday season. The name means, essentially, "Christmas Eve."

Sol: Commonly found at beach bars and nightclubs, Sol is what most Corona drinkers opt for when their usual beer is not on the menu. Frequently served with lime.

Superior: Served in a dark tinted bottle, which helps keep it from getting skunked in a cooler on a sunny day, this full-bodied beer is sold at a discount in grocery stores and is available mostly at bars favoring locals.

Tecate: Most commonly served in cans, Tecate is best enjoyed with plenty of salt and lime. Popular at sports bars.

Victoria: Brewed by Grupo Modelo, the same company that makes Corona and local favorites, this is a hoppy pilsner that isn't generally exported, so it's fun to see it and try a few.

menu, designed by a chef from Nobu Miami, is much better than your typical local beach club fare. Refreshing juices, buckets of beer, and mixed cocktails ensure that there's a delicious beverage for every palate.

The exclusive Coco Maya Beach Club (14th Street at the beach) next to the Blue Parrot Hotel, is the preferred daytime hangout for stylish beach-goers show-

Press Your Luck

Although far from being a real casino destination, the Riviera Maya does offer a few opportunities for tourists with an itch to gamble. A handful of casinos has popped up in the downtown Cancún area, including **Winpot Casino and Sports Book** (Plaza las Americas, 984-109-2166), which offers visitors Vegas-style reel and video slot machines, poker games, a roulette wheel, and a bingo hall. If you're in Playa del Carmen, drop by the back room at **Tequila Barrel** (Quinta between 10th and 12th streets, 984-873-1061, www.tequilabarrel.com) for a quick fix. This sports betting lounge offers bets on games around the world, using Las Vegas odds. Watch on the dozens of TVs or head to the beach, then come back to see if you won.

ing off their new bathing suits, new boobs, or new gym results. It's a great place to sunbathe, listen to lounge music, and feel cool. At night, a DJ spins popular music in front of a dance floor and lounge area and a movie projector plays old Mexican classics.

Family-friendly Kool Beach Club (28th Street at the beach, 984-803-1961, www.koolbeachclub.com.mx), just north of THE ROYAL Resort, is popular with day-trippers, cruise passengers, and downtown Playa beach-goers. There are lounge chairs and beach umbrellas for rent, plus a kids' pool, a restaurant serving seafood and Mexican food, and, of course, cold beer right on the beach. Active folks can play beach volleyball and soccer, ride WaveRunners, or go parasailing, banana-boat riding, kiteboarding, or body surfing. Massage service is provided on the beach or in a shady cabana.

Shopping & Services

While Playa's streets are overflowing with shops, and your hotel concierge can always point you in the right direction for a quick sundry and supply run, a few stops present something unique and atypical. In short, they're pure Playa del Carmen.

Tired of Sauza and José Cuervo and want to try a new tequila? Don Roberto (Quinta at Sixth Street, www.tequiladonroberto.com) is the exclusive seller of cattle breeder, farmer and rodeo promoter Don Roberto Orendain's brand. Popular choices include La Arenita, a white tequila that makes great margaritas, and the higher-end, 100 percent agave Belsanto, which makes for smooth sipping. Although it may not be traditionally Mexican, the Green Fairy absinthe soda that the shop sells is sure to make for an interesting night.

If you're looking for a specific tequila, or just to learn something, Casa Tequila–La Tequilaria (Quinta between Fourth and Sixth streets; Quinta at 14th Street, 984-873-0195) offers one-liter bottles ranging from $7 to $250. Most can be purchased by the shot, making for a fun sampling experiment. Souvenir bottles and flasks are available.

Shops on Fifth Avenue offer goods from across Latin America.

Despite the dominance of MP3s available online, Casita de la Musica (Quinta between avenida Juárez and Second Street) may be the only place you'll be able to easily find the latest Latin and international tracks you've been hearing during your trip. They sell local and international music, including merengue, salsa, Cuban, Mayan, pop, mariachi, and lounge music.

★ Jellyfish Lamp Shop (Fourth Street at Quinta, www.jellyfish.com.mx) spills onto the sidewalk, showcasing the tropical lanterns seen adorning many restaurants and bars. They're made from coconuts or similarly shaped gourds adorned with jewels, whimsical designs, and streamers that make them look like jellyfish with their dangling tentacles. They range from baseball-size lanterns selling for a few dollars to basketball-size works of art selling for more than $100.

PachaMama (south side of calle Corazón) offers Mayan and Mexican artwork, handicrafts, postcards, books, religious art, and great gift items.

The curious Sacbe (Quinta between Second and Fourth streets) has Mayan-inspired artwork, mostly from local artisans. There are artifact re-creations, home décor items, leatherwork, jade carvings, and natural fiber apparel.

The only shops dedicated to rewarding the little ones you left at home (or with a sitter at the hotel), ♪ Caribbean Puzzles (calle Corazón; kiosk at Quinta at 20th Street) offers games, books, puzzles, and other fun stuff for the kiddos. Most of the stock is of the educational variety—nothing makes loud noise or goes fast.

With more than ten thousand books in stock, Mundo Bookstore (First Street between 20th and 25th avenues, 984-879-3004) is a great place to purchase a good beach novel, magazines, regional history books, Mayan literature, and other finds. The store also takes book donations to support local students.

Six blocks straight back from the ferry dock, the local Marsan Market (30th Avenue at South First Street) has fresh meats and fish, fishing supplies, clothing, shoes, fresh fruits, and a wide variety of items found at a typical Mexican market.

Cuban Cigars: Don't Get Ripped Off

For many travelers, the question of where to find authentic Cuban cigars comes up at least once during their trip to the Riviera Maya. A little information can go a long way toward preventing you from losing your hard-earned pesos on fake Cohibas on Playa del Carmen's avenida Quinta.

COUNTERFEITS ABOUND

First, be aware that the majority of so-called Cuban cigars you'll see in Playa are counterfeit, even those sold in cigar stores. If you see a Cohiba sitting in a jar next to a cash register, it is almost certainly fake. The scam here is that the store owners know that visiting Americans will pay high prices for authentic Cubans, so they relabel secondhand cigars (factory rejects) or cheaper brands.

Locally rolled cigars are available in downtown Playa.

Don't buy "Cuban" cigars from any shop or vendor unless the box has a holographic sticker of authenticity attached. The Cuban government now places a holo-gram on genuine boxes (or the three and five packs) of legitimate Cuban cigars. Even the Montecristos at the high-end resorts usually don't have these holograms, and most are just pretty good-looking fakes.

WHERE TO FIND AUTHENTIC CUBAN CIGARS

What's a tourist to do? The best source for authentic Cuban cigars is, believe it or not, the Walmart tobacco shop on the corner of 30th Avenue and 8th Street. You can be assured that not only are they authentic, they are likely the cheapest source in town (you can purchase budget-priced booze while you are there, as well).

La Casa del Habano (Quinta between 26th and 28th streets) is also a reputable source for authentic Cubans cigars and offers a good local alternative if you are opposed to big-box stores. If you choose to stay at a resort, many of them carry a limited number of brands in their store. Some do have authentic Cubans, but be sure to look for the hologram label.

BRINGING CIGARS HOME

It is against U.S. law for U.S. citizens to bring Cuban cigars into the United States or even to purchase and consume them in Mexico, though there is obviously no local enforcement. We do not condone the illegal importing of Cuban products to the United States, and if you do choose to purchase Cuban cigars, it would be wise to smoke them while in Playa.

That said, many U.S. citizens carry cigars back with them in their luggage. Less than 10 percent of travelers arriving in the United States are randomly selected to have their luggage inspected, so the odds are in your favor. Some U.S. citizens have been known to ship unlabeled Cuban cigars back home via an international courier. Be aware that this will be very expensive and there is a good chance that if you ship labeled cigars, they will be confiscated.

Courtesy of SeePlaya.com, a great source for information on the Riviera Maya.

Casa Tequila on Fifth Avenue   Philip Gamon

It's a good place for picking up a unique gift item or just strolling around to sample the local color.

A popular regional chain, Roger's Boots (Second Street between Quinta and 10th avenues) offers handmade leather boots starting at around $100. Custom boots are also available, if you're going to be around a while. They also sell leather bags, belts, fancy belt buckles, hats, holsters, and rifle cases.

Although this may seem like an average little Flower Shop (avenida Juárez between 20th and 25th streets), it may hold the key to an unforgettable evening. Surprise your date with a fresh tropical bouquet. Prices are about half of what you'd expect to pay back home.

Looking for that permanent reminder of a temporary feeling? Screamink Tattoos (10th Street at Quinta, www.screaminktattooshop.com) offers tribal tattoos, Mayan designs, and custom jobs. T-shirts and piercings are also available.

Casa Partagas (Quinta at 14th Street) is a good spot to purchase real Cuban cigars. Ask the staff for an explanation of how to spot the fakes. T-shirts, smoking accessories, and gifts are also sold.

Fitness & Spa Services

Founded by veteran Californian holistic health practitioner Sharon Sedgwick, the modern ★ Spa Itzá (calle Corazón/14th Street near Quinta, on the calle Corazón pedestrian walk, 984-803-2588, www.spaitza.com) takes a traditional approach to body treatments, accenting its services with ancient Mayan healing principles.

Located at THE ROYAL Resort, ★ ROYAL Spa (Constituyentes between

First Avenue and the beach, www.real resorts.com) is open to the public and offers a fantastic temazcal, sweat lodge, a great whirlpool room, plunge pools, and therapy rooms.

Affordable spa treatments are offered at Magic Hands (Quinta between 10th and 12th avenues and Quinta between Sixth and Eighth avenues) amid candlelight and relaxing music. Pedicures and manicures are also offered in this relaxed setting.

At ★ Yoga by the Sea (Eighth Street at the beach, 984-873-0735, www.morethanyoga.com) instructors Arielle Thomas Newman and Ellen de Jonge offer daily hatha yoga classes, yoga retreats, specialized programs, and meditation and relaxation techniques. They have special yoga programs for couples, divers, and golfers.

Authentic Bikram yoga classes are offered every day of the week at Bikram Yoga Riviera Maya (Quinta between 40th and 42nd streets, bikramyogarivieramaya.com).

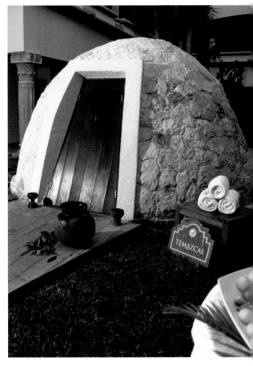

THE ROYAL Resort offers a touch of luxury with the temazcal experience.
ROYAL Resort Playa del Carmen

Where Do Jellyfish Lamps Come From?

Uniquely Playa del Carmen, these gourd lanterns are sold at shops and featured in restaurants and bars throughout downtown Playa. Carved from local gourds and *jícaras,* they're often adorned with tendrils of natural materials such as seeds and shells and sometimes inset with stained-glass panes and marbles.

Local artisans and entrepreneurs are responsible for the manufacturing of these lanterns, which by necessity are all made by hand. The proprietors of the Jellyfish Lamp shop have gone as far as to implement a rigorous training and certification program for local artisans.

Through their program, Maya workers received training for a four-year period before earning the designation of Master Crafter. Starting out, they make the hanging tendrils that fall from the bottom of the lamp. From there, artisans focus on one of three specialties, designing, cutting, and encrusting stained glass, or polishing and finishing the gourds themselves. Four workshops are located throughout the Riviera Maya, including one in Playa del Carmen.

Travelers who don't want to be responsible for toting a lantern back home can also order them online from the Jellyfish Lamp shop (www.jellyfish.com.mx).

20 Luxurious Resorts & Spas for Indulgent Travelers

1. Aventura Spa Palace resort (Puerto Aventuras)

2. Banyan Tree Mayakoba spa resort (Punta Bete)

3. Coqui Coqui Spa Hotel (Tulum)

4. El Dorado Royale—A Spa Resort (Playa Secreto)

5. Fairmont Mayakoba spa resort (Punta Bete)

6. Grand Palladium Kantenah Resort & Spa (Kantenah)

7. Hotel Esencia (Xpu-Ha)

8. Hotel Villa Rolandi Thalasso Spa (Isla Mujeres)

9. La Amada Hotel spa (Playa Mujeres)

10. Live Aqua Cancún resort and spa (Cancún)

11. Mandarin Oriental Riviera Maya spa resort (Punta Bete)

12. Maroma Resort & Spa (Punta Maroma)

13. Maya Spa (Tulum)

14. Mezzanine hotel (Tulum)

15. Occidental Royal Hideaway spa resort (Playacar)

16. Paraíso de la Bonita Resort & Thalasso Spa (Bahia Petempich near Puerto 17, Morelos)

17. Rosewood Mayakoba spa resort (Punta Bete)

18. THE ROYAL Resort Playa del Carmen spa (Playa del Carmen)

19. Spa Itzá (Playa del Carmen)

20. The Tides Riviera Maya spa resort (Punta Bete)

Modern and upscale, The Gym (1st Avenue between Constituyentes and 16th Street, 984-873-2098, www.thegymplaya.com) offers top-of-the-line weight and cardiovascular equipment, fitness classes, and personal training.

Evolve Gym (24th Street, between Fifth and 10th avenues) has top-of-the line machines, tons of weights, and some great classes. They offer Pilates, yoga, spinning, and cardio kick boxing instruction.

48 Hours
in Playa del Carmen

 DAY 1

If your time is limited, pick a hotel on the beach in downtown Playa del Carmen. Mosquito Beach, Playa Maya, or Fusion Hotel would all be good options. No need to go all-inclusive because you won't be spending much time at the hotel anyway. Drop your bags in your room and head straight for the beach.

Head north along the waterfront to the Canibal Royal beach club on the edge of town. Order a bucket of ice-cold Coronas, fresh ceviche, and a whole fried fish. Vacation has arrived.

Spend the afternoon enjoying the sunshine and fresh air, taking frequent dips in the ocean, and applying sunscreen whenever you order another round of drinks.

Temazcal

The word *temazcal* means "bathhouse" in the Nahuatl language of the ancient Aztecs, and the centuries-old temazcal sweat-lodge ceremony hasn't changed much over the years. The ritual, performed by a shaman or trained healer, is designed to serve both spiritual and medical purposes. Native women were known to give birth inside the dark, warm environment of the temazcal, thus making the transition from the womb a bit more gradual. The sweat-lodge ceremony takes place in a stone or adobe hut, dug into the earth and forming a dome large enough for about a dozen participants. Before entering the temazcal, all those who will participate reflect on the four cardinal points and are cleansed with incense. Volcanic stones are heated in a wood fire, carried into the temazcal, and placed in the center of the floor.

Each participant sits behind a clay pot full of water, and the door is closed and sealed, making the inside completely dark and very hot. The leader pours water onto the rocks, creating steam that fills the temazcal and helps partakers to liberate their mind, body, and soul. Ancient chants are repeated, songs are sung, and participants are led through a cleansing ritual. In some versions, regional fruits are passed around to be tasted and rubbed on the skin. Modern-day participants generally wear a bathing suit and can splash water on themselves to regulate their breathing and prevent overheating.

Many people have visions and even see an animal or other creature rising from the glowing rocks. The ceremony leader can help interpret whatever you may see. At the end of the ceremony, it is customary to run to the ocean and bathe in the shallows, letting the cool water wash away the sweat and complete the renewal process. Next, a soothing herbal tea helps lock in the benefits reaped during the ceremony. It's a wonderfully spiritual experience that can leave you energized and refreshed for hours afterward.

Places in the Riviera Maya with temazcal facilities include Maroma Resort & Spa, Punta Maroma (see chapter 3); Ceiba del Mar, Puerto Morelos (see chapter 3); THE ROYAL Playa del Carmen; Cabanas Copal, Tulum (see chapter 1); The Tides, Playa Xcalacoco (see chapter 3); and Ana y José Charming Hotel & Spa, south of Tulum (see chapter 2).

Later that evening, head to Fifth Avenue just in time for Magic Hour—the enchanting hour before sunset when the air cools down, the bars start to bustle, and the parade of vacationers makes its way through town.

Pick a restaurant along Fifth Avenue for a leisurely meal, then enjoy the Playa version of the pub crawl, with a stop at any bar that strikes your fancy. Consider swinging on the barstools at Pez Vela, placing a bet at the sportsbook at Tequila Barrel, or checking out the rooftop lounge at Hotel Básico.

For late-night excitement, head to Coco Bongo and secure a spot upstairs near the DJ booth—the perfect vantage point to watch the action on the stage—and on the dance floor.

The marines and local police are a presence on the beach.

DAY 2 Start your day at Ah Cacao for coffee and pastries. Stock up on snacks for a day of fun in the sun. You've got two choices for your day today. For zip-lining, jungle tours, and Mayan-style water sports, head to the Xplor eco-adventure park, where you'll spend several hours in the trees and on the sand. For a softer sense of adventure, take an expedition with Alltournative Tours and visit a traditional Mayan village, swim in a freshwater lagoon, and maybe even meet a friendly monkey.

For your final night in Playa del Carmen, consider lobster at the Blue Lobster or Big Lobster downtown or walk to Yaxche Restaurant on the north end of Fifth Avenue to sample authentic Mayan cuisine with a contemporary twist. Keep the evening going at the beachfront bar at the Fusion Hotel and witness the fire dancer show.

Ready for more? The Blue Parrot just up the beach is open until 4 AM, with one of the town's largest thatched-roof bars, swinging barstools, and tables in the sand surrounding a dance floor that's always filled with happy revelers. Want to sample more of Playa's nightlife? Take a stroll along the 12th Street Strip and find dance clubs, lounge bars, student bars, and more, all within a few city blocks.

On your final vacation morning, have breakfast on Fifth Avenue, then hit up the souvenir shops close to the town square. If time permits, enjoy one more visit to the beach for a final swim in the Caribbean.

Extend Your Stay

If you're lucky enough to have more than a couple of weeks to spend in the Riviera Maya, you'll have the chance to explore well beyond the traditional tourist attractions.

Kohunlich—These Mayan ruins are located near the border with Belize. Because the location is quite remote, the site is in excellent condition and it's worth the trip.

Bacalar—This ice-blue freshwater lagoon is one of the main attractions in the Mayan Coast. It can be done as a day trip from the southern Riviera Maya, but if you're able to spend several days, there's plenty of other nearby sites to explore.

The Riviera Maya: A Land of Business Opportunity
Contributed by Brenda Alfaro

Great business opportunities abound in the Riviera Maya, and with careful consideration and planning, foreigners can invest successfully in this growth. Doing business in Mexico is not for the faint of heart, however. It requires moxie and experienced advice to be successful. Having a local on your side is always a plus, especially in Latin America, where polite business relationships guide you through the maze of paperwork, labor relationships, and license requirements. Patience is also a must-have virtue to survive the relaxing *mañana* Latin style.

Where do you start to create a business in Mexico? Well, not with the "slick talker and aggressive salesperson" attitude. First, look for someone who has been successful in a quiet way, who obviously has learned the ropes and has created the business and official relationships that have kept her in business.

Second, before stepping into the business community with a substantial investment, research and understand the legal system and labor relationships in Mexico. This is easily done on the Internet. Mexico laws are based on the Napoleonic Code, similar to the laws of France or Louisiana in the United States. Labor relationships are based on the "employee is always right" philosophy. Mexican employees know their rights and use them effectively—as do the lawyers representing them.

Third, understand the importance of a Mexican notary, a powerful appointed position in Mexico. Notaries create most of the official legal documents in Mexico, including establishment of corporations, buy-sell agreements, and real estate transactions. No transaction or legal agreement is considered legal in Mexico unless it has been officially registered. All parties to an agreement must sign it in front of a notary, and that agreement must be registered in the municipality's official records.

Fourth, before completing a business transaction, seek the advice of a person who is completely independent of the parties involved in the transaction and one you trust to translate the agreements to you accurately. I am always amazed when I hear that someone is using a lawyer or notary who was recommended by those who stand to benefit from the transaction, such as a seller or a real estate agent. A good rule of thumb is, "If you would not do this in your country, you should not do it here."

Mérida—The capital city of Yucatán state is a wonderful place to learn more about Mayan culture and experience the slow pace of a modern Mexico city with deep roots in the past.

Havana, Cuba—There are regular flights from Cancún to Havana. Package deals, including airfare and hotel, are available for less than $300, and can be booked at local travel agencies around Playa del Carmen and even many hotel tour desks. Take note, however, that U.S. law prohibits citizens from traveling to Cuba. Adventurous Americans, however, have been known to make the trip without inci-

Fifth, contract an accountant to keep you current with your tax filings and license requirements. Be careful who you contract, and seek the advice of those who have experience here.

Sixth, avoid all lawsuits and labor board actions. Swallow your pride or anger and settle with an employee who is leaving or involved in a legal situation. In the end, it will save you money and stress and allow you to focus on your business at hand rather than revenge or a compelling desire to "win." If you do end up needing a lawyer, find one who actually knows the law and has strong legal contacts.

Seventh, be polite and patient—always! Mexican people are intelligent and are part of a formal, polite society. Do not underestimate their abilities or insult them. Stop, listen, and think before you answer or react. Directness is not a business asset in Mexico. Talk, smile, and never argue or raise your voice. If you do, the costs will be great.

Eighth, follow the rules. It is so much easier when you are always in compliance, which means no extra favors need to be made to run your business. Remember, the person who receives a favor will be out of power in a few months or years, and the new official will expect the same or more—so why begin? And get your FM3, our resident work visa. Don't risk deportation.

Ninth, treat your employees with respect, learn the labor laws, and use employee contracts. Talk with business owners in your field and understand your employee base. Call for references before hiring someone. Identify the "professional labor board employees" who move from business to business, collecting labor settlements. Look prospective employees in the eye—if they do not look back or seem distrustful, do not hire them. Trust your instincts.

Tenth, enjoy the experience. When your patience begins to wear thin, escape to the beach to relax, recharge, and remember why you chose to live and work in this paradise in the first place.

Brenda Long Alfaro and her Maya husband, Jorge Luis Alfaro Mérida, are successful restaurateurs in Playa del Carmen. They own the widely acclaimed Ajua Maya restaurant (see Dining), the Hacienda Maya restaurant, and Ajua Weddings, which offers custom-designed weddings and event services on the Riviera Maya. They also established the Fundación América Maya to provide health care, education, and economic programs to Maya families and children.

dent, because Cuban authorities welcome the U.S. dollars and cooperate by not stamping U.S. passports that are presented upon arrival.

2

The Riviera Maya

SOUTH OF PLAYA DEL CARMEN

TRAVELERS VENTURING FARTHER SOUTH of Playa del Carmen will find a striking variety of options for lodging and recreation, and the farther south you go, the more remote, unspoiled, and adventurous things become. A stone's throw from Playa del Carmen, Playacar is home to nearly a dozen all-inclusive mega-resorts, where travelers from around the world visit to play golf, lie on the beach, and be pampered in every way possible. The beachfront towns of Puerto Aventuras and Akumal beckon scuba divers and fishing enthusiasts with excellent conditions year-round, while the abundant *cenotes*, hidden beaches, eco-adventure parks, and Mayan ruins provide venturesome travelers with the kind of vacation experiences that turn postcards home into exotic tales of intrigue and exploration.

Many of the hotels and resorts south of Playa are all-inclusives, with vast campuses featuring luxurious accommodations, multiple dining options, on-site nightlife, spas, recreational activities, and everything else guests need to spend a week of fun in the sun without ever getting into a car. Other lodging options in this area include local inns; eco-conscious cabanas with an emphasis on nature, rather than luxury; and low-cost hutlike properties fashioned from native materials and devoted to students, traditionalists, and other budget-conscious travelers who want to experience Riviera Maya's splendor much as the locals have been doing for hundreds of years.

PLAYACAR

Just south of Playa del Carmen, off Highway 307, at km 285, the large-scale, gated resort community of Playacar surrounds the ancient Mayan ruins of Xaman-Ha and comprises resort hotels, condos, private residences, shopping

LEFT: Puerto Aventuras is built around a central lagoon filled with dolphins.

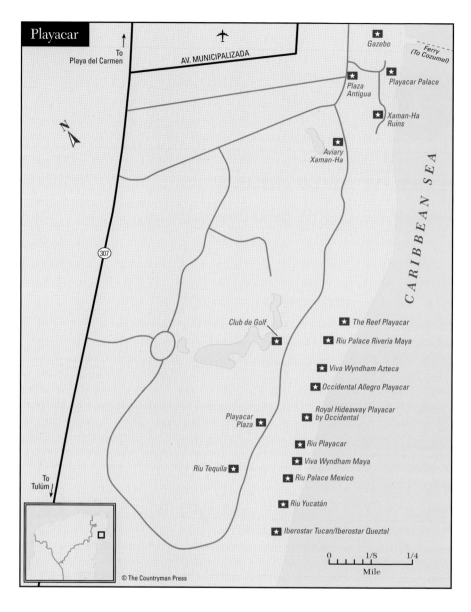

Playacar

To Playa del Carmen

AV. MUNICIPALIZADA

Gazebo

Ferry (To Cozumel)

Plaza Antigua

Playacar Palace

Xaman-Ha Ruins

Aviary Xaman-Ha

307

CARIBBEAN SEA

Club de Golf

The Reef Playacar

Riu Palace Riveria Maya

Viva Wyndham Azteca

Occidental Allegro Playacar

Royal Hideaway Playacar by Occidental

Playacar Plaza

Riu Playacar

Viva Wyndham Maya

Riu Tequila

Riu Palace Mexico

To Tulúm

Riu Yucatán

Iberostar Tucan/Iberostar Queztal

0   1/8   1/4
Mile

© The Countryman Press

plazas, restaurants, a golf course, activities centers, and one of the most pristine stretches of beach in the whole Riviera Maya.

The creation of Playacar was the single most important event in the development of large-scale tourism in the Riviera Maya. Before that, travelers were content with small, locally owned hotels, relatively few services, and European-plan (no meals included) rates. Aside from a few standouts, accommodations were generally simple affairs, with basic amenities and very few luxuries but a strong feeling of tradition and harmony with the surroundings. Strict density restrictions in Playa del Carmen made the town less than ideal for large resort development, and had allowed the town to grow slowly and organically, unlike the rampant development seen in Cancún.

In the early 1990s, though, things started to change. Mexico's real estate conglomerate Grupo Situr purchased a huge plot of barren beachfront land just south of avenida Juárez and christened it Playacar, a term deemed more marketable and English-friendly than the name of the town itself. Since it was out of the jurisdiction of the development restrictions, the Riviera Maya had its first opportunity to build international-class hotels, which needed a larger scale and higher volume of guests to turn a profit.

Today, there are more than a dozen large resorts owned by international corporations and averaging some 300 rooms each. Unlike the small inns and guest houses of a few years ago, these resorts offer a vast array of services and luxuries, including imported linens, efficient air-conditioning, abundant hot water, water-sports centers, on-site scuba training, dry-cleaning service, Jacuzzi tubs, tennis courts, swimming pools, and kids' clubs. Most are operated as all-inclusives, where guests pay one price that includes accommodations plus all meals, drinks, and activities. Many hotels have on-site gourmet restaurants, multiple bars, and even amphitheaters and nightclubs.

The area has become a playground for tourists from the United States, Canada, and Europe. It is an extremely popular wedding and honeymoon destination, and the resorts are quite adept at catering to vacationing couples with welcome amenities (fruit baskets, chilled champagne, flowers), special dinner reservations, and couples' spa treatments. Other common Playacar visitors are families and budget travelers with flexible schedules, who compare prices weekly, waiting for a bargain. Frequently, these travelers will choose their resort based on what special offers are available and tend to be less loyal to the brands or specific hotel properties. Others have had a good experience at one of the resorts and become avid ambassadors for it, claiming that its services and amenities are unbeatable. These travelers wouldn't dream of staying anywhere else and pride themselves on returning year after year, sometimes bringing gifts for their favorite bartenders and waiters.

The main road through the complex, Xaman-Ha Avenue, is made of cobblestone and is lined with manicured tropical plants and an occasional actual Mayan ruin, lending a timeless quality to the otherwise modern resort community. The road parallels the beachfront and splits Playacar into two sides. Phase I, along the water, features a nearly solid line of hotels, though they are mostly low-rise buildings of two or three stories surrounded by tropical vegetation, so the area does not feel overdeveloped or crowded. Phase II, on the other side of the avenue, includes the golf course, hundreds of vacation villas and private homes, and several hotels that are not directly on the beach. These hotels shuttle guests to a beach club, so even though their rooms don't front the beach, their guests are still able to have a beach vacation. Craft stores, restaurants, bars, and tour agencies are housed in various shopping plazas along Xaman-Ha and at Plaza Marina, near the ferry dock. Most guests, however, either take their meals on-site at their all-inclusive resorts or venture into the neighboring town of Playa del Carmen to experience the abundant dining options offered along avenida Quinta (Fifth Avenue) and throughout town. Shopping, nightlife, and other tourist attractions can be found in Playa as well.

During the day, the beach bustles with activity. Some guests stroll along the water, play volleyball, sail, kayak, windsurf, swim, Jet Ski, and enjoy the plethora of

Hotel Choices: All-Inclusive or European Plan

One of the first decisions travelers need to make when planning their trip is whether to stay in an all-inclusive (AI) or European-plan (EP) hotel. AI resorts generally include all food and drinks consumed on-site, plus a variety of nonmotorized watersports, activity programs, and fitness centers. Some even include premium alcohol, gourmet à la carte meals, stocked minibars, and other amenities. EP hotels frequently have their own restaurants and bars also, but guests have to pay for any meals or drinks that they have.

The Riviera Maya has a growing number of all-inclusive resorts, practically pioneering the concept in Mexico. Most of the large-scale full-service beachfront resorts are operated as AIs, while the smaller independently run hotels along the beach and near Playa del Carmen's avenida Quinta are operated on an EP basis.

Overall, the decision on whether to choose for an AI or an EP is up to the traveler. There are positives and negatives to both choices.

AI RESORTS ARE GENERALLY GOOD IF:

You don't want to do much planning. AIs are generally higher priced than hotels because you are getting all meals, activities, and alcohol included. However, the food and activity choices can become boring.

EP HOTELS ARE GENERALLY GOOD IF:

You are a little more adventuresome. You will pay less on average but will need to make arrangements for food, activities, and alcohol yourself. Since you'll likely be spending more time away from the hotel, you will get a more authentic Mexican experience.

Now let's get into the details.

FOOD

Obviously, meals are included at AIs, whereas they are extra for those staying in hotels. AIs generally have limited choices, and, unless you go for the very expensive resorts, the quality of the food can range from poor to very good. Most AIs have a main dining room where meals are served buffet style and a small selection of à la carte restaurants on-site available for little or no extra charge. Reservations are usually required for the à la carte restaurants and can be difficult to get if the resort is busy. It is not unusual for guests at AIs to report that they get tired of the food choices by the end of their stay.

On the other hand, most Playa hotels have limited menus, meaning you'll either have to go grocery shopping at the local supermarket or eat out at the surrounding restaurants. The quality and prices of the restaurants varies widely, but exploring the town looking for a good place to eat can also be a lot of fun.

DRINKS

AIs include unlimited drinks, including water, juices, sodas, beer, and mixed drinks, which is one of their main selling points. This is unfortunately not always as good a deal as it sounds. In Mexico, the same brands of liquor are available in different "grades," where each grade carries a different level of alcohol. The liquor you find in the AIs is generally of the lowest grade, and some guests report that drinks sometimes taste watered down.

If you stay at an EP hotel, you will generally purchase your drinks at local bars, restaurants, or from the in-room minibar. The prices for liquor differ by location, but you are generally assured of quality. If you really want to save money, take a trip over to Walmart and stock up on the cheapest liquor in town.

ACTIVITIES
Most AIs have a variety of activities tailored to their clientele: sports, exercise classes, dance classes, arts and crafts, pool games, and team sports are common offerings. It is less common for EP hotels to have these options available.

One problem with AI-sponsored activities is that these resorts tend to draw a very diverse crowd. Visitors are encouraged to research their resort fully, since you will generally spend most of your time there and you will likely end up socializing with other guests.

BRINGING THE FAMILY?
Although parents should always know where their children are, the setup of an AI resort, with their kids' clubs and activity programs, may allow parents to give children more freedom than they would get in a hotel that has a lot of casual traffic. This can be a big plus for AIs when parents and children have different ideas of what activities they are interested in. Again, parents should never get too lax with their children's safety while on vacation.

CONVENIENCE
Many people like the convenience of not having to carry money to pay for meals and activities. This is a nice perk of AIs.

ROOMS
There is a wide range of room quality at both AI resorts and EP hotels. If having a very nice room is important, you should make sure you do your research carefully. Don't make the mistake of thinking that an AI will automatically be nicer than a nearby EP hotel; the quality of both varies greatly.

COST
Although many believe that AIs are cheaper than EP hotels, this may vary depending on the vacationer and what kinds of activities they do while on vacation. Travelers who spend most of their time at the resort and partake of the free activities will probably find that an all-inclusive is the more economical choice. Vacationers who plan to take several tours and spend a lot of time outside the resort will probably find that an EP hotel is the lower-cost alternative.

Still unsure? Here's a helpful rule of thumb: if you have read this far, it means you like to do your research and enjoy learning about new things and should almost certainly stay at an EP hotel.

Content provided by SeePlaya.com, a great online source for insider's information on the Riviera Maya.

activities, while others seek respite in a lounge chair or hammock and read and snooze to the warm breezes. To the north of Playacar is the town of Playa del Carmen, reachable by bicycle (loaners available at most hotels) or a short taxi ride. To the south is a mile-long stretch of deserted beach decorated with massive boulders, which starts at the Gala Resort and ends at the Xcaret resort and ecopark.

Guests at Playacar resorts can spend an entire week without leaving the complex and have all their needs and whims catered to. Others, however, like to visit Playa del Carmen in the evening to go shopping, stroll the tourist plazas, try some local foods, and enjoy the nightlife.

Checking In
Best places to stay in and around Playacar

It can be a bit difficult to differentiate among the all-inclusive resorts of Playacar. For the most part, the hotels share a common beach, which is just about perfect anywhere along the stretch. The hotels themselves are large-scale affairs, with comparable pools, gyms, restaurants, bars, and activities programs. Nearly all the rooms offer good air-conditioning, plenty of hot water, comfortable bedding, private balconies, minibars, and standard amenities. Most have bicycles for guest use, which makes the couple-mile trip into Playa del Carmen a breeze. The main considerations and differentiating factors are the size of the resort, whether or not it's adults-only, whether it's on the beach or the golf course, and your budget. Rates range from $100 per person per night up to $250. As the price goes up, generally, the rooms are larger, the grounds are better maintained, food and beverage quality is higher, and the vibe is more exclusive.

Adjacent to the Cozumel ferry dock and the Playa del Carmen town plaza, the chic Playacar Palace (north end of paseo Xaman-Ha, www.palace resorts.com) is a good spot for travelers seeking the luxury of Playacar but with ready access to downtown Playa. Playacar's original flagship resort, the structure was first large hotel built around Playa and was completely renovated in 2005.

Luxury and all-inclusives don't always go together. But at the adults-only, 13-acre, 200-room ★ Occidental Royal Hideaway (paseo Xaman-Ha, 984-873-4500, www.royalhideaway.com), the two meld like piña coladas and sunset—which, by the way, are included in the rate. The lavish property has meandering rivers, waterfalls, tropical gardens, six pools (three reserved for quiet relaxation), and several restaurants and bars. Men are required to wear long pants, closed-toe shoes, and collared shirts for dinner.

Spanish-owned ★ Riu Hotels and Resorts (paseo Xaman-Ha, 1-888-666-8816, www.riu.com) has five all-inclusive properties on Playacar's southern end. Guests staying at one hotel can enjoy the facilities at the others, including the nightclub, which is located at the party-friendly Tequila (well, that makes sense!). Other resorts include upscale Palace Mexico, hacienda-style Yucatán, budget-friendly Playacar, and the Lupita set in the middle of the golf course back from the beach.

Also near Playacar's southern, the all-inclusive Iberostar Resort Complex (paseo Xaman-Ha, 984-877-2000 or

15 Adults-Only Resorts for a Kid-Free Getaway

1. Aura Cozumel Wyndham Grand Bay resort (Cozumel)

2. Aventura Spa Palace resort (Puerto Aventuras)

3. El Dorado Royale—A Spa Resort (Playa Secreto)

4. Excellence Playa Mujeres resort (Playa Mujeres)

5. Excellence Riviera Cancún resort (Puerto Morelos)

6. Iberostar Grand Hotel Paraíso resort (Playa Paraíso)

7. Le Reve Hotel & Spa (Punta Bete)

8. Mahékal Beach Resort (Playa del Carmen)

9. Mandarin Oriental resort (Punta Bete)

10. Occidental Royal Hideaway resort (Playacar)

11. Hotel Reina Roja (Playa del Carmen)

12. THE ROYAL Resort Playa del Carmen (Playa del Carmen)

13. Secrets Capri resort (Punta Maroma)

14. Temptation Resort Cancún (Cancún)

15. Sabor Cozumel Resort & Spa by Wyndham (Cozumel)

1-888-923-2722 from the U.S., www .iberostar.com) includes the Tucan and Quetzal resorts, each with 350 rooms. The resort is a sun-worshipers mecca, with a great rock-free beachfront, multiple pools, and outdoor Jacuzzis.

The all-inclusive Viva Wyndham Resorts (paseo Xaman-Ha, 1-800-996-3426 from the U.S., www.vivaresorts .com) include the smaller Mexican colonial-style, 234-room, kid-friendly Azteca and the more contemporary 400-room Maya. Guests may choose to dine at any of the seven restaurants at the two resorts, although several require reservations.

Playacar Beach Properties (984-873-0418 or 1-866-862-7164 from the U.S., www.playacarbeachproperties .com) has an inventory of more than 50 condos and villas in Playacar, including locations on the beach, on the golf course, and around the development. Their Web site lists all of properties and amenities and helps you select one that may suit you.

XCARET TO PAAMUL

South of Xcaret, visitors get their first glimpse of the wild side of the Riviera Maya. No longer will you see souvenir stands, gas stations, and convenience stores every few miles. Here a thick jungle canopy has kept tourism development at bay, while palm trees, unexplored Mayan ruins, and tiny traditional villages dot the landscape. To visit this part of the Yucatán, travelers either take a shuttle bus from the airport or rent a car so they can go where they choose. Public bus service is spotty and will

Xcaret offers a sense of the Mayan past. Riviera Maya Destination Marketing Office

Mi Casa Es Su Casa—Vacation Home Rentals

By Chip Rankin

For years, shrewd travelers to Mexico have chosen private condos and homes over hotels. As the popularity of these vacation rentals has soared internationally, and development in Riviera Maya has multiplied, there are more options than ever.

Private rentals can often accommodate larger groups at a lower overall price and they feature kitchens and amenities allowing guests to dine in, and greater degrees of privacy than hotels.

As with hotels, quality and pricing levels range from budget to deluxe. You'll want to see as many photos of the actual unit you'll be staying in, have a clear idea of its exact location, and review a full list of amenities and restrictions.

Playa Beach Rentals (www.playabeachrentals.com) is a local outfit specializing in rentals and property management. They manage properties through their offices and reservations are booked directly through their listing service.

HomeAway (www.homeaway.com) has the largest international network of vacation rental listings, including in the Riviera Maya, and has done much to popularize the concept in recent years.

VRBO, or Vacation Rental by Owner (www.VRBO.com), owned by HomeAway, has a separate listing service, given its large, loyal following. Many listings are exclusive, so you'll want to check both sites for a most thorough selection.

An international hotel and tourism expert and owner of travel and destination marketing firm Hollis Travel Labs (www.HollisTravelLabs.com), Chip Rankin first became involved in the business after a particularly memorable holiday in Playa.

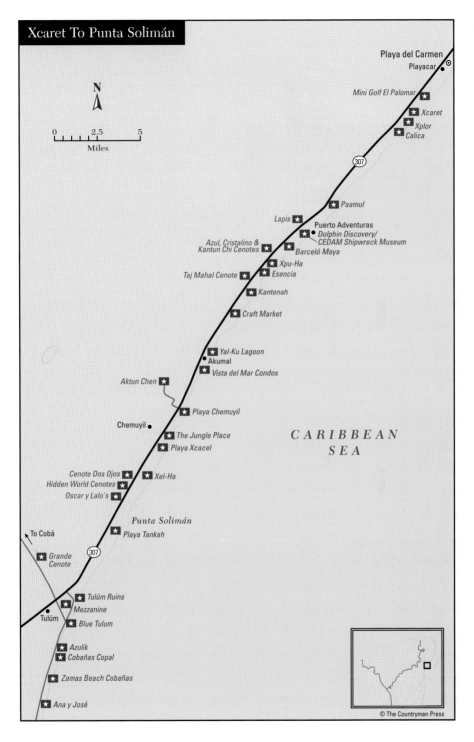

Xcaret To Punta Solimán

N

0   2.5   5
Miles

Playa del Carmen
Playacar

Mini Golf El Palomar

Xcaret
Xplor
Calica

307

Paamul

Lapis

Puerto Adventuras
Dolphin Discovery/
CEDAM Shipwreck Museum

Azul, Cristalino &
Kantun Chi Cenotes
Barceló Maya

Xpu-Ha

Taj Mahal Cenote
Esencia

Kantenah

Craft Market

Yal-Ku Lagoon
Akumal
Vista del Mar Condos

Aktun Chen

Playa Chemuyil

Chemuyil

The Jungle Place
Playa Xcacel

Cenote Dos Ojos
Xel-Ha
Hidden World Cenotes
Oscar y Lalo's

Punta Solimán

To Cobá
Playa Tankah

307

Grande
Cenote

CARIBBEAN
SEA

Tulúm Ruins
Mezzanine
Tulúm
Blue Tulum

Azulik
Cobañas Copal

Zamas Beach Cobañas

Ana y José

© The Countryman Press

let travelers off only along the main road, while most of the hotels and attractions are located along the beach several miles away. Tourists either take their meals on-property at their resort or, if staying at an EP (European-plan) hotel or condo, stop off at the supermarket in Playa del Carmen to stock up on foodstuffs and other essential supplies.

Checking In

Best places to stay in and around Xcaret to Paamul

Located adjacent to the Xcaret ecology park, the 769-room ★ ⊕ Occidental Grand Xcaret (Highway 307, km 282, 987-871-5400 or 1-800-858-2258 from the U.S., www.occidentalhotels.com) is a wondrous all-inclusive playground catering to families and travelers looking for a lot of activities. Rooms at the massive resort are housed in low-rise buildings surrounded by five free-form swimming pools, winding rivers, and tropical gardens.

The RV haven Paamul (Highway 307, km 273, 984-876-2691, www.paamul.com) is gaining in popularity with day-trippers who come to see the sea turtles nest, go snorkeling or diving, or lounge on beach. The main road is lined with RV shelters, some of which have been there for years. Visitors can camp on the beach or stay at the small hotel and there are a few super-casual beachside restaurants. The rocky beach along this shallow bay is not the best for swimming.

Attractions

Formerly just a commercial port and dock for the Cozumel car ferry, the Calica facility (Highway 307, km 280) is becoming a popular stop-off point for international cruise ships and includes a commercial plaza with shops, restaurants, and souvenir stands. Transcaribe (987-872-7671, transcaribemex.com) operates the Cozumel car ferry.

PUERTO AVENTURAS (Highway 307, km 269)

The exclusive resort town of Puerto Aventuras is the only true sheltered marina in the Riviera Maya. It was also the first major development south of Cancún, though it hasn't had the rapid growth seen in Playa del Carmen. If you talk to the locals, they'll tell you this is by design to retain the small-town feel and exclusive nature of the resort. Hurricane Emily passed directly over the marina in 2005, sinking boats, beaching others, and wreaking havoc across town, but thousands of palm trees were replanted, and the area quickly regained its prestorm appeal. In fact, encouraged the town's recovery and resilience, condo sales boomed and the community's challenge became keeping its small-town luster. The economic recession cooled that growth, but Puerto Aventuras should remain popular when real estate surges again.

Visitors enter through a large security gate just off Highway 307. The road winds down to the beach and ends at the 250-slip marina, packed with fishing

Hurricane Emily: An Unwelcome Guest

At 5 PM on July 17, 2005, management at the Moon Palace announced an immediate termination of alcohol sales and room service, instructing guests to stay indoors until further notice. Earlier in the day, the staff had lashed down all the outdoor furniture and plucked all the coconuts from their trees. The guests, many from the northern United States, Canada, and Europe, were complete strangers to tropical weather and immediately lost any romantic notions of hurricane parties or the amusing thrill of riding out a storm. It was an ominous sign of what was to come as the largest Atlantic hurricane ever recorded in the month of July was bearing down on the Riviera Maya.

Just after midnight, Hurricane Emily, a category 4 storm, ripped across the southern tip of Cozumel Island, enveloping the Punta Sur lighthouse in the eerie calm of the eye. The hammocks at the Reggae Shack swung wildly until the wooden poles supporting them collapsed in a heap, followed by the palapa roof of the bar. Up the east side of the island, angry waves licked at the walls of Mezcalito's restaurant as wind-driven rain lashed into the kitchen. A 160 mph gust of wind tore at the roof, pulling it apart bit by bit and spitting it into the ocean. Hundreds of trees along Rafael Melgar Boulevard, the main road along the western beachfront, fell, almost in unison, as the storm continued east. At 1 AM the clock tower in the town square clanged a single time, but the howling wind and distant sirens made it impossible for anyone to hear it.

As the eye moved across the Cozumel channel, the normally ubiquitous ferry boats were nowhere to be seen. The angry storm stirred up massive waves as it traced a path for Puerto Aventuras, hungry for the luxury yachts docked at the marina. Waves crashed over the bulkhead, flooding into shops, restaurants, and hotels. The roof of the Copacabana (now Catalonia Royal Tulum) hotel came crashing down, exposing the lobby to the full force of the storm. Luckily, all the guests were huddled in the relative safety of the hotel's ballroom. A huge metal navigational buoy broke free from its anchor and barreled toward shore, beaching itself in front of the Riu Palace in Playacar. Concrete and wooden utility poles across the region snapped like twigs while billboards along Highway 307 advertising XX Beer and Xcaret park were crumpled like paper in a fist.

Thousands of people hunkered down in shelters from Cancún to Tulum. Several hundred sought refuge in the convention center at the Mayan Palace, thousands more crowded into the Playa del Carmen municipal gym, and some 600 others waited and prayed from inside the concrete walls of a bordello on the outskirts of town. Locals and visitors in Cancún rode out the storm together in the tiny rooms of an elementary school. When one room flooded, the group had to brave the elements and run to another. Shortly thereafter, the door to that room was torn from its hinges.

The eye passed right by Paamul, rumbling the mobile homes and testing their window seals with driving rain. Palm trees were gouged from the ground, and rain-soaked sand whipped into the trailers, sounding like thousands of BBs being shot into beer cans.

continued next page

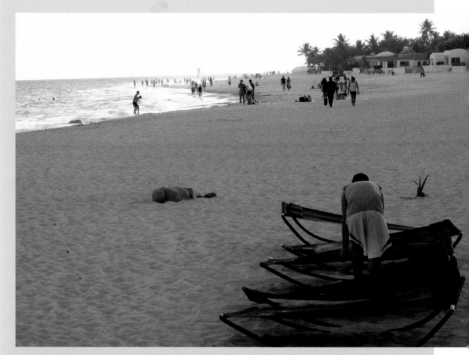

The beaches south of the ferry dock have been restored to their prehurricane condition.

As the night wore on, bloggers tapped away on computer keyboards in sheltered Internet cafés, updating Internet users around the world of the storm's progress. Their missives grew less frequent as powerlines fell and connection became impossible. A key Telmex cell phone tower swayed in the wind, then bent and fell, cutting off yet another mode of communication.

It was still drizzling when dawn broke, but the heavy winds were gone and the furious sea had calmed. Locals and visitors alike crept from their shelters and spilled into the streets to survey the damage. Along avenida Quinta in Playa, many shops suffered from broken glass and ruined merchandise. Water was nearly waist deep along Constituyentes. Many homes in the humble residential area north of the tourist zone had collapsed and lay in ruin, and distraught locals sat on the beach and on the street, numb from shock and unsure of where to go. Swimming pools were filled with sand and debris, street signs littered the streets, the beaches were full of trash, *palapas* were torn down, and uprooted or stripped trees outnumbered healthy ones.

The National Guard arrived early to begin clearing the streets and cleaning up the heavily touristed areas, including Quinta. There were widespread power outages, but some stores were open, selling food, water, and other supplies. Hotel guests and staff worked side by side to clear broken glass, sweep out floodwaters, and repair damages.

It quickly became apparent that things were not nearly as bad as they could have been. Although powerful, the storm was compact and fast moving, so it did not cause as much damage as it could have. Cozumel, Puerto Aventuras, and Akumal were the hardest hit, with thousands of trees downed and many roofs torn off and buildings flooded. The beach in Playa Paraíso was badly eroded, but in Tankah, just down the coast, there seemed to be more sand than before. Two gas stations lost their roofs and were in shambles, but no fires had broken out. Local farms suffered greatly, with the summer's corn, papaya, and citrus crops enduring major losses.

It was clear that the Riviera Maya had learned the hard lessons since being caught severely underprepared for Hurricane Gilbert in 1988. The large-scale evacuation effort had worked. A convoy of 500 buses had moved 60,000 tourists to safety in less than 12 hours. Some hotels in the Riviera Maya sent guests to sister properties in Cancún, while others were sent to shelters in Vallodolid, Mérida, and elsewhere. Hundreds of petrochemical workers were evacuated from rigs and oil platforms in the storm's path.

The storm claimed the lives of four people in Jamaica, and two men working on oil rig evacuations were killed when their helicopter crashed in the Gulf of Mexico. A German dive instructor living in Playacar also died when he was electrocuted as he prepared his home for the storm. Miraculously, no other major injuries or deaths were reported.

The airports in Cancún and Cozumel opened the day after the storm, and hotels and restaurants opened as quickly as they could. Some were back in business in days, while others took weeks or even months before they were ready again. The people of the Riviera Maya kept their faith, helping each other make it through the hard times. New palm trees were planted, *palapas* were constructed, signs replaced, homes built, and lives repaired. No doubt Hurricane Emily was strong, but she was no match for the determination, the will, and the community spirit of the Riviera Maya.

boats, dive boats, sailboats, and pleasure yachts. The marina channels wind through an open-air pedestrian plaza, lined with restaurants, shops, bars, pharmacies, Internet cafés, and a few grocery/convenience stores. A Dolphin Discovery location is built into the marina, and visitors can stroll the plaza while watching the dolphins cavort, swim, and even jump out of the water. Given how pleasantly landscaped and maintained everything is, it's surprising how few places there are to stay. There is a nine-hole golf course, a museum, a crafts market, tennis courts, and a beautiful beach where the reef is close to shore.

Checking In
Best places to stay in and around Puerto Aventuras

With a romantic design inspired by a traditional Mexican hacienda with a contemporary flair, the 1,266-room Aventura Spa Palace (Highway 307, km 270, 984-875-1100, www.palace

resorts.com) is an adults-only, all-inclusive resort occupying 85 tropical acres along the beach. Built around a natural ocean inlet, the resort is ideal for protected-water snorkeling, swimming, and sunbathing. Most guests are vacationing couples celebrating a honeymoon, anniversary, or other special occasion.

Adjacent to the white sandy beach and the commercial marina, the luxurious Omni Puerto Aventuras Hotel Beach Resort (800-843-6664 from the U.S., www.omnihotels.com) is located at the center of activity in town. Despite offering just 30 rooms, the amenities would seem appropriate for a hotel five times its size.

On a beach south of the marina and one mile from Puerto Aventuras'

main plaza, the very upscale ★ Casa del Agua (Highway 307, km 268, www.casadelagua.com) has four rooms right on a perfect, quiet beach in a residential area. Formerly a private residence, the house is contemporary Mexican, with handcrafted furniture, colorful Mexican textiles, and original artwork throughout. A good option for guests seeking simplicity, luxury, romance, and privacy.

Upscale and family-friendly, the 324-room all-inclusive ⚓ Catalonia Riviera Maya (avenida Xcacel, Lot 1, off Highway 307, near km 271, www.cataloniarivieracancun.com) gives guests a taste of the Mexican Caribbean while still providing high-end resort luxuries.

Local Flavors

Taste of the town—restaurants, cafés, bars, bistros, etc.

Most restaurants in Puerto Aventuras are located around the central marina plaza, overlooking the Dolphin Discovery waterway, and most have small interior dining rooms and patios with shaded tables. All in close proximity, it's easy to walk from one to the next, checking to see what looks good. Prices

are a bit higher than in other areas of the region due to the resorts' exclusive nature and lower volume of visitors.

Notable options include Dos Chiles, offering good Mexican food, shrimp, fajitas, and tacos in a casual outdoor eatery, and The Pub, a popular sports bar surrounded by shade trees and serving inexpensive breakfast, pizzas, fresh fish, tacos, enchiladas, and shepherd's pie. Open for lunch and dinner, the pricier Tiramisu, specializes in Italian food including beef lasagne, pizzas, pastas, and a good selection of ice cream and desserts.

Attractions & Activities

Aventuras' attractions are also found around the marina. The small CEDAM Shipwreck Museum, operated by the Club de Exploraciones y Deportes Acuáticos de México (Water Sports & Exploration Club), responsible for locating and protecting the region's wrecks. Founded in 1959 by Pablo Bush Romero, it displays many artifacts recovered from shipwrecks in Mexico and around the world, revealing how they've been excavated and materials recovered and restored. Free to the public (donations accepted).

25 Romantic Spots for Couples

1. Aura Cozumel Wyndham Grand Bay resort (Cozumel)

2. Aventura Spa Palace resort (Puerto Aventuras)

3. Azulik clothing optional hotel (Tulum)

4. Excellence Playa Mujeres resort (Playa Mujeres)

5. Hotel Esencia resort (Xpu-Ha)

6. Hotel Lunata (Playa del Carmen)

7. John Gray's Place restaurant & bar (Playa del Carmen)

8. La Casa del Agua restaurant (Playa del Carmen)

9. La Habichuela restaurant (downtown Cancún)

10. Le Reve Hotel & Spa (Punta Bete)

11. Live Aqua Cancún resort (Cancún)

12. Mahékal Beach Resort (Playa del Carmen)

13. Mandarin Oriental Riviera Maya resort (Punta Bete)

14. Mayan Beach Garden hotel (Mahahual)

15. Mosquito Beach Hotel (Playa del Carmen)

16. Occidental Royal Hideway resort (Playacar)

17. Hotel Reina Roja (Playa del Carmen)

18. Rosewood Mayakoba resort (Punta Bete)

19. THE ROYAL Resort Playa del Carmen (Playa del Carmen)

20. Secrets Capri resort (Punta Maroma)

21. Temptation Resort Cancún (Cancún)

22. The Glass Bar restaurant & bar (Playa del Carmen)

23. Ula Gula restaurant & bar (Playa del Carmen)

24. Villa Las Brisas bed and breakfast (Isla Mujeres)

25. Wyndham Cozumel resort (Cozumel)

More tactile guests can interact with the dolphins at ✔ Dolphin Discovery (www.dolphindiscovery.com), and there are several different packages, offering everything from simple contact to being propelled through the water by two dolphins.

The well-respected Riviera Maya Parasail Adventures (984-873-5683, www .rivieramayaparasail.com) offers activities for vacationers seeking a bit of adventure, including "dry parasailing," in which tandem and solo riders take off from the back of a boat and soar high above the water.

XPU-HA (Highway 307, km 264)

Several different access roads lead from Highway 307 to Xpu-Ha beach, making for fun exploration of the various areas. The picturesque beach is very low-key, with a wide bay, coconut palms, and a shallow reef, making it a good spot for snorkeling. To find the best spots, walk to the north near the Xpu-Ha Palace Resort,

Nobody can resist a kiss from a dolphin. Delphinius & the Wilkerson Family

where the water is calm and the access is easier. The beach to the south is not as sandy, with some rocks, vegetation, and seaweed. There are a few small family-run restaurants serving fresh fish and cold drinks on the beach, one renting snorkeling equipment and WaveRunners. For overnight stays there are several major resorts and a handful of cabanas and villas for rent. On the west side of the highway, across from the Xpu-Ha turnoff, are a pair of small but swimmable cenotes.

Checking In

Best places to stay in and around Xpu-Ha

A unique resort built on 50 secluded beachfront acres, ★ Hotel Esencia (Highway 307, km 264, 1-877-528-3490 from the U.S., www.hotelesencia.com) has hosted many celebrities and is more an opulent private residence than hotel. Once the home of an Italian duchess, it has 29 luxurious rooms and ultra-cool Italian-Mexican décor. The property has large breezy terraces, an idyllic beachfront, high ceilings, an organic spa, a fitness center, and an on-site *cenote*. Rooms feature premium bedding, liquor (including full-size bottles), and iPods.

Private guesthouse ★ Al Cielo Hotel (Highway 307, km 264.5, www.alcielohotel.com) has four rooms built right on the beach, with easy access to the water. There's a small beach club and a gourmet restaurant specializing in fresh seafood and meat. An on-site spa offers shiatsu, Reiki, reflexology, and face and skin treatments.

The ♂ ♂ Barcelo Maya Resort Complex (Highway 307, km 265, direct entrance from the highway, www.barcelo.com) comprises more than 2,000 rooms in five different hotels (Tropical Beach, Maya Beach, Caribe

Live Like a Celebrity for a Week

If hotels and condos aren't your thing and you want to experience the Riviera Maya with first-class luxury and privacy, consider renting a beach house for your visit. Akumal Villas (678-528-1775, www.akumal-villas.com) manages a collection of some of the finest private rental homes and villas in the area, with properties in Puerto Aventuras, Akumal, Jade Bay, South Akumal, Soliman Bay, and Tankah. These homes have one to six bedrooms and feature swimming pools, hammocks, full kitchens, purified water, safes, balconies, satellite TV, and other amenities. Full-time maids, caretakers, and on-call chefs and massage therapists are also provided.

Beach, Colonial Beach, Maya Palace). They're very popular for group trips, corporate incentive travel, family reunions, weddings, honeymoons, and other occasions. The complex' scale makes it a great place for first-time Riviera Maya travelers who would feel most comfortable surrounded by similar vacationers, rather than submersing themselves in the local culture.

The all-inclusive, 144-room ☀ Xpu-Ha Palace (Highway 307, km 265, www.palaceresorts.com) offers beachfront accommodations to families and couples who refuse to travel without their pets.

The beach cabanas at Hotel Esencia are perfectly designed.

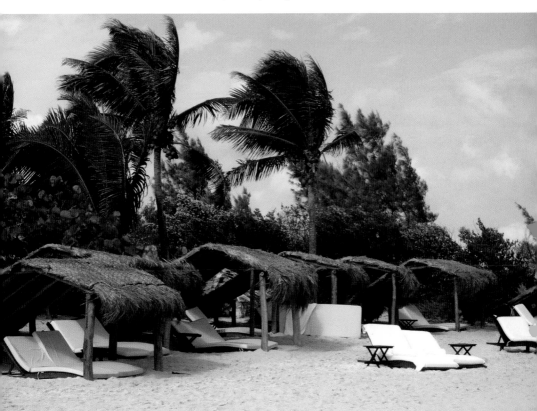

Local Flavors

Taste of the town—restaurants, cafés, bars, bistros, etc.

On the grounds of the Al Cielo hotel, the casually upscale beachfront ★ Restaurante al Cielo (Highway 307, km 264.5, www.alcielohotel.com) has a palapa roof and several tables right next to the sand. The internationally trained chef prepares shrimp, seafood paella, Angus beef, duck, quail, and lamb. No credit cards.

Run by a former Four Seasons chef, ★ Sal y Fuego (www.hotelesen cia.com) at Hotel Esencia specializes in seafood. Many signature dishes at this upscale restaurant use organic ingredients native to the area.

The small family-owned La Playa has several tables in the shade or right on the beach.

KANTENAH

A small sign on Highway 307 at km 262 points the way to Kantenah beach, which is a couple miles down a washboard road. There are many coconut trees and a quiet bay with a shallow reef for snorkeling. Near the beach, there is a large handicrafts market with better prices than in Cancún or even Playa del Carmen, and there's another one on the highway, at km 259.5, with a large assortment of pots, rugs, and blankets.

Checking In

Best places to stay in and around Kantenah

The adults-only, 133-room, all-inclusive El Dorado Seaside Suites (9 Highway 307, km 262, 984-875-1910, www.karis mahotels.com) is a popular destination for honeymooners, couples, and even families seeking to experience the Riviera Maya's less populated areas without sacrificing first-class service, comfort, and convenience. Three restaurants serve Asian, Mexican, and seafood specialties (and no buffets) and several bars are sprinkled throughout the property. El Dorado Guests can pay a day-use fee to visit the clothing-optional Hidden Beach hotel next door.

The 414-room all-inclusive, family-friendly ♂ ➴ Grand Palladium Kantenah Resort & Spa (Highway 307, km 260, 984-877-2100. www.fiesta-hotels .com) features Mayan-inspired architecture, suitable to its natural surroundings. A staff biologist monitors the hotel's impact on the environment and advises on ways to preserve native flora and fauna. As a result, there are many trees, tropical gardens, and native animals on the property. A half-mile stretch of open beach is perfect for jogging, sunbathing, and sun worshipping.

The 42-room, all-inclusive, clothing-optional, and upscale Hidden Beach Resort (Highway 307, km 262, 984-875-7000, www.hiddenbeach resort.com) is boasts a pool, hot tub, and beach cabanas. Guests can enjoy nude dining, sunbathing, and ocean swimming (though it's mostly rocky). The hotel's gourmet restaurant serves three meals per day, either in the shaded dining room or alfresco, next to the pool. There is a swim-up bar, where bartenders (clothed, for the most part) are happy to mix up special drinks. At night, guests head to the on-site mini-discotheque for nude salsa lessons, dance music, and socializing.

This is not a swingers resort, and doesn't allow public displays of anything not allowed at a clothed hotel. Singles welcome.

AKUMAL (Highway 307, km 255)

Five separate highway exits lead to this marina town, whose name translates into "Place of the Turtles." It is known as a family-friendly resort area with calm and shallow coves, dozens of nearby dive sites, superior sportfishing, pleasant pedestrian plazas, quality restaurants, lively bars, and a variety of accommodations options. The area consists of three separate bays: Half Moon, Akumal, and Aventuras. The late author John D. MacDonald wrote several of the books in his famous Travis McGee series of boat bum/private detective novels while lounging on these beaches.

The area is still a nesting ground for sea turtles, and they are now closely protected by the government and privately funded preservation organizations. Visitors can take guided tours to see the turtle nests and, if the timing is right, see the turtles lay their eggs or watch the hatchlings return to the water. An information center at the main entrance can book tours, provide directions, and reserve accommodations ranging from simple hotel rooms to large private villas. There are several grocery stores, an Internet café, a dive center, a kiteboarding office, and handicrafts available near the main entrance. There's free parking in a safe lot just before the gate if you're just visiting for the day. The best beach within a short walking distance is just beyond the dive shop.

Checking In
Best places to stay in and around Akumal

Accommodations at the sprawling beachfront ★ Vista del Mar Condos & Hotel (Half Moon Bay, 984-875-9060 or 1-888-425-8625 from the U.S., www.akumalinfo.com) range from a basic hotel room to a three-room condo at the water's edge that's darn near luxurious.

With 241 rooms and a broad white-sand beach, the all-inclusive ✦ Akumal Beach Resort (Highway 307, km 255, 983-875-7500, www.akumalbeachresort.com) is ideal for families and couples seeking casual and comfortable surroundings without superfluous luxuries.

Open since the early 1990s, the family-friendly all-inclusive ✦ Gran Bahia Principe (Highway 307, km 250, 984-875-5000, www.bahia-principe.es) is a massive upscale complex (more than 2000 rooms) that includes the Tulum, Akumal, and Coba resorts and a central plaza with resort shops, tour desk and most popular nightlife attractions. It's also home to the 27-hole, Robert Trent Jones, II-designed Bahia Principe golf course.

Set upon Yalku Lagoon, the nine-room Posada Que Onda (on Caleta Yalku street, north of Half Moon Bay, 984-875-9102, www.queondaakumal .com) offers charming and affordable accommodations with a large pool and the beach a ten-minute walk away. The on-site Italian restaurant serves seafood and homemade pasta under a large *palapa* roof.

Local Flavors

Taste of the town—restaurants, cafés, bars, bistros, etc.

Just inside the main entry gate to Akumal, you'll find a cluster of restaurants and shops. ✦ ★ Turtle Bay Café (984-875-9138, www.turtlebaycafe.com) offers a little of everything in a small, homey building with a large *palapa* out front. With several ceiling fans, it's often one of the cooler spots in town and frequented by local ex-pats and villa owners.

The ultracasual and delightfully rustic beach bar ✦ ★ La Buena Vida (on the beach of Half Moon Bay, www.akumalinfo.com) has chair swings, a long happy hour, good music, and an upstairs indoor dining room with a nice view of the beach and serves seafood, burgers, and steaks. Treehouse seating 20 feet in the air is accessible via ladders and waiters will even climb up carrying traysful of drinks.

The casual La Lunita Restaurant (at La Tortuga Condos on the beach-

A waiter delivers drinks to one of the elevated tables at La Buena Vida.

front a half-mile south of the marina, Half Moon Bay) serves international and Mexican dishes for breakfast and dinner.

The author and staff of the Buena Vida restaurant in Akumal.

Spinning through Life on Spiral Island

A unique chapter in Puerto Aventuras history ended when Hurricane Emily rumbled through the marina in July 2005.

The story began in 1998, when British ex-pat, artist, and musician Richie Sowa (or "Reishee," as the locals call him) moved to the Riviera Maya with a dream of living a life of relaxation and simplicity while stressing recycling and low-impact survival. To that end he started collecting empty water bottles (he had accumulated more than 250,000 of them when the storm hit) and loading them into fishing nets, which were arranged in a spiral pattern to create an artificial island, which he cast adrift in Puerto Aventuras. He planted mangroves and fruit trees, added some 10 tons of sand, and built a house from discarded wood, bamboo, and thatched palm.

The island, sometimes called Bottle Island, reached the size of half a basketball court and could be maneuvered around the marina with an outboard boat motor attached to one end. It had a solar cooker (with reflectors laid out in a spiral) and a self-composting toilet and was home to several cats, dogs, and sometimes ducks. Richie's island was featured on *Ripley's Believe It or Not!* in 2000. His self-stated long-term goal for the project was to "use the waste from this world as a foundation to create a tranquil piece of paradise and sail around the earth on a floating island with the message of love and faith."

During the hurricane, Richie and his animal friends took shelter on the mainland. When morning dawned, his island lay in ruins, ripped apart and beached on the sand. He planned to transport the island by truck to nearby Soliman Bay and reconstruct it. But as of 2011, reports had him in the San Francisco Bay Area in the United States, starting from scratch but keeping his dream afloat.

CHEMUYIL (Highway 307, km 249)

Not really a touristy town, the dusty beachfront village of Chemuyil hosts many of the service workers for nearby Akumal and other developments. It has a gated entry, and the guards are not necessarily welcoming of foreign adventure-seekers, but if you can't get enough of the Riviera Maya beaches and you won't be content until you see them all, you should be able to talk your way in and make your way to the beach for a look.

The beach itself is relatively clean, and the water is very calm and shallow since the reef comes all the way to the surface and acts as a breakwater keeping out the waves. A couple of private campsites and some basic hotels accommodate the few backpackers, naturalists, and escape artists who find their way here, and there's a handful of beachside restaurants and bars.

Checking In

Best place to stay in Chemuyil

Known in the native Mayan language as *kuxi k'aax*, ★ ⟿ the Jungle Place (East of Highway 307, km 248; just inland from Chemuyil, www.thejungle

place.com) offers two bungalows set on a 20-acre nature preserve, home to dozens of spider monkeys and royal toucans. The units are surprisingly upscale, with stone walls, hardwood furnishings, air-conditioning, and a nature-friendly but contemporary vibe.

XCACEL (Highway 307, km 247; between Chemuyil and Xel-Ha)

A popular nesting ground for loggerhead and green turtles, Xcacel has very few services and no electricity. The area is a nature preserve with skunks, snakes, and other protected animals, plus a combination of beaches, *cenotes*, mangroves, and jungle terrain. The turtles are most common in the warmer part of the year, from May to October. If visiting during this time, it's very important to avoid the nests and not bother any of the turtles. A *cenote* large enough to swim in is on the southern end of the beach (walk to the right, as you're facing the ocean). A small path leads from the beach to the *cenote*; look for a small wooden sign. To the north, the reef comes close to the beach, making it a good spot for snorkeling. A primitive camping facility offers a place to pitch a tent.

PUNTA SOLIMAN (Highway 307, km 240)

A restful beach good for jogging, sunbathing, and shell collecting, Soliman is the kind of place where you feel compelled to arrange your Corona bottles and lime on the table and take a picture with the sundown in the background. In fact, this beach has become famous for being the site featured in a popular series of Corona beer commercials.

Local Flavors

Taste of the town— restaurants, cafés, bars, bistros, etc.

Set right along the highway directly across the street from the Soliman Bay entrance, Oscar y Lalo's (Highway 307, km 240, 984-804-6973) serves delicious fresh seafood, including great ceviche and fish fillets. The best thing on the menu is the fried whole fish, large enough for two.

Top 10 Jobs for Foreigners

1. Bartender
2. English teacher
3. Hotel activities staff/animation (all-inclusives)
4. Hotel front desk, guest services, or concierge
5. Real estate sales
6. Restaurant host/hostess
7. Scuba instructor
8. Time-share representative/sales
9. Tour guide
10. Waiter/waitress

Get a Job and Stay Awhile

Although it's not always easy to make the transition from tourist to local, it is possible. With a bit of determination and luck, you can find a job and live in paradise. The Mexican government requires that all foreign workers have an FM3 visa, which your employer must obtain for you. Fluency in Spanish is required, though exceptions are sometimes made. And don't expect to make anything near what you could earn back home: Minimum wage in Mexico is about $10 per day, and most jobs available to foreigners generally pay around $1,000 per month. Depending on the job, sales commission, bonuses, room and board, and other perks can help sweeten the pot. The cost of living can be much less, but only if you plan on living like a local. If you're looking for a permanent vacation and expecting to work during the day and then party at tourist clubs every night, you'll probably need additional financial resources.

TANKAH (Highway 307, km 237; between Xel-Ha and Tulum)

Tankah is a small bay that was once an important ceremonial site for the ancient Maya, and there are minor ruins in the area, though they are still being explored and are not open to the public. The main road parallels the beach and is home to several guesthouses and inns, and one of the largest is Casa Cenote, which is between the beach and a large freshwater lagoon called Manatee Cenote, rumored to have a manatee living in it (though not even the locals have seen one in recent years). The cenote has a channel that leads underground, below the road and the hotel, and ends 100 feet offshore from the beach. Only experienced cave divers should do the swim, however.

Checking In

Best places to stay in Tankah

The tiny Blue Sky Resort (Highway 307, km 237, on the beach, just past the *cenote* in Tankah, 984-801-4004, www.blueskymexico.com) has six modern rooms and a small pool in the courtyard, right by the beach. An on-site restaurant serves a varied international menu and is open to the public.

A charming collection of casitas, Casa Cenote (998-874-5170) sits on the beach between the calm waters of Tankah Bay and Manatee Cenote. The rooms are along the beach and have terra-cotta tile floors, local artwork, and ceiling fans; some also have air-conditioning. The main hotel has a small restaurant and bar with a *palapa* roof and grill and several plastic tables on the beach.

TULUM (Highway 307, km 230)

The dusty but incredibly fast-growing town of Tulum lies about 80 miles south of the Cancún airport. The Riviera Maya officially ends where Highway 307 intersects the road to Cobá, and just north of there is the turnoff to the Tulum ruins.

Turn west at the crossroads, and the town of Cobá, a picturesque lagoon, and the Mayan ruins of the same name are about an hour away. For a traditional Mayan meal, stop at the Restaurante Campestre Las Cabañas, about 10 minutes before you get to town. Go south and you'll be in the Mayan Coast, also called the Sun Coast (see chapter 4), where the road bypasses Laguna Bacalar as it skirts the Sian Ka'an biosphere and heads toward Kohunlich and on to Chetumal, and eventually to the beach town of Xcalak and the border with Belize.

Many of the resorts do not have power-line electricity and rely on solar power or generators to keep the lights on and the beer cold. It is common for rooms not to have electric lighting and for hotel staff to light candles along the walkway, and even in the rooms. Guests at these hotels are encouraged to bring flashlights, mosquito repellent, and nature guides, and to leave their mobile phones, laptop computers, and urban mindset behind.

Buses depart for Tulum from Playa del Carmen from the bus station near the town square every hour and cost $2. A *colectivo* shuttle van departs Playa from Second Street between 15th and 20th avenues and will drop passengers off anywhere along the way between Playa and Tulum for $2, even if the drop-off is off the main road. The van fits eight people and departs as soon as it is full, from 7 AM to 8 PM.

There are two bus stations on Tulum Avenue, across the street from each other on the southern edge of town, between Alfa and Jupiter streets. Buses depart hourly for Playa del Carmen, Cancún, Mérida, Chetumal, Bacalar, and other towns in the region.

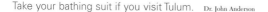

Take your bathing suit if you visit Tulum. Dr. John Anderson

Checking In

Best places to stay in and around Tulum

Notable hotels and guesthouses can be found on the beachfront to the north and south of Tulum, as well within the pueblo, or downtown area, of Tulum itself.

La Vita è Bella (on the Tulum beachfront, 1½ miles north of the turnoff to Tulum pueblo, www.lavitae bella-tulum.com) is composed of 10 villas strung along the beach, quite luxurious given the Tulum's casual atmosphere. The hotel offers in-room massage service, and an on-site restaurant serves Italian and Mexican food.

Just a stone's throw from the Tulum ruins, the Thai- and Mediter-ranean-influenced beachfront hotel, restaurant, and lounge ★ Mezzanine (1 mile north of the crossroads from Tulum, 984-804-1452, www.mezza nine.com.mx) oozes with style, with provocative décor and deep-rooted romantic appeal. A smallish *cenote*-like plunge pool and a cozy bar and lounge front its four hotel rooms. At night, tiki torches and red and orange candles bathe the entire pool deck and dining room in a sensual amber glow. The bar has become a trendy spot for traveling hipsters and locals alike. Every Friday, visiting DJs from Europe and around the world spin house- and chill-out music for as many as 250 people.

Downtown, Blue Tulum (984-871-1000 or 1-866-636-4882 from the U.S., www.bluetulumresorts.com) enjoys a privileged setting at the center of Tulum's beachfront hotel zone. As the only local large-scale property, it can appear a bit garish, but if you overlook the size and slightly corporate feel, it's an amazing hotel that truly offers a complete getaway. Small villas house 96 rooms, featuring rain showers, Italian linens, and butler service. It offers three gourmet restaurants, and a lavish day spa featuring a Mayan Temazcal sweat lodge, meditation classes and other treatments. Due to a rocky waterfront and aggressive waves, ocean access is offered at nearby beach club.

Located one block off the main strip in Tulum pueblo, the small and stylish Hotel Latino (Andromeda Street at Colonia Centro, 984-871-2674, www.hotel-latino.com) has a façade vaguely reminiscent of Hotel Deseo hotel in Playa del Carmen. There is a small pool, and rates include the use of a bicycle.

The center of low-budget info and activity for Tulum pueblo, The Weary Traveler (Tulum Avenue between Jupiter and Acuario streets, tulum .wearytravelerhostel.com) has a nice shaded courtyard and snack bar, a common refrigerator, and acceptable rooms with bunk beds. The hostel offers discounted tours, gear rental, traveler camaraderie, and is known as a good place to party with other backpackers.

Uno AstroLodge Tulum (on the Tulum beachfront, near Punta Piedra beach, 984-134-7180, www.unoastro lodge.com) is all about spiritual healing, global positivity, and energy balance. Rooms have a New Age vibe and there's a small kitchen for guest use. When not lounging on the perfect beach, guests can enjoy a variety of therapeutic treatments, including a full-body massage accompanied with Egyptian harp music, Reiki, yoga classes, and a moonlight temazcal ceremony.

More bohemian beachfront venues can be found south of Tulum pueblo on the Punta Allen road. The adults-only, clothing-optional resort, Azulik (½ mile south of Tulum pueblo,

VIDAS—Helping Pets and People in the Riviera Maya

A group of volunteer animal lovers called International Veterinarians Dedicated to Animal Health (VIDAS) travels each year to the Riviera Maya, providing education and free veterinary care in an effort to fight pet overpopulation, which leads to starvation, disease, and other health problems. They work with local communities to improve the lives of pets and the people who love them. Their first trip, in 2002, involved two vets and six students and resulted in the sterilization of 100 cats and dogs over five days in Playa del Carmen. Since then, more than 5,000 animals have been sterilized and vaccinated throughout the Yucatán peninsula. If you'd like to help the group by sponsoring a pet, making a contribution, or otherwise participating, log on to www.vidas.org.

551-084-2820 or 1-877-532-6737 from the U.S., www.azulik.com) features 15 beachside huts made from local hardwoods. Each sports a waterfront deck, private bathroom with hot water, and wooden bathtub situated smack in the middle of the room. Candles and matches are provided, as no room has electricity. The beach right behind the hotel is rocky with many sea fans that wash in with the tide, but there are sandy access points good for swimming a short walk away.

The 47-room, clothing-optional ⇨ Cabañas Copal (½ mile south of Tulum, 551-084-2820 or 1-877-532-6737 from the U.S., www.cabanas copal.com) is eco-conscious and rustic. The lobby and restaurant have electricity, but not the rooms. A beach bar serves cold drinks at the water's edge and has hammocks for guests to relax in while enjoying the day. Rooms are simple, with thatched roofs and heated water, but all water must be trucked in or pumped from a well, so guests are encouraged to use it sparingly. The staff advises that geckos, hermit crabs, iguanas, and even nonpoisonous snakes are sometimes seen on the property, but are treated like guests and shouldn't be feared. A traditional Mayan spa

is on-site, offering a range of authentic treatments and a temazcal.

The 22 rooms at ★ (ᵖ) Zahra (1 mile south of Tulum, 984-806-4406 or 1-877-532-6737 from the U.S., www.zahra.com.mx) have thatched roofs, but with ceiling fans, electric lights, hot water, in-room spa services, room service, and wireless Internet access, they're not entirely rustic. There are beaches on two sides of the hotel and many palm trees. An on-site restaurant, often showcasing live music, serves traditional Mayan and Mexican food.

Situated on a small quiet beach, Zamas Beach Cabañas (3 miles south of Tulum, 415-387-9806 from the U.S., www.zamas.com) takes its name from the Mayan word for "sunrise" and has 15 *palapa* bungalows. Wind- and solar-generated power stays on until late at night. An open-air restaurant features Mayan-inspired dishes, Mexican specialties, wood-oven pizza, and fresh seafood, including lobster.

With a self-styled jungle-chic vibe, (ᵖ) La Zebra Beachfront Cabanas & Cantina (3.7 miles south of Tulum, 998-112-3260, www.lazebratulum.com) seems a landmark of an imagined and storied 1980s Tulum—even though

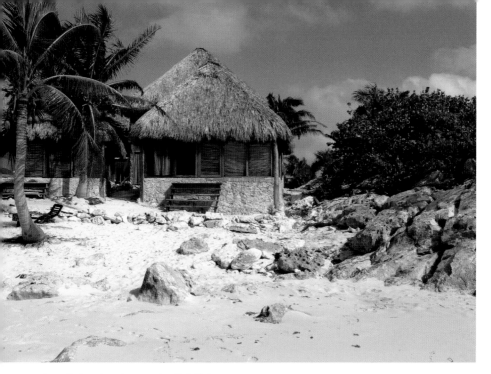

A rustic beach cabana at Azulik in Tulum

there was nothing like it in Tulum's hippie heyday. Its owners, the same Aussies who own the slick Mezzanine Hotel up the beach, say that it's understated. Nevertheless, premium bed linens, ceiling fans, large beds, hole-free mosquito nets, wireless Internet access and local artwork ensure an air of casual luxury. The nine cabanas are staffed by a group of sisters who delight guests with their hearty Mexican cooking and drinks at the on-site cantina. Outdoor pit-roasts are featured on the giant charcoal grill each Sunday. Guests and visitors are invited.

Past the simple hotels and Mayan-style huts of the main Tulum hotel zone, where the road is encroached by palm trees and brush, the upscale day spa and seven-room ★ Coqui Coqui Spa Hotel (5 miles south of Tulum, 998-112-5428, www.coquicoquispa .com) offers guests a true escape without sacrificing comfort or style. The

home, known locally as the Xtabay Estate, offers a lifestyle designed to enhance the harmony between body, mind, and soul. Guests can reserve a single room or the entire home, decorated with Mexican artifacts, handmade furnishings, tapestries, and a variety of European and Asian accents.

The 14-room Ana y José Charming Hotel & Spa (5 miles south of Tulum, 998-887-5470, www.anayjose .com) offers clean, comfortable, and well-designed rooms. Its beach club has developed a reputation as being a party scene and frequently has day-tripping revelers from Playa del Carmen and beyond, which can add to the excitement in an otherwise fairly remote spot. Electricity stays on 24 hours.

Nearby, the 10 serene beachfront casitas of Shambala Petit Hotel (984-125-6474, www.shambalapetithotel .com) serve as a haven for couples and close friends seeking to disconnect with their regular lives and reconnect with each other, nature, and themselves. The hotel offers traditional Mayan-style rooms with palapa roofs and mosquito nets, plus yoga classes, Thai massage, scuba trips, wedding planning, and a pristine beach.

Operated by the same team that runs Playa's über-popular Ba Ba Club and Lounge, the Om Tulum Hotel Cabanas & Lounge (6 miles south of the Tulum crossroads, 984-8794784, www.tulum-playa.com) brought the same trendy casual attitude to Tulum in early 2008. Nine cabanas and a beach club front a picture-perfect white sand beach. Guests and visitors gather at the lounge, open nightly until 2 AM, to listen to chill-out music, enjoy cocktails, and make new friends. Rooms have electricity until 1 AM and free Internet service. Rooms can be reserved online, but all local charges are cash only.

Local Flavors

Taste of the town—restaurants, cafés, bars, bistros, etc.

Il Giardino (Satelite Avenue at Sagitario Street, 984-806-3601) serves moderately priced Italian food, including lasagne, pasta, and fresh fish, in a tropical garden setting.

Meanwhile, staking its figurative flag in the ground, El Pequeno Buenos Aires or the Buenos Aires Grill (Tulum Avenue at calle Beta, 984-871-2708, www.pequenobuenos aires.com) claims to be the only steakhouse south of Puerto Aventuras. It serves moderately priced Angus beef, grilled lobster, shrimp, fish, and vegetarian food.

A typical local restaurant serving very inexpensive breakfasts, lunches, and dinners, Taqueria Gringa (Tulum Avenue between Jupiter and Acuario streets; across from the Weary Traveler) features tacos, enchiladas, quesadillas, and other local fare on plastic tables.

The casual and inexpensive La Palapa del Chino (Tulum Avenue between Osiris and Beta Sur, 984-804-3647) offers a twist on the typical menu, serving inexpensive Chinese and Mexican food daily.

Find fresh vegetarian and vegan dishes at the coffee shop Elemental (Centauro Sur, 984-120-5340, www.ele mentaltulum.com), everyday from 8:30 AM–10:30 PM. The menu features fresh salads, wraps, noodles, and curries.

If you're spending the day at the beach, most of the featured lodging options also have great little beachfront cafés.

Spa

Beachfront ★ Maya Spa (next to Cabañas Copal in the Tulum beach hotel zone, 551-084-2820, www.maya -spa.com) offers daily yoga classes, lucid dreaming courses, and a temazcal, a Mayan-style sweat lodge. Local shamans perform traditional Mayan treatments, and local healers use native plants and herbs to perform various healing ceremonies. Other services include body wraps, Reiki, aesthetic treatments, Mayan massage, and flotation chamber therapy.

How Green Was My Getaway?

Evaluating Ecological and Sustainable Marketing Claims   *By Chip Rankin*

Around 2006, it suddenly became stylish for hotels and tourism businesses to be environmentally sensitive. Terms like *green, sustainability, carbon offsets,* and *eco-friendly* began to appear with increasing frequency.

Once companies saw marketing advantages in being environmentally and culturally conscious, the claims came fast and furious. Many are genuine. Many are superficial. And many lay in between.

No hotel or company on Earth has perfected its sustainability programs, so a business making a genuine effort today, and seeking to improve it, represents progress.

If you're booking a trip and want to stay in sustainable properties, it can be hard to determine just how valid a company's marketing might be. Here are a few rules-of-thumb that should help you determine if the marketing claims are sincere.

Seek specific details. If a hotel or business is actively making an effort to engage in true sustainability programs, they'll be glad to be specific about their efforts. You'll often see them articulated on their Web site. If not, sending an e-mail asking about specific examples can usually reveal what you want to know.

Make sure they aren't just focused on your sacrifice. If green programs are based on your willingness to make a sacrifice, then that business isn't doing very much. All hotels want you to limit the number of items you send through their laundry, and to reduce your consumption of their energy and resources. It costs them less. And while it's great that they may want to educate you about recycling once you return home, that doesn't take much effort on their part. If they aren't actively engaging in daily practices and programs themselves, then their marketing claims are hardly genuine.

It's not all about LEED certification. In the U.S., a LEED-certified (Leadership in Energy and Environmental Design) building shows the builder's observation of environment principles. But LEED is an American program, and is often unrecognized overseas. Even with certification, ongoing operations involving energy conservation, recycling, use of environmentally safe cleaning agents and buying food and resources from local producers can have a much larger impact.

Be forgiving with smaller, established "ecological" hotels. Although all the above points hold true, the term *ecological* has been in use for a long time in Latin American and the Caribbean, signifying a smaller, rustic, low-impact property. Some hotels of this type continue to use the term without intentionally making any new specific efforts toward sustainability. Often, it's the context of the word that changed on them. But even without specific programs, these smaller hotels have a much smaller environmental footprint and overall negative impact than the large concrete box resorts found along the beach.

> *Chip Rankin is an international hotel and tourism expert and owns Hollis Travel Labs (www.hollistravellabs.com), a travel and destination marketing firm. His adventures in hotel development and beach tourism began in Cancún and Playa del Carmen.*

BOCA PAILA, SIAN KA'AN & PUNTA ALLEN

Very few travelers will ever have the chance to visit a place as remote—and as starkly beautiful—as the Sian Ka'an biosphere reserve in their entire lives. Meaning "gift from the sky" or "the sky's beginning" (depending on which translation you believe), Sian Ka'an was officially designated a nature reserve in 1986. It spans more than 1.25 million acres, 10 percent of the land in the state of Quintana Roo, and it is an official UNESCO World Heritage site. Don't expect to find picnic tables, public bathrooms, concession stands, or beach bars—this is not a nature park like Xcaret or Xel-Ha. This land is remote and does not have any of the facilities or services that one sometimes associates with a "park." Once Sian Ka'an became a federal reserve, all development was frozen, and all activities are strictly regulated, which is designed to protect the wild diversity of flora, fauna, and geography encompassed in the reserve. There are more than 300 species of birds (including herons, ibis, roseate spoonbills, and parrots), 100 types of mammals (such as wild cats, monkeys, coatimundis, and deer), and such land features as barrier reefs, mangrove swamps, lagoons, marshes, and tropical forests. There are also more than 25 Mayan relics, small native villages, and ruins of abandoned ranches, hotels, restaurants, and homes.

The goal of the reserve is to provide a place where nature can thrive on its own, without the negative impacts that come with the presence of humans and the development that always seems to follow. A portion of the biosphere is completely restricted, but much of it is open to exploration, as long as visitors follow the reserve's strict rules of low- or no-impact adventuring. A rocky and sometimes sandy road passes through the area, and vehicles may not depart from the path. There is no inland fishing or scuba diving, though snorkeling is allowed since it has less impact on the reefs. A handful of fishing lodges and rustic hotels operate in the reserve, though they must provide their own water and electricity since there are no utilities in the area.

There is a $2-per-person fee to enter the park, and all travelers must check in at the visitors center. Jeeps and four-wheel-drive vehicles are recommended as the road is heavily rutted, rocky, and sometimes muddy. Taking a regular rental sedan on the road makes for slow going and may violate your renter's agreement, nullifying any sort of insurance you have purchased, so it's best to check in advance. There are plenty of picturesque and totally deserted beaches where you can stop for a bit of beachcombing, picture-taking, and stretching. Unfortunately, since the beach is not tended to like at the resorts, years of washed-up trash remains piled at the high-tide mark, making a silent yet very compelling case for the need for more awareness of garbage-dumping in the world's oceans.

At the southern end of the road, you'll reach the tiny village of Punta Allen. And no, some gringo named Allen doesn't own the town. The name comes from the Mayan word *allin*, which means "crocodile." The village is home to 600 inhabitants, said to originate from 90 original families. There are a handful of lodges, a couple of restaurants, a bar, and a general store called Tienda Socorro, where travelers can purchase basic supplies.

With mangrove swamps, shallow lagoons, and a barrier reef that comes quite close to the beach, this region is a favorite for birdwatchers, anglers, and

⊱ 25 Eco-Friendly Spots for Eco-Conscious Travelers

1. Aktun Chen nature park (near Akumal)

2. Alltournative Expeditions (Playa del Carmen)

3. Azulik clothing optional hotel (Tulum)

4. Banyan Tree Mayakoba resort (Punta Bete)

5. Cabañas Copal hotel (Tulum)

6. Caverna de los Murcielagos *cenote* (Hidden Worlds Cenotes near Tulum)

7. Cesiak Centro Ecologico tour (Boca Paila)

8. Chankanaab Park (Cozumel)

9. Crococun Crocodile Farm & Zoo (Puerto Morelos)

10. EcoColors excursions (Cancún and throughout the region)

11. Friends of Sian Ka'an Tour (Sian Ka'an)

12. Garrafón Park (Isla Mujeres)

13. Home of the Whale Sharks excursion (Isla Holbox)

14. Hotel Bucaneros (Isla Mujeres)

15. Hotelito Casa Las Tortugas (Isla Holbox)

16. Hotel Laguna Bacalar (Laguna Bacalar)

17. Island of the Birds excursion (Isla Holbox)

18. Maya Spa (Tulum)

19. Rancho Buenavista (Cozumel)

20. The Explorean jungle retreat (Kohunlich, near Belize)

21. The Jungle Place lodge (Chemuyil)

22. VEA Excursions (Sian Ka'an)

23. Xaman-Ha Aviary (Playa del Carmen/Playacar)

24. Yaax-Che Jardin Botánico (Puerto Morelos)

25. Yalahau Cenote (Isla Holbox)

shell collectors. Crocodiles and manatees also make their home here, which adds to the excitement and your chance for a once-in-a-lifetime natural encounter. Jimmy Buffett fans will recognize this area as the setting for the singer's novel *A Salty Piece of Land*, which chronicles an American expatriate cowboy who sails with his horse to the fictitious island of Punta Margarita (sound familiar?) in Ascension Bay and becomes a fishing guide.

Speaking of fishing, the shallow flats, coves, and tiny coastal islands of Sian Ka'an, Punta Allen, and Ascension Bay offer some of the best fly- and light-tackle fishing in the world. Popular catches include barracuda, bonefish, and the coveted permit, which range from 2 to 20 pounds. Many of the lodges host fly-tying sessions for anglers who want to tie their own flies. If you're not familiar with fly-fishing techniques, local guides can teach you how to do it. If that's not your thing, you can fish in many of the same spots using light tackle. Most fish are caught by sightcasting, where the guide or the angler stands on the boat and searches the water for signs of fish, and then makes pinpoint casts to land the fish. At other times, anglers will wade into the waist-deep water and cast into the schools.

7 Active Ideas for Adventurous Travelers

1. Bike Rentals (Akumal, Playa del Carmen)

2. Bikram Yoga Riviera Maya (Playa del Carmen)

3. Horseback Riding (Cozumel, Isla Holbox, Paamul, South of Playa del Carmen)

4. Ikarus Kiteboarding (Playa del Carmen)

5. Selvatica park (Puerto Morelos)

6. Xplor park (Xcaret)

7. YucaTreks Far Out Adventures (Playa del Carmen & throughout the region)

Getting There

Take Highway 307, the main highway along the Riviera Maya, south from Playa del Carmen to the town of Tulum, about 45 minutes away. At the main Cobá crossroads, one stoplight past the turnoff to the Tulum ruins, turn east and follow the paved road a couple of miles to the end, and then turn right, to the south, and parallel the beach. After passing the Tulum beach hotel zone (which includes Cabañas Copal, Azulik, Ana y José, and so on), you'll cross a usually empty guard post marking the unofficial beginning of the Sian Ka'an biosphere reserve. Three miles later, you'll come to an arch across the road and the official, always-manned biosphere entrance. All vehicles must stop to be logged in and pay a $2-per-person fee to enter. Once inside the park, follow the road along the beach for another 10 miles (about 45 minutes' worth of bumping up and down), and you will reach Boca Paila, marked by twin bridges (one wooden, one concrete, built in 2005) over the lagoon. Twenty miles into the trip, you'll come across a small unmarked Mayan temple partially hidden in the scrub brush next to the road, on the west side of the road. Several miles later, the road ends at the town of Punta Allen. Once you've left Tulum, the next gas station is in Punta Allen, which is 40 miles and about an hour and a half away (in good conditions), so don't leave without filling up.

Colectivo shuttle service is available from Tulum to Punta Allen departing from a garage on Highway 307, two blocks north of the Weary Traveler. It leaves daily at 2 PM.

Checking In

Best places to stay in and around Boca Paila, Sian Ka'an & Punta Allen

Accommodations are eco-friendly "lodges," which means simple, no airconditioning, no bathtubs, no swimming pools, and few luxuries. Travelers in these parts tend to be nature enthusiasts, backpacking adventurers, serious anglers, and others who are comfortable in tents, wooden cabanas, and other no-frills accommodations. For the hearty few that are up to the task, staying the night in the biosphere can reveal wondrous parts of the jungle that are rarely seen by others. The hotels in the area offer shuttle service from Cancún or the Riviera Maya, with advance notice required. Credit cards are not accepted, except for advance reservations in some cases, so plan ahead.

Clean rooms, Mayan-style meals, and world-class bonefishing make ★ Bonefish Bum Lodge (northern edge of Ascension Bay, 984-877-8532 or 1-888-584-1453 from the U.S., www .bonefishbum.com) one of the world's best places to spend a week on the water, watching for the telltale flash of a bonefish as it turns to take a fly.

Just when you think you can't take the bumpy road through Sian Ka'an anymore, you arrive at Pesca Maya (3 miles north of Punta Allen, 998-845-6501 or 1-800-894-5642 from the U.S., www.pescamaya.com). The lodge is built on the land of the Chenchomac (Mayan for "land of the foxes") ranch, a former coconut plantation. It has a large, well-built *palapa* restaurant and bar, which serves as the library, fly-tying station, and social center.

Ascension Bay Bonefish Club (on the edge of Ascension Bay, Punta Allen, 984-877-8532 or 1-800-819-0750 from the U.S., www.ascensionbay.com) hosts only six anglers per week, in a

small house built right on the beach. All-inclusive packages run Friday to Friday and include transfers from Cancún, lodging, meals, and six days with a private fishing boat and guide.

Let It Be Inn (Punta Allen, 984-877-8506, www.letitbeinn.com) also limits its roster to six anglers at a time and is about as secluded and private as it gets. Hosts Rick and Rosie Montgomery run the tiny lodge, cook the restaurant's delicious meals, help plan fishing trips, and take care of anything else guests may need.

Eco-friendly lodge ⇌ Cesiak (2 miles north of the Boca Paila bridge on the road from Tulum to Punta Allen, 984-871-2499, www.cesiak.org) is located on a 15-acre beachfront ranch that housed an upscale resort until 1982. Opened in 2000, Cesiak's eco-conscious rooms are housed in tents on wooden platforms and have terraces, hardwood furniture, and great views.

The rustic Casa Cuzan (on the southern edge of Punta Allen, 983-834-0358, www.flyfishmx.com) offers 12 fan-cooled, thatch-roofed cabanas; a restaurant (think lobster, fish, Mexican/ Mayan cuisine); and great access to the area's best fishing spots.

Activities & Tours

Housed at the Cesiak eco-lodge camp in Boca Paila (see Lodging), ⇌ Cesiak Centro Ecologico (984-871-2499, www.cesiak.org) offers an all-day Sian Ka'an tour and a sunset bird-watching tour, both include visits to a Mayan ruin and boat tours.

Led by a bilingual guide, the ★ ⇌ Friends of Sian Ka'an Tour (www.amigos desiankaan.org/eng) takes guests on a driving tour through the reserve, a boat trip through the mangroves, and a visit to a freshwater spring.

If you have only one day to visit Sian Ka'an but want to fit in as much as possible, try VEA Jeep Safari (984-875-5040 or 1-866-646-6202 from the U.S., www.jeep-safari.com), including a Jeep ride to the biosphere entrance, a boat tour to see dolphins, swimming, snorkeling, bird-watching, and beachcombing.

3

The Riviera Maya
NORTH OF PLAYA DEL CARMEN

ALSO EXTENDING NORTH OF PLAYA DEL CARMEN, the Riviera Maya is dotted by more exclusive destinations resorts, such as those in the grandiose and exotically modern Mayakoba development, and the growing town of Puerto Morelos, which today is much like Playa was way back in 1990.

PUNTA BETE REGION

Marked by the large wood-and-stone entrance of the Mayakoba megadevelopment, Punta Bete is just 4 miles north of Playa del Carmen, at km 296–298, making it popular for visitors who want to stay somewhere out of the way but still be close to the action of town.

Checking In
Best places to stay in and around the Punta Bete Region

This area is dominated by the 1,600-acre master planned luxury resort development Mayakoba (Highway 307, km 297), whose name translated roughly into "Village of Water" in Mayan. The complex features a mile-long white sand beach, the 18-hole El Cameleón Golf Course designed by Greg Norman, and three exclusive hotels each with its own custom spa. Each hotel presents a distinct design and luxury atmosphere and all Mayakoba guests and residents are encouraged to travel between the three via a series of pristine jungle-lined waterways and sample a wider variety of spa and dining options.

The 107-room Banyan Tree Mayakoba (984-877-3688 or 1-800-591-0439 from the U.S., www.banyan

LEFT: Many parts of the Riviera Maya retain their slow pace and local charm.   Philip Gamon

15 Stylish Spots for Trendsetters

1. Ba Ba Club & Lounge (Playa del Carmen)

2. Canibal Royal Beach Club (Playa del Carmen)

3. Diablito Cha Cha Cha lounge (Playa del Carmen)

4. Hotel Básico and Básico Terrace Bar (Playa del Carmen)

5. Hotel Deseo and Deseo Bar (Playa del Carmen)

6. In Fashion Boutique Hotel (Playa del Carmen)

7. Kartabar (Playa del Carmen)

8. Live Aqua Cancún resort (Cancún)

9. Mamita's Beach Club (Playa del Carmen)

10. Mandala Bar (Playa del Carmen)

11. Mandarin Oriental Riviera Maya resort (Punta Bete)

12. Mezzanine hotel (Tulum)

13. Mosquito Beach Hotel (Playa del Carmen)

14. Reina Roja hotel (Playa del Carmen)

15. Rosewood Mayakoba resort (Punta Bete)

tree.com) has a modern Asian-meets-Mayan motif, and aspires to connect guests to the elements. The hotel and most of the villas are set back, inland from the beach, along a series of canals and waterways winding through the hotel and connecting it to the larger resort. All rooms are stand-alone villas, each complete with a private garden, pool, and outdoor bathtub.

The 401-room, family-friendly ★ Fairmont Mayakoba (1-800-441-1414 from the U.S., www.fairmont .com) features a home-style Mexican décor, with dark wood, stone, and a palette of gold, soft reds, and oranges throughout. Given its remote location, many guests would assume that the hotel is all-inclusive, but it isn't. There are, however, several excellent restaurants and bars on-site.

The striking and unusual 128-room ★ Rosewood Mayakoba (984-875-8000 or 1-888-767-3966 (U.S.) , www.rosewoodMayakoba.com) successfully maintains its jungle ties through its connection to the elements, use of

local materials and integration of tropical flourishes. A network of striking manmade canals wind throughout the resort through a wide variety of villas. Rooms on and near the beach tend to be crowded together, while accommodations further back, especially the adults-only island suites, are almost entirely quiet.

With a barefoot-chic décor, the stylish 25-room boutique Le Rêve Hotel & Spa (984-109-5660, www .hotellereve.com) mixes modern design elements with tropical flourishes. The restaurant showcases an evolving, chef-prepared menu utilizing many fresh ingredients, local products, and international flavors. There is a fitness center on-site and yoga classes are available on the beach. Packages available to rent the entire hotel for private celebrations including weddings, retreats, family reunions (children under 16 are permitted when the entire hotel is reserved), and gay-friendly events.

The 128-room Mandarin Oriental Riviera Maya (Highway 307, km 298,

984-877-3269 or 1-800-526-6566 from the U.S., www.mandarinoriental.com) introduced a new level of sophistication to the region's ultra-luxury, all-inclusive category. The architecture is thoroughly modern, with smooth lines and cool colors. Interiors utilize native hardwoods, stone, and other local accents. Guests have easy access to three championship golf courses, including the El Cameleon course, located next door.

Small and very upscale, ★ The Tides Riviera Maya (Highway 307, km 294, Playa Xcalacoco [just south of Punta Bete], 987-877-3000 or 1-866-332-1672 from the U.S., www.tides rivieramaya.com) is one of the more likely places to spot a vacationing celebrity or business tycoon. Far from pretentious, though, the resort formerly known as the Ikal del Mar, strives to harmonize with nature rather than completely shut it out and prides itself on the fact that no trees were cut down during construction. A thatched palm

Playa Xcalacoco

Some small Mayan ruins and a coconut grove mark the small, secluded beach of Xcalacoco, which is just south of Punta Bete. There are a couple of palapa restaurants that serve seafood and Mexican dishes, and campers can set up their temporary home at the Xcalacoco campsite, which has solar power and public showers.

pavilion at the hotel entrance passes as the lobby, and the 30 guest rooms and royal villas are housed in free-standing modernized versions of Mayan-style huts scattered along a winding sand trail that leads from the powdery white beach to the jungle. The villas and furnishings are made from local stones and hardwoods.

PLAYA DEL SECRETO & PLAYA PARAÍSO (Highway 307, km 308–312)

Playa del Secreto and Playa Paraíso combine to form one of the largest stretches of mostly undeveloped beach remaining in the area. Several spots along the shoreline are frequented by sea turtles, which lay their eggs in the balmy summer months. The area is dominated by the massive Iberostar resort complex, which includes five separate but connected all-inclusive resorts, a convention center, and an 18-hole golf course.

Checking In

Best places to stay in Playa del Secreto, Playa Paraíso & Punta Maroma

Playa del Secreto & Playa Paraíso
The 432-room, all-inclusive, adults-only El Dorado Royale—A Spa Resort by Karisma (Highway 307, km 312, Playa

Paraíso, 998-872-8030, www.karisma hotels.com) bills itself as "laid-back luxury," and it seems to be an appropriate description for a resort best known for its in-room hot tubs and patio hammocks. Spanning 450 acres of prime beachfront land, the hotel has a mile-long beach (called Punta Brava) marked by white sand, a few rocks, and hundreds of palm trees. The on-site European day spa offers a variety of traditional European and regional Mayan treatments.

Five resorts share amenities at this massive all-inclusive ♂ ★ Iberostar Playa Paraíso Complex (Highway 307, km 309, 984-887-2800 or 1-888-923-2722 from the U.S., www.iberostar .com), with more than 1,900 rooms in Iberostar's Paraíso Beach, del Mar, Lindo, and Maya hotels. Varied architectural themes are exhibited across the resorts, with rooms varying in price, décor, and amenities. Guests at all properties are encouraged to visit the shared beach, which is almost a mile long, and to visit select pools, restaurants, and bars located throughout the property. Also on-site, the Iberostar Playa Paraíso Golf Club features 18 holes of golf designed by P. B. Dye, son of renowned course designer

Pete Dye. In addition to the facilities offered at each individual hotel, a central shopping and entertainment center contains a nightclub, a sports bar, a spa, and a variety of stores. Guests of the most luxurious and adults-only Iberostar Grand Hotel Paraíso have access to all complex features, but also enjoy a level of privacy and luxury not found in the other hotels.

Home to what may be the largest and most impressive entryway of any hotel in the Riviera Maya, the aptly named ♂ Mayan Palace Riviera Maya (Highway 307, km 310, Playa Paraíso, 984-206-4000, www.mayanpalace.com .mx) is equally inspiring once inside. With such a grand entrance, it's a bit surprising that the resort has only 336 rooms. Although the architecture may be inspired by the traditional Mayan

Top 10 See-and-Be-Seen Hotels of the Riviera Maya Area

1. Playa Palms at the Blue Parrot (Playa del Carmen): With an open-air dance floor and fire dancers at your back door, you can't go wrong.

2. Fairmont Mayakoba (Punta Bete): The huge stone entryway makes you wonder what's inside; only the privileged few know for sure.

3. Live Aqua Cancún: Cancún's one and only lounge hotel, with 24-hour DJ and unlimited top-shelf tequilas.

4. Hotel Básico (Playa del Carmen): The prosperous days of 1950s Latin America glorified with a rooftop bar, oil-tank swimming pools, and rooms with neon lights.

5. Hotel Deseo (Playa del Carmen): Up the unmarked stairs, it's the hip hangout for the Playa elite.

6. Hotel Esencia (Xpu-Ha): The former estate of an Italian duchess can be yours, for a price.

7. Maroma Resort & Spa (Punta Maroma): If it's good enough for Tom Cruise and Katie Holmes, you'll probably enjoy it also.

8. Mezzanine Hotel (north of Tulum pueblo): Swanky digs, topless beaches, and DJ parties in the shadow of the Tulum ruins.

9. Reina Roja (Playa del Carmen): The crimson queen brings shades of Amsterdam's Red Light District to downtown Playa.

10. Paraiso de la Bonita (north of Puerto Morelos): With a $3,000-a-night penthouse, you never know who you may rub shoulders with at the swim-up bar.

Several roadside shops along the highway sell souvenirs. Mike Stone

building style, with thatched-palm roofs, low-rise buildings, and heavy use of local materials, the standards of luxury are significantly higher than even the Mayan gods could have imagined. The beach is beautiful but rocky, so be prepared to pick your way through the rough terrain if you want to go swimming. There is an on-site 18-hole Jack Nicklaus golf course, tennis courts, and kids' club, which provides complimentary childcare in a fun environment. Since the property is so large, some guests complain about the walking distances from one attraction to another, but the landscaping and the natural beauty seem to keep most happy.

Punta Maroma

Six miles south of Playa Paraíso, quiet Punta Maroma has the kind of sugar-sand beach so often featured in postcards and travel agency brochures. The beach, more than 100 feet wide in many parts, is bordered by coconut palms and sea oats, and there are very few rocks and light waves, making it a great place for swimming and snorkeling. There are a few upscale resorts, villas, and private homes, but it has an uncrowded, timeless, and faraway feel to it, making it an ideal spot for a tropical escape.

Recognized as one of the top hotels in the world, the 65-room ★ Maroma Resort & Spa (Highway 307, km 305; enter through the Venta Club entrance, 998-872-8200 or 1-866-454-9351 from the U.S., www.maroma hotel.com) deserves its stellar reputation, with repeat guests making up a large percentage of the monthly reservations. The resort occupies some 25 acres of land, giving it an uncluttered and private feeling hard to find in the region. Unlike many Riviera Maya resorts, Maroma is not the kind of place where visitors hang out in their cutoffs and tank tops, swilling margaritas, and playing volleyball in the pool. Guests are much more subdued, and there is even a dress code at the restaurant for dinner. Don't get the feeling that it's stuffy, though. It's definitely still relaxed, just upscale.

The resort is down a gravel road and on an absolutely perfect beach. The jungle encroaches from all sides, and jungle animals seem ever-present, including iguanas, birds, and even arboreal turkeys, which call loudly from the trees at dusk. At night, a thousand candles line the walkways, giving the hotel a romantic and faraway feeling. The on-site Maya/Zen spa specializes in Reiki, facials, mud baths, aromatherapy, body scrubs, crystal therapy, and other types of body treatments. Massages are also offered at a beachside hut or in the hotel's lookout tower, perched four floors above the jungle canopy, making it one of the tallest points around.

A beachside temazcal (sweat lodge) is the place to be at dusk, when guests are led through a 90-minute sweat-lodge ceremony, followed by a refreshing dip in the sea. Another treatment, a flotation chamber, allows guests to float weightless in a hyper-salted water tank. A 45-minute rest in the chamber is supposed to be equivalent to an eight-hour sleep. An on-site gym has a full-time personal trainer, yoga and Pilates classes, and modern equipment. The restaurant, next to the beach, serves grilled fish, fresh seafood, lobster, salads, natural fruit juices, ceviche, and nightly specials. Try the *agua de chaya* for a refreshingly sweet alternative to water.

The resort is closed for upgrades

Celebrity Guests at Maroma Resort

Tim Allen • Tony Blair • Tom Cruise • Claire Danes • Danny DeVito • Cameron Diaz • Matt Dillon • Minnie Driver • Farrah Fawcett • Enrique Iglesias • Brad Paisley • Sean Penn • Robert Plant • Prince Charles • Sharon Stone

each August. The four-bedroom Villa Pisces has its own private pool and feels much more like a beachhouse than part of a hotel.

A lavish resort complex on 71 acres of pristine beach just south of Playa Maroma, the 285-room ★ ♂ Secrets Capri (Highway 307, km 298, 987-873-4880, www.secretsresorts.com) is adults only, all-inclusive, and appeals to active couples wanting to experience a broad range of recreational options while submerged in the comforts of a high-end resort. The architecture is a combination of Mediterranean and colonial Mexican, with graceful arches, tile work, and tropical plants throughout. Guests are welcomed into the lobby with a glass of champagne and a chilled towel before descending a grand staircase to the pool deck area. This is a popular spot for weddings and honeymoons, and it offers an on-site wedding planner.

PUERTO MORELOS (Highway 307, km 320; 20 miles north of Playa del Carmen)

If you want to know what Playa del Carmen was like 20 years ago, just take a look at modern-day Puerto Morelos, which where the Riviera Maya officially begins. The quiet town square ringed by a few restaurants and shops, the natural beach, the unpaved roads, the encroaching jungle—it's almost exactly how Playa used to be. The road from the highway to town is a straight shot through 2 miles of scrub brush and mangrove swampland before ending at the town square. Most of the development is within a couple blocks of the square, which has a beachside restau-

Maroma's Lomi-Lomi Massage

The Lomi-Lomi massage is one of the oldest and most powerful forms of healing. It works gently yet deeply into the muscles with continuous, flowing strokes, offering a complete nurturing of the body and gifting the recipient with a deep sense of relaxation and well-being. This flowing massage allows for a very close bond between the energy of therapist and the client energy, using long and slow movements and a very loving touch to relax you to the inner core, helping you to let go of old beliefs, patterns, and behaviors. Some people cry, others laugh, and others have a near out-of-body experience as they descend into a very deep state of relaxation.

rant, several open-air sidewalk restaurants, a couple of Internet cafés, a coffee/pastry shop, and a few souvenir stores, pharmacies, money exchange offices, and dive shops. Along the beach you'll see a leaning lighthouse and a fishing pier where the boats dock when they're not pulled up onto the beach. Less than a half-mile offshore is the barrier reef, and you can see the waves breaking where the coral meets the surface, which indicates a great spot for snorkeling when the seas are calm. The roads leading north and south from town are dusty and unpaved, but they lead to some of the nicest natural beaches in the area. To the north are a collection of rental homes and small hotels, plus a couple of recently developed large-scale resorts. To the south, the road curves behind an army base and then a shipping and industrial area before meeting the beach again near the entrance to a laid-back budget hotel and a clothing-optional "lifestyle" resort.

A gambling-boat operator had petitioned to operate a casino boat from the port to take travelers to international waters, but the petition was denied, and the area retains its calming and relaxed feeling. A ferry transfers vehicles from Puerto Morelos to Cozumel. For more information call 998-871-0008.

Getting There

Puerto Morelos is located at the midpoint between Cancún and Playa del Carmen. The turnoff from Highway 307 was marked with just a speed bump only a few years ago, but now there's a traffic light, turning lanes, several shops, and even a road sign. Another road, just north of the Crococun Zoo, leads to the north end of town and the Secrets Excellence and Paradisus hotels. From there the road winds and turns as you head south, passing by private homes and small family-run hotels. In several spots, heavy marine rope has been laid across the street as a sort of makeshift speed bump. After a few miles, the road ends at the town square. There are frequent buses from the Cancún and Playa del Carmen bus stations that will drop you off at the crossroads, and from there it's a 2-mile hike to town or a $3 taxi ride. A new bus station was built in 2008 on Highway 307, just south of the main crossroads next to the 7-Eleven convenience store, with regular departures to Tulum, Playa del Carmen, and Cancún. Although it may not be generally encouraged, it's also fairly easy to hitch a ride along the road that leads to town. Since the road basically goes to only one place, it's a pretty fair bet that anyone headed down that road is going somewhere close to where you are.

Puerto Morelos

180

Cancún International Airport

To Cancún

N

0 2.5 5
Miles

JOSE MA. MORELOS

AV. NINOS HEROES

To 307

6 7 8
Town Square
5
4
3 TULÚM
2
1

9 I. MUJERES

AV. ROJO GOMEZ
AV. RAFAEL MELGAR

COZUMEL

CARIBBEAN SEA

Ferry Dock (To Cozumel)

Bahía Petempich
Paraíso de la Bonita

307

Crococun Crocodile Farm & Zoo

Ceiba del Mar
Puerto Morelos

Selvatica Central Vallarta RUTA DE LOS CENOTES
Selvatura
El Rey Polo Club
Yaax-Che Botanical Garden
Cenote Verde Boca del Puma Siete Bocas
Lucero
Rancho Loma Bonita

El Dorado Royale
Playa del Secreto & Playa Paraiso
Mayan Palace

Iberostar Resort Complex / Paraiso Beach

Maroma Paradise Beach Club
Tres Rios Eco Park Punta Maroma
Secrets Capri

CARIBBEAN SEA

Mayakobá

Ferry

Punta Bete
Tides Riviera Maya
Xcalacoco
La Reve

Playa del Carmen

Xcaret

CARIBBEAN SEA

Ferry

Isla Cozumel

To Tulúm

San Miguel de Cozumel

1. Marland Travel
2. Internet Café
3. Money Exchange
4. Church
5. Pharmacy
6. Police Station
7. Groceries
8. Fishing & Snorkeling Tours
9. Hunab-Ku

© The Countryman Press

Checking In

Best places to stay in and around Puerto Merelos

Bahia Petempich

With fewer than 100 rooms and suites, the very high-end, all-suite ★ Paraiso de la Bonita Resort & Thalasso Spa

(Highway 307, km 330, 998-872-8300 or 1-866-751-9175 for reservations from the U.S., www.paraisodelabonita .com) has 1,100-square-foot standard rooms with ocean views. The service is impeccable, and the staff does an excellent job of making guests feel special. The architecture and décor are unusual, with a combination of African, Asian, Balinese, Caribbean, European, and Mayan inspirations. The beach is raked clean, but the tides are full of seaweed, making swimming less than pleasant.

The Feng Shui–friendly ♂ Azul Beach Hotel by Karisma (Highway 307, km 330, 998-872-0808, www .karismahotels.com) is an up-market all-inclusive boutique resort located just a few miles north of Puerto Morelos, past the gated entrance to Bahia Petempich on an idyllic beach. The lobby has marble floors and minimalist décor, with lots of whites and blues, and calming music playing in the background. The 98-room hotel welcomes families and even has an activities program for kids. Unlike many all-inclusives, the hotel features gourmet menu options and the bars serve premium liquors.

If you venture into the Desire Resort & Spa (Highway 307, km 326, 998-872-8280, www.desireresorts.com), you'll quickly see that it is not for the prudish. In fact, if you're not a swinger or at least open to the swinger lifestyle, you're best off choosing another place to spend your vacation. If, however, you're into that kind of thing, this stylishly done resort deserves a serious look. It is known in the "lifestyle" circles as one of the best hotels around for swingers who enjoy traveling to the tropics to meet others, have fun, and cast away their inhibitions, assuming they had any to begin with.

The resort accepts only adult couples. Billed as "clothing optional," the 110-room all-inclusive hotel caters much more to the sexually liberated set than the run-of-the-mill nudist or "naturist." Public displays of affection, even extreme affection, are allowed and, in some designated areas, encouraged. And even though there's a strict "no means no" policy, it's clear that there are lots of yeses going on.

There is a great beach, and the local officials look the other way (literally), allowing guests to be on the beach in the buff, though it's generally frowned upon in most other areas. There are two pools and a huge Jacuzzi with room for 30 people (I'm sure you could fit more if you tried), which seems to be the center of attraction most days. Next to the dance bar there is a "play room" where the most sexual activity takes place.

Puerto Morelos Proper

Halfway between the Cancún airport and Playa del Carmen, the 126-room Ceiba del Mar (Highway 307, km 320, 998-872-8060, www.ceibadelmar.com) is set along the beach just north of Puerto Morelos. Surrounded by jungle on a large plot of land and with architecture combining traditional Mayan and contemporary Mexican design, the resort is laid out with meandering paths in a sort of villagelike atmosphere. Its guests never feel too crowded. There are two large, beautiful pools, rooftop sundecks, an upscale lobby, and a European spa that uses organic spa-care products.

Designed as a place of tranquility and relaxation, with an emphasis on privacy, personal service, and romance, the romantic, adults-only Excellence Riviera Cancún (Highway 307, km 323; northern end of Puerto Morelos, 998-872-8500, www.excellence-resorts .com) has 440 suites featuring a Jacuzzi tub, making spending time inside even more appealing. There are six swimming pools, a fitness center, three outdoor Jacuzzis, a beauty salon, and a large full-service European spa with a soothing, gardenlike atmosphere.

On a northern beach between Bahia Petempich and the town square, the simple and inexpensive Hotel Ojo de Agua (Highway 307, km 321,

Avenue Javier Rojo Gómez at the beach, 998-871-0202, www.ojo-de -agua.com) serves somewhat as a home base for local beachfront activity. The hotel's 36 rooms, decorated in contemporary Mexican style, have air-conditioning or fan and kitchenette.

South of Puerto Morelos

Rancho Sak Ol (Highway 307, km 318; southern end of Puerto Morelos, past the Army base and shipping facility, 998-871-0181, www.ranchosakol.com), formerly known as Rancho Libertad, offers an alternative to the large corporate-owned hotels for travelers seeking simplicity and serenity over luxury and indulgence. Fourteen mini-malist rooms feature suspended beds, air-conditioning (downstairs units), and purified drinking water, and face a rocky yet calm and natural beach that is practically deserted—a good spot for more hotels. You can look to the north and see a half-sunken barge that has been there for years.

Local Flavors

Taste of the town—restaurants, cafés, bars, bistros, etc.

This casual beachfront Ojo de Agua Restaurant & Bar (avenida Javier Rojo Gómez; on a northern beach near Excel-lence Riviera hotel, 998-206-9179, www .ojo-de-agua.com) offers a breakfast buf-fet, fresh seafood, and Mexican dishes, as well as a daily happy hour from 3 to 4.

A second location for Playa del Carmen favorite, the upscale Yaxché Restaurant (at the back of the La Ceiba Hotel, facing the main street) is one of the few places around with air-conditioning. It serves traditional Mayan cuisine for lunch and dinner, including turkey, *tikin chic* (baked fish wrapped in banana leaves), and great steak amid replicas of Mayan relics, tropical plants, and carved stone.

In the town square, the second-story, air-conditioned The Old Fisherman

15 Party Spots for Tequila Drinkers, Mingling Singles, and the Party Crowd

1. Beer Bucket bar (Playa del Carmen)
2. Canibal Royal Beach Club (Playa del Carmen)
3. Casa Tequila–La Tequilaria store and shot bar (Playa del Carmen)
4. Coco Bongo nightclub (Cancún & Playa del Carmen)
5. Coco Maya Beach Club (Playa del Carmen)
6. Diablito Cha Cha Cha lounge (Playa del Carmen)
7. Don Roberto tequila store (Playa del Carmen)
8. Hotel Deseo and Deseo Bar (Playa del Carmen)
9. Hotel Reina Roja and bar (Playa del Carmen)
10. Jimmy Buffett's Margaritaville Café (Cozumel)
11. Mamita's Beach Club (Playa del Carmen)
12. Mandala Bar (Playa del Carmen)
13. Mezzanine hotel (Tulum)
14. Santanera bar (Playa del Carmen)
15. Señor Frog's bar (Cancún, Cozumel & Playa del Carmen)

(north side of the town square) offers fresh lobster, *chiles rellenos,* hogfish in butter, grouper, and other seafood dishes, plus grilled steak and chicken. Waiters are longtime local residents who can give you advice on tours and activities.

The most prominent restaurant near the town square, Pelicanos (southeast corner), is also the largest, offering a selection of Mexican and American breakfasts for less than $5, and for lunch and dinner, it's seafood or nothing. Try the fried whole fish, the shrimp ceviche, or the grilled shrimp, and you can't go wrong.

Small and inexpensive, Le Café D'Amancia (southwest corner) serves sandwiches, fresh breads, cheesecake, fruit, espresso, cappuccino, and coffee.

Nearby, Monchis (get it?) sells coffee, sandwiches, ice cream, and other snack items, mostly to go, as well as a selection of T-shirts and other souvenirs. (You won't find items that are much different than at other area shops, but many of them are made locally, so you can feel good about your purchase.)

Offering a view of the luxury yachts docked at the marina, the casually elegant La Marina (on the Marina El Cid, 998-871-0184) serves lobster, fresh fish, and other seafood specialties.

Activities & Tours

Part traditional polo field, part real estate development, El Rey Polo Country Club (8 miles down the Ruta de Cenotes Road in Puerto Morelos, www.elreypolocountryclub.net) hosts regular polo tournaments that are quite high in quality and draw players and spectators from around the country. The larger development encompasses 73 rustic home lots, clubhouse, dressing rooms, golf driving range, horse stables, and children's play area. It seems wildly out of place deep in the Mayan jungle, but is a curious place to visit and ponder what may come if the region keeps growing so rapidly.

The friendly folks at Fishing & Snorkeling Tours (northeast side of the town square, next to the beach) can arrange fishing and diving trips along the Puerto Morelos coastline, and, with their own fleet of shaded 25-foot boats and local guides, they can custom-create a trip that suits your fancy. It's preferred that you make your reservations the day before so the staff can get all the necessary equipment and supplies, though impromptu trips can be arranged as long as you're flexible.

Operating out of the Ojo de Agua hotel, Puerto Morelos Adventure Tours (998-884-2316, www.snorkelincancunrivieramaya.com) offers active tours in the area. Top trips include a two-hour snorkeling trip that includes lunch, beer, equipment, and a visit to a handicrafts market; an ATV tour that visits two *cenotes,* a Mayan village and market; and a *cenote* and reef snorkeling excursion, which includes visits to caves, *cenotes,* and a marine park.

The humble Puerto Morelos Church (west side of the town square) may not have any historical significance, but its Spanish-only services are open to visitors and it offers an authentic glimpse into life for locals.

★ Selvatica (Ruta de Cenotes, km 19, 998-847-4581, www.selvatica.com.mx) also runs adventure tours through a 300-acre nature preserve (see chapter 5).

4

Other Destinations
Near Playa del Carmen

MEXICO'S ENTIRE CARIBBEAN COAST is marked by popular, and lesser known, tourism destinations. Although the region known as the Riviera Maya is set smack in the middle of the coast, it doesn't technically include them all. The diving mecca of Isla Cozumel, the burgeoning resort city of Cancún, the bohemian island town of Isla Mujeres, the remote Isla Holbox, the unpopulated Isla Contoy, and the adventurous Mayan Coast all make noteworthy overnight side or day trip destinations.

Most travelers to the Riviera Maya arrive via Cancún, which is one of the world's most popular mega-resorts. The small islands to the north of Cancún offer an abundance of relaxation, sunshine, and pristine beaches without the crowds so often associated with area vacations. Cozumel, meanwhile, is a scuba diver's dream, where shore, wall, and night dives can all be done in a single day.

ISLA COZUMEL (11 miles from Playa del Carmen by boat)

Isla Cozumel was once considered the sacred home of Ixchel, the Mayan goddess of fertility and childbirth, and Maya women from around Mesoamerica would travel to pay homage and pray for their unborn children. Several religious shrines have survived over the years and can still be visited today. Measuring 28 by 10 miles, Cozumel is only 5 percent developed and is mostly open land, ripe for exploration on Jeep, horseback, or moped. It's a mecca for scuba divers and snorkelers, who revel in the amazingly clear waters, easily accessible reefs, and first-class dive operators.

The ferry from Playa lands at the town square of San Miguel, the island's only town, on its western shore. From nearly every beach hotel on this side of the island, guests have a spectacular view of the sunset as it slowly dips into the

LEFT: Be sure to bargain when shopping for local goods. Brian E. Miller Photography/www.lomimonk.com

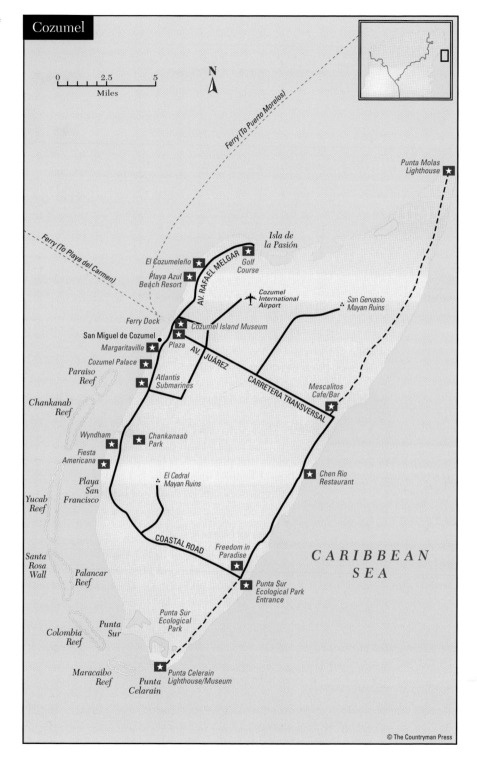

Cozumel

0   2.5   5
Miles

N

Ferry (To Puerto Morelos)

Ferry (To Playa del Carmen)

Isla de
la Pasión

El Cozumeleño
Playa Azul
Beach Resort

AV. RAFAEL MELGAR

Golf
Course

Cozumel
International
Airport

San Gervasio
Mayan Ruins

Ferry Dock
Cozumel Island Museum

San Miguel de Cozumel
Margaritaville
Plaza

AV. JUÁREZ

Cozumel Palace

Paraiso
Reef

Atlantis
Submarines

CARRETERA TRANSVERSAL

Mescalitos
Cafe/Bar

Chankanab
Reef

Wyndham
Chankanaab
Park

Fiesta
Americana

Playa
San
Francisco

El Cedral
Mayan Ruins

Chen Rio
Restaurant

Yucab
Reef

Santa
Rosa
Wall

COASTAL ROAD

Freedom in
Paradise

Palancar
Reef

Punta Sur
Ecological Park
Entrance

C A R I B B E A N
S E A

Punta Sur
Ecological
Park

Colombia
Reef

Punta
Sur

Maracaibo
Reef
Punta
Celarain

Punta Celerain
Lighthouse/Museum

Punta Molas
Lighthouse

© The Countryman Press

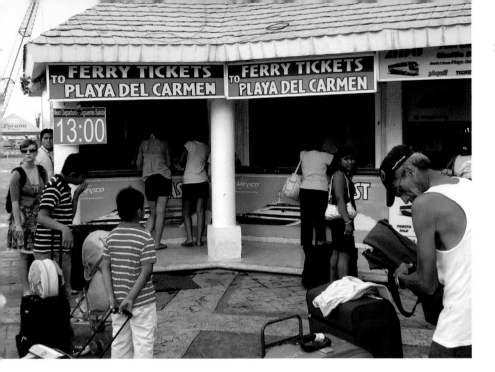

Buy your ferry tickets in advance if you want, or just before you board.

Caribbean. Dozens of shops, restaurants, bars, and other attractions are within an easy walking distance of the ferry dock. A few hotels are downtown and the rest are along the beaches to the north and south of the square. The eastern side of the island faces the open ocean, and the water is much rougher, with less reef and much less development. Visitors can drive around the south side of the island, hugging the shoreline almost the entire way. It's a great way to get away from the crowds and feel like a real explorer, though you are never more than 15 minutes away from a cold beer and tasty plate of food. A few Mayan ruins are run as federal parks, with information centers, gift shops, and certified multilingual guides.

Checking In

Best places to stay in and around Isla Cozumel

The all-inclusive 176-room diving resort ⚓ ★ Cozumel Palace (southern hotel zone, km 2.5, 987-872-9430, www.palaceresorts.com) was extensively refurbished in 2005, sprucing up the pool, guest rooms, lobby, restaurants, and all common areas. Although right on the water, its shoreline is exposed reef, so a small beach was built up above the rocks. Snorkeling is excellent right at the hotel, with barracuda, parrot fish, colored coral, sea anemone, sea urchin, lobster, and other marine life.

One of Cozumel's original hotels, the 252-room El Cozumeleño (northern hotel zone, km 4.5, Santa Pilar Beach, 987-872-9530 or 1-800-437-3923 from the U.S., www.elcozumeleno.com) remains one of the most

The Mexican navy on display just offshore from the Cozumel Palace

popular spots for families and others looking for affordable, all-inclusive beach vacations.

At the southern end of the island, the casual 224-room Fiesta Americana Cozumel Dive Resort (southern coast road, km 7.5, 1-800-FIESTA1 from the U.S., www.fiestaamericana.com) has traditional Mexican décor and is popular with families, serious scuba divers, and other guests valuing ready access to the best dive sites over proximity to downtown (20 minutes away by car). The hotel's beach club lies across the street from the main building.

The ✎ Wyndham Cozumel (southern coast road, km 12.9 Zona Hotelera Sur, 987-872-9300 or 1-888-293-0293 from the U.S., www.wynd

hamcozumel.com) is 15 minutes south of town and offers 404 luxurious rooms and suites, a half-mile beach, kids' club, spa, and extensive resort amenities. Its adults-only Sabor (www .saboresorts.com) section features dedicated guest rooms and a private pool. Wyndham offers its adults-only, all-inclusive boutique Aura (www.aura resorts.com) and members-only Regency Club (www.regencyclub cozumel.com).

The 50-room, hacienda-style Playa Azul Beach Resort (northern hotel zone, km 4, San Juan Beach, 987-872-0033, www.playa-azul.com) offers its guests unlimited play at the Cozumel Country Club golf course, just a few minutes away.

Local Flavors

Taste of the town—restaurants, cafés, bars, bistros, etc.

Most of your meal options can be found downtown, on or within walking distance of the town square.

★ Pasta Prima (a block south of the plaza on the right-hand walkway) is a favorite for visiting dive clubs, honeymooners, and even locals searching for an authentic Italian meal. Visitors enter from the street level and climb a stairway so narrow it seems like a replica from a Mayan ruin. The dining room is on an open-air patio overlooking the city streets, with the ocean just beyond. It bustles most nights, and there is frequently a wait for a table, though it is always worth the time.

Facing the ferry dock on the west side of the town square, ★ Las Palmeras is fun spot to pass time waiting for the boat to Playa del Carmen. Famous for its fishbowl margaritas (served ice cold, potent, and delicious), it offers breakfast, lunch, and dinner and has covered seating with open windows and walls, allowing in the ocean breezes.

For more than 25 years, inexpensive ★ Casa Denis has served some of the best food in town, especially fish, tacos, enchiladas, shrimp, and steak. They also have *sopes*, a traditional dish from Acapulco served on thick, soft corn tortillas with lettuce, cheese, refried beans, and meat toppings.

There are also several good choices when you leave downtown and explore the island. A great place for a lunchtime stop, ★ Chen Rio Restaurant (7 miles up the coast on the island's east side) has limited menu, with fried whole fish the main specialty, served by a rare beach on Cozumel's west coast with calm waters. No credit cards.

One of the fancier and pricier restaurants on the island, Pepe's Grill (one block south of the town square) is the traditional spot for a first or last meal on Cozumel. The chef prepares tender steaks, fresh seafood, and Mexican specialties. It may be best known, however, for its Mayan coffee, containing Xtabentún, a local orange schnapps. Waiters make the after-dinner drinks tableside, and as they're prepared, the whole restaurant watches as the liquor is set aflame and poured into the coffee.

The casual outdoor café Plaza Leza (south side of town square) specializes in inexpensive fajitas and steak, and the smell from its grills will catch you as you walk by. After dinner, linger awhile with a cup of coffee or a tropical drink and sidewalk parade. On Sunday nights, it's a great place to watch the music and festivities that take place at the plaza's gazebo.

Local favorite Mezcalitos (at the intersection of the cross-island road and the northern end of the road that goes along the eastern shoreline) serves Mexican dishes and snacks, and has a full bar. Everyone here is doing the same thing—cruising around the island—so it's easy to meet other travelers and pick up tips on hidden beaches and good places to go.

Bars & Nightlife

While restaurants welcome patrons to linger over drinks, most nightlife takes place in chain establishments located on Rafael Melgar Avenue between the town square and the cruise-ship dock.

Built on the water, ★ Jimmy Buffet's Margaritaville Café (Rafael Melgar Avenue by the cruise-ship dock, www.margaritaville.com) is a Parrothead paradise, with beachfront tiki bar, beach music (including plenty of Buffett hits), burgers, seafood, and an open-air dance floor. Patrons are passionate about their beach-bum hero, and impromptu sing-alongs are commonplace.

A block south of the town square, this Hard Rock Café (Rafael Melgar Avenue at Second Street, 987-872-5271, www.hardrock.com) is one of the chain's smallest outposts. Live music is featured most nights and visitors enjoy checking out rock memorabilia and buying T-shirts.

The Hard Rock Café in Cozumel fits in well with the local scene.

With one atop the other, two Mexican mainstay tourist bars by the cruise-ship dock make bar-hopping easier than ever. Just take the escalator down from Señor Frog's (www.senor frogs.com), and you're at Carlos 'n Charlie's (www.carlosandcharlies.com). Frog's is more nightlife oriented, with a stage, dancing waiters, and full-time party atmosphere, while Carlos 'n Charlie's is more of a restaurant, with a more subdued atmosphere until late at night, when it becomes a bar. Depending on the day and how many cruise ships are in town, these tourist havens can be packed or empty, raucous or tame. Both serve consistent Mexican food, seafood, and pasta.

Located away from downtown, the come-as-you-are daytime beach bar Freedom in Paradise (southern coast road at the southern tip of the island, www .bobmarleybar.com), has no electricity, doesn't accept credit cards, and is rather ramshackle, but it's a must-see waypoint for travelers circumnavigating the island.

Beach Clubs

Long considered Cozumel's best beach, ★ ⚓ ☼ Playa San Francisco (southern coast road, km 15, 987-872-0754) is still its most popular. It's been the site of thousands of weddings and remains a favorite place for watersports, seafood, and cold beers.

At Mr. Sancho's Beach Club (southern coast road, km 13, 987-876-1629, www.mrsanchos.com), a lively beach club on a picture-perfect white-sand beach south of town, visitors can swim, snorkel, ride ATVs or motorcycles into the jungle, or partake of other playful activities. The beach is public property, but facilities have a fee.

The well-established Playa Mia Grand Beach Park (southern coastal road, km 15.5, 987-872-9030, www.playamia.com) is like a tropical island recreation paradise. Visitors pass the day kayaking, sailing, parasailing, sunning, swimming, and applying sunblock. It's noted for its small zoo, floating climbing wall, and underwater replica Mayan relics submerged for snorkelers' enjoyment.

Way South: The Explorean Kohunlich

Set almost at the border of Belize, **The Explorean** (km 5.65 carretera Chetumal Escarcega, Ruinas Kohunlich, 983-201-8350, www.explorean.com) is a remote all-inclusive jungle retreat for guests truly looking to escape and connect with nature. The low-rise hotel utilizes stone, thatched roofs, and native materials to blend with the jungle surroundings. It is located adjacent to the Kohunlich Mayan ruins, 30 miles from the Chetumal International Airport and approximately 200 miles from the Cancún airport. It emphasizes adventurous activities, with one excursion per day included in the rate, including jungle treks, hiking, Mayan ruin tours, kayaking at a nearby lagoon, cycling, rappelling, and bird-watching.

Meals are taken at the hotel restaurant, **La Palapa,** with a thatched-roof dining room and an open terrace, perched above the swimming pool and jungle canopy. The 40-room hotel features a modern take on jungle chic, with Mayan artifacts, handcrafted furnishings, and furnished terraces with sofas and hammocks where guests can sit and enjoy the natural landscape. Rooms don't have TVs or telephones, but do have air-conditioning, safes, and complimentary turndown service.

It's popular with sophisticated and adventurous adults, who generally stay for a few days while touring Mayan ruins and taking eco-friendly tours. With no nightlife in the area, most guests retire fairly early after an evening of star-gazing and listening to the nighttime fauna.

Attractions

Created in 1980 to protect the region's marine life, and flora and fauna along the shoreline, ★ Chankanaab Park (southern coast road, km 9.5, 987-872-0914, www.cozumelparks.com) is Cozumel's main beach and nature park. Crystal clear water, with more than 100 feet of visibility on most days, makes for excellent snorkeling and scuba diving, and the beach offers easy water access, slow currents, and exciting shore dives, where statues of Christ and the Virgin Mary beckon from the shallows. The park boasts a lush botanical garden, a reproduction Mayan village, and a dolphin and sea lion discovery lagoon.

★ ⇌ Punta Sur Lighthouse Park (Southern Coast Road, km 27, 987-872-0914, www.cozumelparks.com), a 100-hectare ecology reserve and beach park, encompasses white-sand beaches, mangrove swamps, lagoons, and thick jungle.

Cozumel's primary Mayan site, the ★ San Gervasio Mayan Ruins (Cross-Island Road, km 7.5, 987-872-0914, www.cozumelparks.com) were an important destination for Maya women seeking to honor Ixchel, the goddess of fertility. The site, spanning a couple miles, has several different temples and small pyramids, and is home to many tropical birds and iguanas (see chapter 6).

★ Cozumel Island Museum (Rafael Melgar and Fourth Street, www.cozumelparks.com) documents the island's story through a series of re-creations, drawings, and artifacts. Displays range from Mayan days, 16th-century discoveries by Juan de Grijalva and Hernán Cortéz, the pirate years, and the War of the Castes to the present day.

U.S.-owned ⚐ Cozumel Mini-Golf (First Street South at 15th Avenue, 987-872-6570, www.czmgolf.com) is open until 11 PM, making it a fun place to enjoy the outdoors, sip a cocktail, listen to music, and practice your putting skills.

Rancho Buenavista (987-872-1537, www.buenavistaranch.com) offers two-hour horseback tours through some of the island's most rugged and picturesque landscapes.

CANCÚN (45 miles north of Playa del Carmen)

Although it's officially too far north to be part of the Riviera Maya, many visitors choose to stay a night in Cancún for a taste of the world-class shopping, great restaurants, powdery beaches, and over-the-top nightlife. The hotel zone is about 14 miles long, with dozens of hotels and every tourist service imaginable. The less commercial downtown area offers great local restaurants, a large bus station, and many shops and nightspots. The main tourist area is at the elbow of the 7-shaped tourist strip, near the convention center. Within a short walk, there are two malls, 20 restaurants, more than a dozen nightclubs and bars, pharmacies, cigar shops, grocery stores, souvenir shops, and—yes—even strip clubs. An 18-hole waterfront golf course is just a few minutes away, and there are even some impressive Mayan ruins just miles from the convention center.

Hurricane Wilma battered the hotel zone with 150 mph winds, 25-foot waves, and an 11-foot storm surge when it stalled out over the city for nearly 12 hours in late 2005. Beachfront resorts suffered major damage and there was serious beach erosion, but the hotels immediately rebuilt and Mexico's number one tourist town has reemerged with a larger beach and new hotel and condo towers dwarfing those that came before them.

Checking In

Best places to stay in and around Cancún

Most Cancún hotels (and all listed here) are located in the aptly named hotel zone. There are scores of resorts across different price categories that offer something to suit almost every type of traveler.

Known for its near perfect location on the beach and in walking distance to the convention center and main tourism entertainment district, ★ Dreams Cancún Resort & Spa (boulevard Kukulcán, km 10, Punta Cancún, 998-848-7000 or 1-866-237-3262 from the U.S., www.dreamsresorts

.com) has the best beach in this part of Cancún, hidden in a sheltered cove. There's no easy public access to the beach, making it especially safe and relaxing. Although it's all-inclusive, guests are not required to wear wristbands and instead sign all meals/drinks to their room. The staff goes out of its way to provide great service, even though tips are included in the room price.

For something a few miles removed from the central tourist area, ★ Live Aqua Cancún Unlimited (boulevard Kukulcán, km 13, 998-840-6010, www.feel-aqua.com) is set on a perfect beach across from a new shopping center. Thoroughly contemporary in every way, the all-inclusive hotel showcases sensory touches such as aromatherapy kits in each room, 24-hour lounge

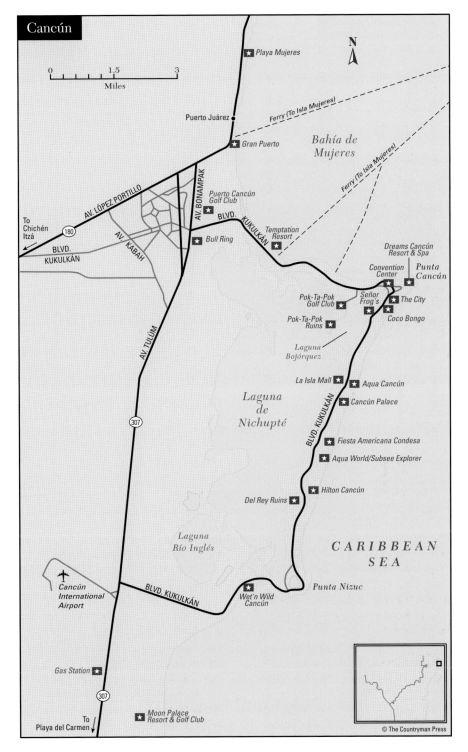

Cancún

0   1.5   3
Miles

Playa Mujeres

N

Puerto Juárez

Ferry (To Isla Mujeres)

Gran Puerto

Bahía de Mujeres

AV. LÓPEZ PORTILLO

AV. BONAMPAK

Puerto Cancún Golf Club

BLVD. KUKULKÁN

Temptation Resort

Ferry (To Isla Mujeres)

To Chichén Itzá

180

AV. KABAH

Bull Ring

BLVD. KUKULKÁN

Dreams Cancún Resort & Spa

Convention Center

Punta Cancún

Pok-Ta-Pok Golf Club

Señor Frog's

The City

AV. TULÚM

Pok-Ta-Pok Ruins

Coco Bongo

307

Laguna Bojórquez

Laguna de Nichupté

La Isla Mall

Aqua Cancún

BLVD. KUKULKÁN

Cancún Palace

Fiesta Americana Condesa

Aqua World/Subsee Explorer

Hilton Cancún

Del Rey Ruins

Laguna Río Inglés

CARIBBEAN SEA

Punta Nizuc

Cancún International Airport

BLVD. KUKULKÁN

Wet'n Wild Cancún

Gas Station

307

To Playa del Carmen

Moon Palace Resort & Golf Club

© The Countryman Press

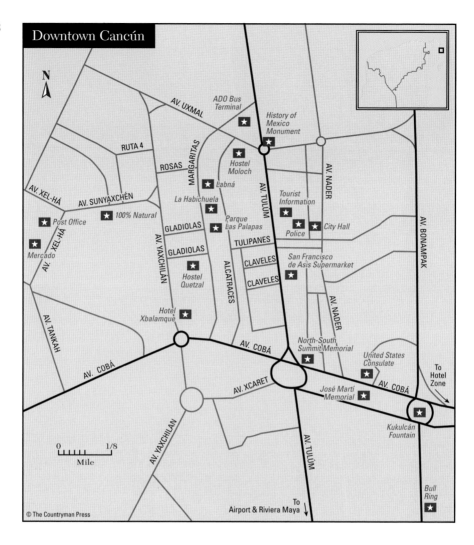

Downtown Cancún

music, and phosphorescent pillows at the beachside lounge. On-site restaurants feature celebrity chefs and have become the hip spots in town for the see-and-be-seen crowd. Guests, however, get preferential reservations. Other highlights include an upscale spa, a "garden of secrets" nature walk, wine and mescal bar, and poolside lounge area with sun cabanas.

Cancún Palace (boulevard Kukulcán, km 14.5, 998-881-3600, www.palaceresorts.com) is one of the liveliest resorts in the Palace chain,

appealing to spring-breakers, singles and young couples, though many families make it their home base also. A huge pool winds across the back of the hotel, with poolside games and dozens of people wading through the water to and from the swim-up bar with plastic cups full of exotic cocktails.

For those who complain that Cancún has no charm, the all-inclusive Fiesta Americana Grand Condesa Cancún (boulevard Kukulcán, km 15.5, 998-881-4200, www.fiestaamericana .com) may change their mind. With the

The all-inclusive Live Aqua Cancún is one of the city's most luxurious hotel resorts.
Live Aqua Cancun

tallest palapa in all of Cancún, the resort evokes a grand imagination of a Mexican village. Inside, a slick mix of traditional Mexican hacienda décor is accented by local touches and modern upgrades. The lobby is cooled with ocean breezes, and the beach is composed of flourlike sand.

And for travelers that would gladly trade native charm for some good old-fashioned American hedonism, enter Temptation Resort Cancún (boulevard Kukulcán, km 3.5, 998-848-7900, www.temptationresorts.com). This real-life "Temptation Island" is like a booze-fueled topless reality show, without the cameras. Although some nudity is allowed, it is not a "lifestyle" resort, meaning that sex in public is prohibited. In fact, though there's a sexy vibe throughout the complex, the all-inclusive resort somehow retains a touch of class and elegance with upscale rooms and well-kept facilities. The hotel beach is powdery white with a waveless waterfront, though nude ocean swimming is strictly prohibited.

Local Flavors

Taste of the town—restaurants, cafés, bars, bistros, etc.

Restaurants are plentiful in the hotel zone and on the main strips in downtown Cancún, making it easy to find options in or near your hotel. However, there are several destinations worth a special trip.

The indoor air-conditioned dining room at ★ La Habichuela (25 Margarita Street, 998-884-3158, www.lahabichuela.com) is quite pleasant and suitably upscale to impress any date, but the true joy of this place in downtown Cancún is the back patio, where the trees, plants, Mayan replicas, and twinkling lights create a majestic setting for a long, slow meal. The specialty of the house at this restaurant is the Cocobichuela, featuring a coconut stuffed with lobster in a cream sauce. It has a unique flavor and goes great with ice-cold beer.

Although it's hardly an authentic cantina, ★ Pericos (Yaxchilán 61, 998-884-3152, www.pericos.com.mx) throws a nightly fiesta that sure is fun. There are folkloric dancers, funny skits, conga lines, a live mariachi band, and even dancing masked little people. The menu features a selection of Mexican standards, including fajitas, tacos, enchiladas, and grilled steak or shrimp.

Built on stilts over the water in the Nichupté lagoon, across the main road from the beach in the hotel zone,

★ Lorenzillo's Lobster House (boulevard Kukulcán, km 13, 998-883-1433, www.lorenzillos.com.mx) advertises its lobster all over town and lives up to its hype. Choose from tails or whole live lobster and pick your meal from the tank. It's a great place to watch the sunset, and at night you can see the city lights and the stars at the same time. The dining room fills up nearly every night, so go early or call ahead if you want one of the coveted waterside tables on the outer deck.

Right next door to Lorenzillos, The Plantation House (boulevard Kukulcán, km 13, 998-883-1254) offers a more buttoned-up approach to seafood and the over-the-water dining. The wait staff has a well-practiced Southern sense of service, and food, including grilled shrimp and lobster, is prepared fresh.

The sprawling grounds of the all-inclusive Fiesta Americana Grand Condesa

Fiesta Americana Grand Condesa Cancun

The show at Coco Bongo lasts until sunrise. Coco Bongo

Bars & Nightlife

One of the city's top nightspots sits across from the convention center. But to call ★ Coco Bongo (boulevard Kukulcán, km 10.5, 998-883-5061, www.cocobongo.com.mx) a bar would be woefully inadequate—to even call it a nightclub is somewhat of a joke. It's more like an entertainment center, where travelers congregate to celebrate life and get a bit crazy. There's often a line wrapping around the corner, but it goes fast, and you can start making friends before you even get inside. There you'll find a central bar area ringed by stadium-like seating, an upper deck with another bar and more seating, and an elevated stage, where most of the club's nonstop action happens. From celebrity impersonators and high-flying acrobats to live rock music, there's always something happening on stage or hanging from the rafters above the main bar. The atmosphere is very convivial, with a strong spirit of communal fun.

The legendary ♂ ★ Señor Frog's (boulevard Kukulcán, km 9.5, 998-883-1092, www.senorfrogs.com) keeps packing in the partiers, night after night. No matter what time of the year or what day of the week it is, you'll find a mix of young and old, locals and visitors, partying hard and dancing even harder. The bar host keeps things moving with games, contests, and sing-alongs, while the waiters and shot-girls make sure nobody goes thirsty. It's open for meals during the day, but around 10 pm the tables get pushed back and the dancing starts.

Megaclub The City Cancún (Punta Cancún, boulevard Kukulcán, km 10.5, 998-848-8380, www.thecitycancun.com) features a swanky Miami Beach–style cabana bar and a massive indoor discotheque complete with laser light shows, smoke machines, and live performances. There are nine bars, big-name DJs, and a four-level dance floor. The whole place can accommodate more than 4,000 partiers, making it one of the largest nightspots in all of Latin America.

Hurricane Wilma—
Mexico's Costliest Natural Disaster in History

Three months after Hurricane Emily tore through the Riviera Maya in July 2005, Tropical Storm Wilma formed in the Atlantic Basin, churning and sputtering for a few days without much strengthening or fanfare. On Wednesday, October 19, though, things changed quickly. Within 24 hours, the storm had developed into a massive category 5 hurricane, reaching a minimum central pressure of 882 millibars and sustained winds of 175 mph, making it the most intense hurricane on record in that part of the world. The U.S. State Department issued an urgent evacuation notice for all U.S. citizens in the region. By the morning of Thursday, October 20, the MTV Latin Music Video Awards in Xcaret had been canceled and music performers and celebrities crowded the Cancún airport with thousands of tourists, all trying to get a flight back home. Meanwhile, the storm was poised offshore, forecast to veer to the east and spare the region, but not yet showing signs of the turn.

By late afternoon, winds from the outer bands of Hurricane Wilma began lashing the coast of Cancún and the Riviera Maya. Palm trees were bending and the waves were crashing, even though the storm was still 150 miles offshore. At dawn on Saturday, October 21, 10-foot waves were pounding into the seawall on the western shore of Cozumel, shooting sprays of water 30 feet into the air. The outer bands were tearing at the trees and rooftops and some signs had already blown down. Up and down the Riviera Maya and Cancún, hotels prepared for the worst and visitors and residents were bused to shelters while the military patrolled the streets, ensuring everyone had a place to ride out the storm. As the hurricane's eye neared the coast, the area braced for a direct hit, with landfall predicted to be somewhere between Playa del Carmen and Cancún.

At 10 AM on Friday, Cancún police reported the city's first death. A local woman was on her roof cleaning debris and a power line fell and electrocuted her. At 2 PM, the wall of the eye passed over the northern tip of Cozumel, while all across the region, the situation deteriorated rapidly. Gary Walten, an Akumal resident and owner of LocoGringo.com, was seeking shelter in his home while talking on the phone to CNN, which broadcast the conversation to the world. Wolf Blitzer asked him to hold his phone near the window so the audience could hear the sound. The noise was howling at a near-deafening volume, described by one survivor as "one thousand cats, screaming in pain." Water was washing across the main street through the Cancún hotel zone, and avenida Quinta in downtown Playa del Carmen was a shallow river, with whitecaps cresting between storefronts. Most of the windows were boarded up; those that weren't were shattered. Cars were washing down the street in downtown Cancún and in the back streets of Playa and Puerto Morelos.

By sundown, the eye had stalled over the Cancún hotel zone, creating the worst-case scenario for the region, as the rainfall continued relentlessly. The wind created a 50-mile-long wall the strength of a Force 2 tornado, and the storm surge inched higher and higher. Reports of an exploded gas tank and associated injuries made their way across the Internet, with readers praying for the safety of their loved ones, stranded in shelters across the area. Water was waist deep along the Cancún hotel zone and had completely washed out the road leading from Tulum to Punta Allen. Through the night, things only got worse. Witnesses in Playa del Carmen reported seeing 200-gallon water tanks, stoplights, plate glass, and even automobiles flying through the air. Water had washed completely over boulevard Kukulcán in Cancún, connecting the ocean and the lagoon and making one solid sea of water.

At sunrise on Saturday, October 22, weary-eyed residents and tourists, many kept awake by the screeching winds and rising waters, peeked out the windows and were horrified by what they saw. The devastation was worse than anyone had imagined. Mexico's president Vincente Fox had already declared the entire region a disaster zone. To make matters worse, the storm was still stalled, meaning the misery would last at least another 12 hours. Nearly every hotel in Cancún had lost dozens, if not hundreds, of windows, while the ocean in Playa del Carmen had risen to meet avenida Quinta, forming a sea of water 3 feet deep along the town's main tourist district. By 3 PM, the winds had receded to below hurricane strength for the first time in 24 hours, though the conditions were still too severe for anyone to leave the shelters. Food and water were running scarce and reports of looters being arrested in Cancún did little to calm any fears. Across the entire region, waves of up to 25 feet continued to crash ashore, ripping apart everything in their path.

By Sunday, rumors of "total devastation" swept across the Internet, while Hurricane Wilma left the Yucatán and made a beeline for the Florida coast, where it went on to cause $11 billion in insured damages. Back in the Riviera Maya, thousands of travelers were stranded, with no way to get home. The Cancún airport was damaged, and some tourists paid up to $400 for a taxi to Mérida to catch a plane out. Tour operators scrambled to take care of their passengers and get them home. Some stranded survivors waited in line for two hours to use a payphone to tell loved ones that they were alright. Over the next week, the Mexican government passed out roofing materials for rebuilding houses and thousands of bottles of water and also cleared the streets. Generous locals prepared food for hungry tourists. Residents and visitors banded together to start cleaning up.

Within weeks, most of the damaged buildings had been cleared or were in the process of being rebuilt. The Capitan Lafitte, just north of Playa del Carmen, was declared a total loss. Cozumel's beachfront and Cancún's hotel zone took the brunt of the storm, with some hotels having to replace hundreds of windows and replace soft goods in all of their rooms. But over the following months, the beaches regained their natural splendor. Restaurants along Quinta in Playa put on fresh coats of paint and rebuilt their *palapas*. The large all-inclusive resorts along the Riviera Maya built back bigger and better than ever.

Thankfully, Hurricane Wilma claimed only five lives in all of Mexico. Once again, the region proved itself to be incredibly resilient, even in the face of great challenges. By 2006, the crowds were returning in droves, proving that the Riviera Maya is not only a destination full of history and stories of a splendid past, but also a world-class travel destination with unlimited drive for the future.

PLAYA MUJERES (9 miles north of Cancún)

Everything at the Playa Mujeres has been done big, by design. The master-planned resort welcomed its first guests in 2007 and though it's near Cancún, it's isolated and feels like a separate destination.

Travelers who journey beyond Cancún's northern outskirts will find lush tropical landscaping framing a lavish grand entrance. Within the complex are two upscale luxury hotels, both with spas, an 18-hole Greg Norman–designed championship golf course, and an inland 176-slip marina. Both hotels are modern and elaborate with a focus on luxury and comfort. People wanting escape the world in style would find it easy to hide away for the week.

If you prefer finding the perfect beach over than luxury, this is not your destination. The ocean beyond the resort is deeper than you'll typically find in the region, making for darker waters than some may expect. The beaches are kept clean, and while better than almost all U.S. beaches, they're more underwhelming that most beaches along the Mexican Caribbean.

Getting There

From Cancún's hotel zone, take boulevard Kukulkán to downtown Cancún. Turn right on boulevard Bonampak, heading toward the ferry to Isla Mujeres. From downtown Cancún, continue 9 miles to the gated entrance to Playa Mujeres.

Checking In

Best places to stay in and around Playa Mujeres

Two resort hotels make up the accommodations within Playa Mujeres. The 450-room, all-inclusive Excellence Playa Mujeres (Prolongación Bonampak, Punta Sam, 998-872-8600 or 1-866-540-2585 from the U.S., www.excellence-resorts.com) puts tropical grandeur and playful pomp on display in its ornate lobby with massive chandeliers and a promenade staircase leading down to the resort grounds. A modern, tropical chic pool and bar set the tone for this upscale, adults-only resort. Set right alongside the resort's seven winding pools, all ground-floor rooms feature swim-up access and some suites feature rooftop Jacuzzis.

With its crisp lobby, showcasing many plush textures and shades of white, upscale boutique, La Amada Hotel (Prolongación Bonampak, Punta Sam, 998-872-8730 or 1-888-692-6232 from the U.S., www.laamadahotel.com) makes no bones about its designer leanings. Palm trees and local vegetation offset the bright white building and sands of the landscaped grounds. Honeymooners, couples, and guests docked at the adjacent La Amada Marina (www.laamadamarina.com) make use of the hotel's restaurants and bars.

ISLA MUJERES (15 miles north of Cancún, by boat)

Once a sacred pilgrimage site for the Maya, 5-mile-long Isla Mujeres is now a top spot for travelers seeking sunny days, pristine beaches, good food, tropical bars, and a casual lifestyle not found on the mainland. Spanish conquistador Francisco

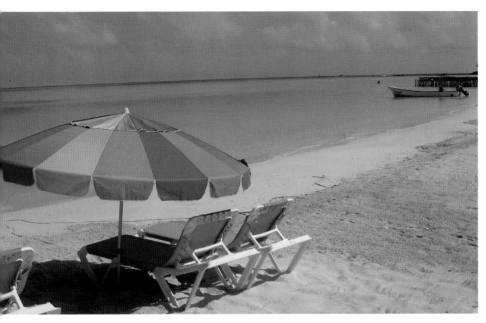

Parts of Isla Mujeres are still remote and unpopulated. Chip Rankin

Hernandez de Córdoba named the island when he visited in 1517, looking for gold and other riches. He didn't find precious metals, but did discover a large number of Mayan statuettes of women, once used in religious ceremonies. He named the spot Isla Mujeres, meaning "Island of the Women." Later visitors included pirates such as Jean Lafitte, followed more recently by hippies and bohemians who used it as a place to get away from civilization and commune with nature. Today, the island's narrow roads are best explored in golf carts, which are available for rent by the hour or by the day. Draws include tranquil beaches, charming restaurants and bars, local shopping, snorkeling, fishing, and diving.

Getting There

Ferries depart every 30 minutes to Isla Mujeres from Gran Puerto (www.gran puerto.com.mx), located in the neighborhood of Puerto Juárez, and the nearby older port, which still officially goes by the name Puerto Juárez. Start times and evening schedules vary.

The shiny new port complex

Buy Local for Local

Taking its individuality seriously, Isla Mujeres still frowns on international chains. Aside from a few small hotel groups, the only international brands permitted on island to date are the 7-Eleven convenience store and Grupo Anderson's Official Multi-Brand outlet, both across from the ferry dock. Even the Multi-Brand store is a concession to local policy. The corporation owning Carlos'n Charlie's and Señor Frog's may sell official souvenirs, but it hasn't been allowed to use either brand name on its public signage nor open a restaurant or bar on island.

Isla Mujeres

Downtown Isla Mujeres

Car Ferry
(To Punta Sam)

Hotel Na Balam ★

★ Hotel Secreto

CARLOS LAZO

Post
Office ★

HIDALGO

ABASOLO

MADERO

MORELOS

BENITO JUÁREZ

AV. GUSTAVO RUEDA MEDINA

Tourist
Office ★

Passenger Ferry Pier ★

Car Ferry Pier ★

N

Bahía of
Mujeres

Soggy Peso ★

Isla
Tiburón

Salina
Chica

Laguna
Makax

Dolphin Discovery ★

Hotel Villa Rolandi ★

Salina Grande

CARIBBEAN
SEA

Turtle Farm ★

Passenger Ferry
(To Gram Puerto &
Puerto Juárez)

AV. GUSTAVO RUEDA MEDINA

0   0.5   1
Miles

Garrafon
Park ★

Lighthouse
★

Manchones ★ ★
Cruz de
la Bahia

Mayan Punta
Temple Sur
Ruins

© The Countryman Press

(complete with parking garage, convenience store, and McDonald's) is located 5 miles north of Cancún, while the older Puerto Juárez is just several blocks beyond it. Unless you want to indulge nostalgia for the old route, Gran Puerto offers the simpler bet.

And if you want a little local color on your trip, bypass the air-conditioned cabin, and head to the rooftop deck seating. Most days, once the boat gets going, you'll be treated to the sounds of a local musician covering tropical and popular classics—often in unintentionally entertaining ways. Be sure to have a few dollars (or 10 to 20 pesos) on hand for when they pass the hat.

Checking In

Best places to stay in and around Isla Mujeres

Accommodations options range from backpacker to boutique and offer several unique spots that make Isla Mujeres a unique stop for any budget.

Ideal for budget travelers, the friendly ★ Hotel Bucaneros (downtown, 998-877-1222, www.bucaneros .com) exudes a genuinely local vibe. The inn's 16 rooms are simple, but attractive and clean, and some have air-conditioning. Restaurants and bars are in easy walking distance and the beach is a 10-minute walk away.

Set on a perfect white sandy beach, the more elaborate ♂ Hotel Na Balam (calle Zazil-Ha, no. 118, Playa Norte, 998-877-0058, www.na balam.com) is adorned with Mayan décor, lush jungle foliage, and hammocks ideal for napping in the warm breeze. The hotel specializes in weddings, yoga retreats, and hosting other special groups.

Straight out of a trendy magazine photo shoot, the minimalist 12-room ★ Hotel Secreto (Punta Norte, 998-877-1048, www.hotelsecreto.com) overlooks a secluded cove of Half Moon Beach and presents its guests with a sense of privacy and exclusivity that can be hard to find on in the region. A great spot for a romantic hideaway, it regularly picks up visitors who found their original Isla accommodations more rustic than charming.

Guests arrive to the opulent ★ Hotel Villa Rolandi (East beach, 998-877-0500, www.rolandi.com) via a private yacht from Cancún. Its sincere and insightful staff, opulent yet quirky rooms, elegant restaurant jutting over the sea, and private beach all

Isla Mujeres is just a short boat ride from Cancún, visible on the horizon. Chip Rankin

Hotel Secreto in Isla Mujeres is a hip getaway for couples.   Chip Rankin

ensure supreme satisfaction.

The six-room seaside bed-and-breakfast Villa Las Brisas (2½ miles from Playa Norte, www.villalasbrisas .com) offers a relaxing respite from the hurried world, with no phones, TVs, or alarm clocks. From May to July, sea turtles nest on the hotel beach.

Local Flavors

Taste of the town—restaurants, cafés, bars, bistros, etc.

Plenty of quality restaurants and cafés can be found in downtown Isla, including La Adelita (avenida Hidalgo, downtown), featuring a grilled menu and a selection of 150 tequilas; Chi-Chi & Charlie's (Playa Norte) serving inexpensive burgers, cocktails, and sunset views; and the romantic ★ Zazil Ha at the Na Balam hotel (calle Zazil-Ha, no. 118, Playa Norte, 998-877-

Exclusive and indulgent, ★ Casa de los Sueños (on the road to Garrafón, 998-877-0651 or 1-866-705-1691 from the U.S., www.casasuenos.com) is more like a grand private villa than a hotel. It offers 10 rooms and suites with ocean views, premium bedding, and unique décor.

0058, www.nabalam.com), offering delicious vegetarian and regional specialties under a large palapa roof by the beach.

Removed from town and set on a dock behind the hotel of the same name, the gourmet restaurant ★ Casa Rolandi (998-877-0500, www.rolandi .com) is known to draw the Cancún elite who boat over just for seafood, steak, shrimp, and Mexican specialties and an excellent wine list. The owners also have a delicious outpost downtown, Rolandi's Pizzeria (calle Hildalgo), which is very popular but doesn't offer the same romance or the view of the hotel.

Texas Barbecued Ribs for Sunday Brunch at the Soggy Peso

If Sunday morning finds you on island, swing by this hidden bar (www.soggy peso.net) for an amazing Bloody Mary and succulent barbecue lunch. The owner, a former fine dining proprietor from Austin, fires up his smoker every Saturday, smoking beef ribs for 24 hours for this weekly brunch. When they're done, juicy meat falls right off the bone and visiting Texans routinely declare them "best ever!" The ribs sell out, so get there right at noon and don't dawdle.

Bars & Nightlife

Popular with both locals and tourists, Buho's (avenida Carlos Laza, Playa Norte; by the Maria del Mar hotel, www.cabanasdelmar.com) is Isla's de facto happy-hour beach offering cocktails made with tropical fruit and a playlist mixing reggae and American rock.

For some daytime drinking, and a change of pace from downtown, head to the ★ Soggy Peso Bar & Grill (avenida Rueda Medina, south of the naval base on the bay side of the island, 998-274-0050, www.soggypeso.net). This ultra-casual Jimmy Buffett–friendly *palapa* bar is open from noon until around 8:30 PM, offering ceviche and other special treats. Marked only by a small handmade sign, it's hidden behind a house on the right a few miles south of downtown.

If there's a big game on, try Sergio's (adjacent to the town plaza), a sports bar offering beer, burgers, and tacos.

A typical beach restaurant in Isla Mujeres

Attraction

Set on the southeast tip of Isla Mujeres, Garrafón Park (Punta Sur, km 6, www.garrafon.com) marks Mexico's the easternmost point. Each New Year's Day, locals flock to this spot to be the first of their countrymen to see the sun in the new year. With the Yucatán Peninsula's highest cliff, the park gets its name from the Spanish word for "canister," either because the site used to be a fuel depot or because the bay is shaped like a water bottle's curved neck, depending on who you believe. It has several restaurants, souvenir shops, an ice-cream parlor, a swimming pool, a protected snorkeling area, a sundeck, and a hammock area, and there is also a museum and an ancient Mayan lighthouse relic. Visitors can rent snorkeling equipment, clear-bottomed kayaks, or Snuba or Sea Trek suits to experience the underwater realm.

ISLA HOLBOX (105 miles northwest of Cancún)

Holbox (hol-bosh), a narrow island 7 miles off the Yucatán's northern shore, is one of the region's lesser known and underappreciated destinations. Mayan for "black hole," its year-round population is less than 1,500, including descendants of the island's original eight families. Stories claim pirates settled it, using it as a hideout, mingling with the locals, and deciding to stay.

The island is a come-as-you-are hideaway for ultracasual vacationing. If the Riviera Maya is the land of *mañana* (tomorrow), then Holbox would be sometime next week. It's doubtful anyone has ever worn a tie here, unless it was a joke. Most locals don't even wear shoes, given the powdery sand roads. In fact, the mayor led an effort to pave the streets a few years ago, but locals voted it down.

Life has remained pretty simple in the Riviera Maya.   Philip Gamon

Since the island faces the Gulf of Mexico, it doesn't have the turquoise water common in the Riviera Maya. It's more of a greenish murky color, though some areas are clear enough for snorkeling. Due to currents and the island's location, thousands of shells wash on shore at each high tide. Complete with no breaks, many are highly prized by gatherers.

There are no cars, just electric carts, bikes, and mopeds. Locals operate the handful of restaurants, bars, and inns. Others go fishing and lobstering and sell their catches each day at the beach. There are no banks or ATMs; most businesses accept only

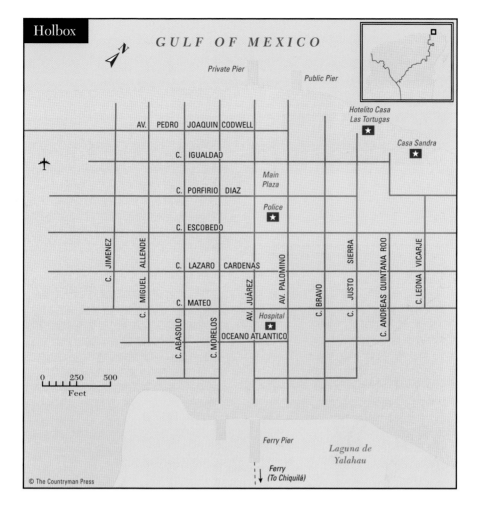

cash. Tourists while away the day on the beach or go windsurfing, sailing, fishing, snorkeling, and diving.

Yalahao Lagoon, on the sheltered side of the island, features a mangrove swamp, flamingos, schools of dolphins, and a freshwater spring just up from the beach. It's a popular gathering spot for locals and tourists alike. In the times of the Maya, it was believed to have curative properties, and natives would come from miles away to rejuvenate and refresh.

Getting There

The island of Holbox is a three-hour drive from Cancún and a further 7 miles off-shore. Visitors typically arrive via ferry or private water taxi from the mainland village of Chiquila, which they travel to by buys or private car.

If you take a chartered flights, the airstrip is just a few blocks from the town plaza. The company Aerosaab (Playa del Carmen, www.aerosaab.com) offers plane charters starting around $500.

Helpful Links: Isla Holbox

HolboxIsland.com—Highlights hotels, tours, transportation, restaurants

Cancun.com/Holbox—Covers restaurants, attractions, hotels, shopping, tours

HolboxWhaleSharkTours.com—Overview of the island, its attractions, whale-shark tours

Checking In

Best places to stay in and around Isla Holbox

Not long ago, overnight visitors to Holbox needed to be comfortable sleeping on hammocks and taking quick showers before the water ran cold. While this remains common, several small hotels now offer cold air-conditioning, comfortable beds, and an artistic tropical style for guests seeking a little panache. If you need Jacuzzi bathtubs and Italian sheets to end your day, you're best off visiting the island on a day trip and returning to your upscale hotel in Cancún or the Riviera Maya.

The cheapest way to stay the night is to rent one of the Mayan-style beach *palapas* on the island's north side. For around $10, you get a place to put your things and a hammock under the stars or in a small hut. Bathrooms are communal and in poor shape. Renting a room in a local house is another low-budget solution. To go this route, ask any cab driver, waiter, or another local, and they're sure to know someone with a room for rent. This typically ranges from $15 to $25 and includes a private room, shared bathroom, and usually a meal or two with the host family.

Travelers seeking slightly more stylish comfort may choose from several local beachfront boutiques pushing the envelope in Holbox.

The 21 suites at the barefoot boutique Las Nubes de Holbox (paseo Kuká on the corner of calle Camerón, 984-875-2300, www.lasnubesdeholbox.com) are tucked away in thatch-roofed bungalows that conceal their upscale, air-conditioned interiors amid a tropic village setting.

Designed and owned by a local artist, the romantic 12-room CasaSandra (calle de la Igualdad, 984-875-2171, www.casasandra.com) showcases handmade décor reflecting Holbox's back-to-nature ambience.

Guests at the ultra-relaxing, rustic chic Hotelito Casa Las Tortugas (Playa Blanca, 998-875-2129, www.holboxcasalastortugas.com) can swing in hammocks outside their 12 eclectically designed suites and bungalows or retreat inside to curl up in Egyptian cotton sheets.

Local Flavors

Taste of the town—restaurants, cafés, bars, bistros, etc.

All centered around the town square, restaurants welcome locals and visitors as they mingle and compare menus. Several restaurants display samples of their fresh fish and other dishes. Select shops along the square proffer fresh fruit smoothies and ice-cream treats.

Popular stops include Pizzería Edelyn; serving up amazing lobster pizzas, ice-cold beers, and lively atmosphere on a second-story terrace overlooking the town; and the inexpensive, open-air Viva Zapata, offering lobster, whole fish, shrimp, and traditional Mexican fare under a palapa roof. Meanwhile, a slight hint of European flair imbues the romantic Pelicanos with its menu of pastas, lasagne, fresh shrimp and fish, desserts, and quality coffees.

Bars & Nightlife

When the sun goes down, the island quiets noticeably. Visitors stroll the square and the main streets and tend to linger over dinner with a few extra drinks. Lights are dimmed and candlelight provides much of the atmosphere. A few places on and around the square tend to be livelier, but only relative to the quiet town.

★ Habana Nights is the most popular, thanks to its laid-back Caribbean atmosphere and big-screen TVs, especially during key soccer matches and sporting events. The Bar at La Isla Restaurant usually has a good mix of locals and tourists, making it a promising spot to connect and learn about the area. You can oftentimes meet boat captains and snorkeling guides and arrange for a special excursion not offered at the tour desks. Mingle with friends, or maybe even make some new ones, at the Tiki Tiki lounge. The second story terrace overlooks the town square and has a bit of a clubby vibe with lounge music and international bar options.

Activities

Beyond lounging on the beach and grazing at local restaurants, Holbox is best known as the home of the whale sharks, the largest species of sharks in the world often growing as long as a standard 72-seat school bus. Fortunately, they are gentle giants, preferring to passively feed on plankton, so they are quite slow and docile.

From May to September, ★ whale shark sightings are popular and visitors join them swimming Holbox's waters. Many tour operators guarantee that they'll find the sharks or refund your money. Typically, the captain zeros in on a shark and slowly pulls the boat within several feet. Two at a time, snorkelers swim alongside for about 10 minutes. The shark continues to move, so there's a fair amount of swimming involved to keep up, though most people are so engrossed in the experience that they don't notice how tired they're getting. Boats carry about 10 people, so after an hour or so on deck, you'll have another turn to jump back into the water, continuing the interaction.

Some boat captains and tour operators offer private charters. Tours are available that include transportation from Cancún, Playa del Carmen, or even Cozumel. A top operator is Holbox Tours & Travel (www.whalesharktours.com).

Tours and private charters can also be arranged to visit the Island of the Birds, a natural habitat a few miles away, take Sportfishing and Flyfishing excursions, visit the Yalahau Cenote, and go horseback riding.

This bird sanctuary and wildlife refuge is offshore from the northeastern tip of the Yucatán Peninsula. There are no bars or restaurants, no hotels, no roads, and very few facilities. A small group of Mexican marines runs a lighthouse, museum, lookout tower, and outpost, but there are no other full-time inhabitants. It's a popular nesting ground for sea turtles, and occasionally naturists will camp out and care for them and watch for poachers, backed by the marines. There are a few rolling hills and a long deserted beach, ideal for strolling and snorkeling.

Getting There

Visitors can arrive by private boat or with a tour group, but proper authorization in required. The island (www.islacontoy.org) is managed jointly by the local NGO Amigos de Isla Contoy A.C. and by the Secretary of Environment, Natural Resources and Fishing (SEMARNAT) who limit island visitors to 200 per day. If traveling with a tour group, your permit is likely included, but visitors traveling on private watercraft must apply for permits at the park offices in Cancún or Isla Mujeres.

THE MAYAN COAST— SOUTH OF THE RIVIERA MAYA

South of the Riviera Maya, beyond Tulum and the nearby Si'an Kaan reserve, are some curious and quirky hideaways that few travelers venture see, including the stunning Lake of Seven Colors and the emerging town of Mahahual, which just may become the quirky, upscale getaway that today's toddlers favor in 20 years.

LAGUNA BACALAR

About 2½ hours south of Playa del Carmen is Laguna Bacalar, a freshwater lake just east of Highway 307 that feeds into Chetumal Bay. With crystal-clear water and gleaming white sands, it's a rare jewel in the jungle. The lake has a dramatic setting and varying depths, causing the colors to change from spot to spot—hence its nickname, the "Lake of Seven Colors." It is a prime spot for snorkeling, birdwatching, swimming, and photography.

Checking In

Best places to stay in Laguna Bacalar

A full-service hotel with 33 rooms and suites (some air-conditioned), and incomparable views of the lagoon, Hotel Laguna Bacalar (25 miles north of Chetumal, just off Highway 307, 983-834-2206, www.hotellaguna bacalar.com) is an ideal headquarters to explore the area. The crisp white, turquoise, and pink hotel feels much like a charming throwback to '50s Baja California. A terrace restaurant overlooks the lagoon and a sundeck offers direct access to the lagoon itself.

MAHAHUAL

When you arrive in Mahahual you'll immediately notice a laid-back atmosphere, but with a sense that things may be changing. More villas and small inns continue to pop up, and the town is slowly developing a rustic yet upscale tone, similar to Playa del Carmen's early days. There are a few sandy streets, several open-air restaurants, and hotels and private homes are stretched out along the beach.

The shallow reefs of the Chinchorro Banks are known for being the healthiest in the area, with huge sea fans, sponges, anemones, sea cucumbers, arrow crabs, and seahorses. There are also hundreds of species of fish (including large barracuda), sea turtles, and even dolphins, which sometimes follow dive boats and play in the wake.

In 2000, Mahahual completed construction of a cruise ship terminal, and each month there seem to be more arrivals, steadily changing the face of the town. The cruise dock is only five blocks from the town center, and the street's become lined with new restaurants, bars, and souvenir shops. When the boats are in town, the beach is full of day-trippers snorkeling, swimming, riding WaveRunners, and enjoying the day. The rest of the time the village is mellower, with locals talking in the storefronts, tourists lingering in the beachside restaurants, and only a few people relaxing on the beach.

Getting There

To get to Mahahual by car from anywhere along the Riviera Maya, take Highway 307 south toward Chetumal. Fill up with gas when you go through the town of Carillo Puerto, as there are not many stations in this area. Once you pass the village of Limones (about 2½ miles south of Playa), you'll go about 2 more miles, and then you should see a sign for Mahahual and the Cafetal exit. Turn left and head east to the beach. From this point, Mahahual is still about an hour away. About halfway down this road, you'll arrive at a military checkpoint, so don't be alarmed if you see men in uniform carrying machine guns. They may search your car for drugs, but they are courteous and won't cause any problems—as long as you don't. The road is a fairly straight shot through the jungle, finally arriving at the small beach town of Mahahual. Most hotels, restaurants, dive shops, and other attractions are close to the area where the main road meets the beach.

To get to Mahahual by bus, from the Cancún bus station take a bus to Limones, either a direct or a bus to Chetumal that stops there. Be sure to ask, as not all buses to Chetumal stop in Limones. From there transfer to a Mahahual bus, which leaves every hour or so from Limones.

Checking In
Best places to stay in Mahahual

Surrounded by trees and flowering plants, Balamku Inn (3 miles south of the Mahahual town square on the main beach road, 983-838-0083, www.balamku.com) is a great escape for nature lovers and the beach is perfect for tanning and relaxing.

Right in the center of town on the beach, the 10-room La Posaada de los 40 Canones or Forty Cannons Hotel (www.40canones.com) may seem bustling for the area, but relative to more touristy destinations up the coast, is still ultra-relaxed.

On an excellent, remote beach up the coast from Mahahual center, the solar-powered ★ Mayan Beach Garden (El Placer, 15 miles north of Mahahual, www.mayanbeachgarden.com) offers suites and beach cabanas with ceiling fans and direct beach access.

5

Activities

ADVENTURE ABOUNDS IN THE RIVIERA MAYA, and wherever you are, most activities are no more than an hour away from any hotel in the area. Nearly every hotel tour desk can sell you tickets that include round-trip transportation. They're also easy to get to by rental car or even bus, so they make for good self-guided outings as well. Note: Secondary and local attractions are discussed in other chapters in this book, based on the area where they're located.

Nature Parks, Amusement Parks & Zoos

Once a sacred Mayan site, the Mayan-themed ✦ ★ Xcaret (Highway 307, km 287, 3 miles south of Playa del Carmen, www.xcaret.com) recreational park is far and away the top attraction in the area. True to its roots, it has several native ruins on-site, and each evening native dancers put on an incredible show of Mayan dances and rituals. There's an interactive museum, miniature models of many Mayan sites, and a petting zoo.

Visitors can go tubing or snorkeling through an underground river, watch horsemanship exhibitions, see native fish in a saltwater aquarium, watch butterflies in their natural habitat, go scuba diving, lounge on the beach, swim with dolphins, and even visit a re-creation of a native Mayan village. Near the village, an ancient ball court is set up where games of *pok-ta-pok* are played, with rules similar to those that were used more than a thousand years ago. In the game, players try to bounce the ball through an overhead hoop without using their hands or feet. It is said that in ancient times the losers were sacrificed to the gods. Tour buses from Cancún come in hourly, so it's best to arrive early to experience the park before it gets too crowded.

Next door, Xcaret's new park ★ Xplor (Highway 307, km 282, 998-849-5275, www.xplor.travel) caters to the active adventure set, letting them explore its

LEFT: An afternoon sail through Akumal Bay   Riviera Maya Destination Marketing Office grounds through the air, water, and land. Guests can enjoy 2.5 miles of zip lines including water landings, tour through the jungle on amphibious ATVs that they drive themselves, and swim or hand-paddle a personal raft though an underground river surrounded by striking stalactites and stalagmites. Book through a local tour agency or just show up at the ticket office. All-inclusive available.

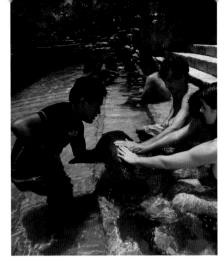

Learn about sharks at Xcaret Park.
Riviera Maya Destination Marketing Office

A 370-acre activity and nature park, ★ Tres Rios (Highway 307, km 300, 7 miles north of Playa del Carmen, 998-887-8077 or 1-800-714-3643 from the U.S., www.tres-rios.com) offers an environment to learn while you have fun. There are mountain bikes for cruising through the jungle, canoe trips, jungle rivers, sea kayaks, snorkeling beaches, freshwater swimming holes, and beach hammocks. Hiking tours and horseback expeditions are offered and take participants through the dense jungle to see *cenotes,* tropical flora, wild animals, and deserted beaches. If you're interested in scuba diving, you can take a resort course that includes an hour of instruction and then an actual open-water dive, with an instructor at your side. Park areas are left as untouched as possible, giving visitors the feeling that they are seeing the land much as the Maya did hundreds of years ago. All-inclusive available.

Nature park ★ Xel-Ha (Highway 307, km 245, 8 miles from Tulum, 998-883-3143, www.xel-ha.com) was once a Mayan seaport, and later a popular snorkeling cove frequented by an adventurous few. Today it's one of the Riviera Maya's largest attractions. Meaning "where the waters are born," Xel-Ha features underground rivers where fresh and salt water come together, an animal nursery, cliff jumping, a tubing area, a dolphin discovery center, massage huts, ocean snorkeling, mountain bike trails, and a hiking area. All-inclusive available.

Mayan for "underground river cave," ★ Aktun Chen (Highway 307, km 107, between Akumal and Xel-Ha, 998-877-8550, www.aktunchen.com) is a 1,000-acre nature park with a large cavern and jungle tour. The main, 600-yard long cave is said to have been a natural bunker for the native Maya, who sought its protection during serious storms. An hourlong guided walk through the park reveals badgers, iguanas, spider monkeys, tropical birds, and wild turkeys. There's also a motorized ATV tour, if you'd rather ride than walk. Along the way, you'll see many tropical flowers, coconut palms, and a gum tree called the *chicozapote.* The cave itself has amazing formations of stalactites and stalagmites, and an amazing underground *cenote,* more than 35 feet deep. Though the cave winds its way several hundred yards through the ground, there are frequent openings and areas where fresh air and the sun shine through, so it's not as claustrophobic as it may sound.

If prefer fauna over flora, you'll enjoy ✂ Crococun Crocodile Farm & Zoo (Highway 307, km 323, near Puerto Morelos, 998-850-3719, www.crococunzoo .com). Formed in 1985 as a commercial croc farm where the animals were raised

Swim with the Dolphins

Ancient Mayans saw the dolphin as a sacred animal and a source of inspiration for the creation of myths and legends. Today, dolphins contribute to aquatic therapies and humanities disciplines, and experience has shown that they only lack the ability to speak.

At Xcaret, dolphins are treated with care and respect, and their well-being is always the main priority. Biologists there, and area veterinarians, meet all the needs of the park's dolphins. They monitor their health, weight, and food, and conduct research on their behavior. In fact, biologists claim that the 40-year life expectancy of a dolphin can increase when living in captivity or semicaptivity (in extensive areas of its natural habitat). Dolphins have actually been born in captivity at Xcaret, and the way in which the baby mammals arrive into this world is quite a sight. They come out of their mother's womb tail first, so as not to drown, and they emerge like torpedoes to the surface as they take in their first breath. Their first year is a delicate time, because dolphins are born without antibodies; however, their mothers feed them for one to two years, building these defenses.

Qualified dolphin trainers, who are constantly learning new skills, spend long hours with the dolphins, forming extremely strong, family-like bonds and communication abilities. Every single approach of the trainer receives an answer from the dolphin: a jump that soars more than 6 feet up in the air, a tail dance, a flipper greeting, a friendly sound, and underwater tricks.

Due to their high cognitive ability, dolphins understand every instruction their trainers give them. Dolphins have the ability to associate, and this allows them to translate signs and develop a series of perfectly synchronized movements. With a "target pole," which functions as an extension of their trainer's hand, dolphins learn to identify instructions until they develop a language that establishes a sophisticated communication with their trainer.

for their skins and skulls, it's been transformed into a preserve, where visitors' admission fees go toward rescuing the crocs rather than killing them. The park now has dozens of other animals, including white-tailed deer, spider monkeys, snakes, spiders, and birds. Except for 300 crocodiles, many animals are tame enough for kids to pet.

A fun little stop-off between Cancún and Playa del Carmen is the 150-acre Yaax-Che Jardín Botánico (Highway 307, km 33, just south of Puerto Morelos). Set up like a museum, with everything clearly marked and explained, this botanical garden and nature preserve has hundreds of species of plants, trees, and flowers. From a hilltop overlook you can see the jungle canopy and the ocean beyond, and a small Mayan ruin called El Altar that dates from the 1400s. There's also a mock-up of an ancient Mayan homestead and a *chicle* camp, where farmers worked to process the rubber gum from the *chicle* tree. Look for the native tree called the *ceiba*, which the Maya called *yaax chen*. Considered a spiritual icon, it was said to connect the three levels of the universe.

Popular with families and nature buffs, the privately run ✍ Xaman-Ha Aviary (paseo Xaman-Ha, behind Plaza Play-acar, Playacar, 984-873-0330, www.ariarioxamanha.com) exhibits more than 50 species of tropical birds, including flamingos, toucans, macaws, and other favorites native to the region. Some are caged, while others roam free in their natural habitat. There are many iguanas, butterflies, turtles, brown squirrels, and freshwater fish.

A small replica Mayan temple marks the entrance to Kantun Chi (Highway 307, km 266.5, 14 miles south of Playa, 1 mile south of Puerto Aventuras, 984-873-0021, www.kantun chi.com), an ecology and adventure park, across from the Barcelo Maya Hotel. Meaning "yellow stone mouth" in Mayan, it has nature trails, swimming holes, caves, and an animal sanctuary. Fauna include raccoons, spider monkeys, and white-tailed deer, along with several endangered local species,

Keep your eye out for iguanas and you may make a new friend.   The Wilkerson Family

which the park is helping to bring back. It has four *cenotes* large enough for swimming and snorkeling, including one called Uchil Ha, or "Ancient Water," said to have been an ancient Mayan religious site. Visitors can go horseback riding, mountain biking, or hiking.

Just across the highway from the Cancún airport, as you head to the Cancún hotel zone, you'll find the 18-acre Wet'n Wild Cancún (boulevard Kukulcán, km 25, Cancún, 998-193-2000, www.wetnwildCancún.com). You can't tell from the road, but it's actually on a huge stretch of perfect white-sand beach. There are wave pools, water slides, a lazy river, tube rides, and many other freshwater attractions. Dolphin-swim programs are offered through Dolphinaris (www.dolphinaris.com), located at the back end of the park.

Cenotes

Cenotes are relatively small and the water does not circulate, so it is important that all swimmers and divers rinse off any mosquito repellent or sunscreen before entering the water.

Remember to bring cash, as most individual *cenotes* have an admission starting around $10, with larger parks and excursions run upward of $60. For general information about cave diving, see chapter 7.

Camino de Cenotes

Across from the main entrance to Puerto Morelos, a gravel road heads inland, under a tall archway etched with CAMINO DE CENOTES at the top, at approximately km 321 of Highway 307. This road is a fairly straight shot for 25 miles, passing through the blue-collar town of Central Vallarta, past several *cenotes,* and on into Quintana Roo's interior. There are dozens of *cenotes* in the area, though most are still inaccessible. The largest is Selvatica, an ecopark complete with bike rentals, zip lines, and canopy tours, and the road there passes other *cenotes* in various stages of tour-readiness. Check for signs as you travel the road, and you could be the first to visit a newly opened one.

Popular stops include ★ ➪ Selvatica (Ruta de Cenotes, km 19, 998-847-4581, www.selvatica.com.mx), which boasts a 160-foot-wide *cenote,* perfect for cooling off and swimming. The park also includes a 300-acre preserve, with bike riding, zip-lining, canopy tours, and lunch. Impromptu visits can also be accommodated. With 24 platforms, the 2-mile-long zip-line circuit is the longest in North America. This trip was named, "one of the 35 great adventures of the world" by *Travel & Leisure* magazine.

At ★ Siete Bocas (Ruta de Cenotes, km 13) there are seven different lagoons, a couple of them large enough for swimming. There isn't yet a road connecting the *cenote* to the main road, so visitors have to walk 25 minutes down a jungle path to reach it.

A small sign marks the turnoff to the medium-size Boca del Puma *cenote* (Ruta de Cenotes, km 14), which has a camping area and room for snorkeling and swimming.

Cenote Verde Lucero (Ruta de Cenotes, km 16) has several different *cenote* openings, with underground caverns connecting them. There's not much to see for snorkelers, but trained divers can traverse underground to the connected lagoons. The *cenote* is about a quarter mile from the entrance. You can park and walk or, if you want to brave it, drive your car right up to the edge.

Hidden Worlds Cenotes

Discovered in 1986, Hidden Worlds Cenotes (Highway 307, 30 miles south of Playa, 2 miles south of Xel-Ha, 984-877-8535, www.hiddenworlds.com) covers nearly 10,000 hectares of land, and the cave system runs for 42 miles, most of it underground. In business since 1994, it hosted the filming of the IMAX movie *Journey into Amazing Caves* and operates as a private scuba and snorkeling park, affording visitors an incredible underwater experience that feels more like being in space than underwater. Visitors choose from several different *cenotes* and caves, depending on their experience, the time they have available, and whether they want to scuba or snorkel.

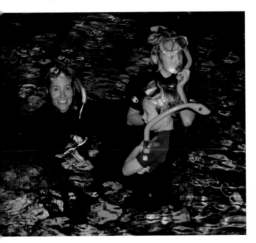

Cenotes offer a rare opportunity to snorkel in gin-clear freshwater. The Wilkerson Family

The first site is called Dos Ojos (Two Eyes), essentially two separate *cenotes* connected by a channel. This is the main site where most of the IMAX footage was shot, and is the third largest underwater cave in the world. Basic dive certification is required, and there is natural light the whole way. The water is unimaginably clear, and if not for the air bubbles, it really would seem like outer space, especially given the otherworldly scenery, unlike anything you would ever see on the land.

The next dive, the Caverna de los Murcielagos (the Bat Cave), has been known to bring divers to tears with its awesome beauty. The cave is as dramatic as it is exquisite, with a sublime combination of steep drop-offs, Disney-worthy stalactites, and elaborate features that have taken millions of years to develop. There are also hundreds of brightly colored tropical fish, elusive cave shrimp, and other critters. The depth is only 35 feet, making it especially safe for scuba newcomers and easily appreciated by snorkelers.

The relatively small and shallow Hilario's Well is best for snorkelers. During a one-hour guided tour, snorkelers encounter stalagmites, stalactites, and other truly awe-inspiring formations.

Other *Cenotes* around the Riviera Maya

One of the region's better-known *cenotes*, ★ Aktún-Ha or The Carwash (just south of Akumal, off Highway 307) is frequented by scuba-diving groups from the United States and beyond. The Carwash is only 50 feet deep, but the caverns are wide and long (nearly 2 miles long), making it very popular for certified cave divers. During the summer the surface is covered with algae, but in the cooler months snorkeling is possible.

★ Cenote Azul (Highway 307, km 266, www.cenoteazultravel.com), half the size of a basketball court, is on a small ranch bordering the highway. Look for the hand-painted sign along the road and slow down fast to avoid slipping on the gravel entryway. The lagoon is a short walk from the parking area and has a rope swing and 10-foot-high cliff, perfect for jumping into the water. An adjacent *cenote*, El Jardín del Eden, offers a similar experience and is a frequent stop for tour groups.

Part of an immense nature preserve and ranchers' cooperative, ecopark ★ Cenote Dos Ojos (Highway 307, km 242) offers several *cenotes* for exploring, snorkeling, and scuba diving. First discovered in 1985 by dive maven Mike Madden, it's been extensively explored and mapped. Most of the *cenotes* connect through underground caverns, which require advanced cave-diving certification to experience.

Cenote Ponderosa (Highway 307, 3 miles south of Puerto Aventuras), a *cenote* and cavern dive, comprises two separate *cenotes*, connected through an underground channel. Wide caverns are easy to maneuver and swim around, helping prevent feelings of claustrophobia. The main feature is an underground air dome called the Chapel, where divers can submerge and breathe natural air, even though they are under the water level.

Chaak Tun Ts'ono'ot (avenida Juárez at 120th Avenue, Playa del Carmen), whose name translates from Mayan as "rain rock *cenote*," has multiple caverns and a stunning cave formation.

Popular with snorkelers and divers, ★ Grand Cenote (2 miles inland from the main intersection in Tulum on the road to Cobá) features amazing underwater stalactites, stalagmites, and other limestone formations. You can swim a ring around the middle island sundeck area. It makes for a great stop-off after a trip to the beach or a long drive back to Playa from Cobá.

A group of four *cenotes* and caverns, the Taj Mahal (Highway 307, 3½ miles south of Puerto Aventuras, just past Xpu-Ha) is known for a cavern called the Beam of Light Room. This spot is less crowded than many of the others, making it a good place to linger over a picnic lunch. The connected Sugarbowl *cenote* has a large cavern open to the daylight, which creates mind-numbing rays of light under the water.

Water Sports & Activities

At ✴ ★ Dolphin Discovery (1-800-417-1736 from the U.S., www.dolphindiscovery.com), you can interact with live dolphins at one of three locations (Villa Pirata, Isla Mujeres, 998-877-0207; avenida Juárez, downtown Cozumel, 987-872-6605; Puerto Aventuras, on the marina, 998-849-4757). Several 45-minute packages are available, from viewing sessions where participants pet the creatures and observe tricks to swimming sessions where guests are pulled through the water by a dolphin. For all programs, the minimum age is eight. Children ages eight to 11 must be accompanied by a paying adult. No pregnant women or people with physical or mental limitations are permitted.

★ Ikarus Kiteboarding (Quinta at 16th and at 20th streets, Playa del Carmen, 984-803-3490, www.ikaruskiteboarding.com), which is PASA and IKO certified, offers lessons, equipment rental, and sales of windsurfers, skateboards, and kiteboards. It also has bathing suits, backpacks, T-shirts, and other beach games.

A great trip for snorkelers of all levels who want to wet their fins in the Caribbean, three-hour ★ Snorkeling Tours (Tank-Ha Dive Center, Quinta between Eighth and 10th streets, Playa del Carmen, 984-879-3427, www.tankha.com) depart on a 25-foot boat with a sun shade. Advance reservations are highly recommended and can be made by phone or by stopping by the Tank-Ha shop.

With Atlantis Submarines (carretera a Chankanaab, km 4, Cozumel, 987-872-5671, www.atlantisadventures.com) guests see the amazing reefs of Cozumel, including Santa Rosa and Palancar, from the comfort of a chair. The air-conditioned sub submerges 100 feet deep and passes by many of the same sites that scuba divers visit.

Sub See Explorer (boulevard Kukulcán, km 15.2, Cancún, 988-848-8300, www.aquaworld.com.mx) also offers an underwater ride through the reefs and undersea channels. Off the coast of Cancún, you can see living coral reefs, sea sponges, sea fans, angel fish, parrot fish, grouper, rays, sea turtles, moray eels, and other marine life.

Located off the west coast of Isla Mujeres, ★ MUSA or Museo Subacuático de Arte (Isla Mujeres, www.musacancun.com) is an artistic snorkeling site ranging from about 10 to 20 feet deep. Featuring sculptures of people and common objects by artist Jason deCaires Taylor (www.underwatersculpture.com), it was started in 2009 to draw visitors away from the fragile coral reefs while providing infrastructure for new coral growth. Already stunning, plans call for it to become the world's largest underwater sculpture gardens. As of press time, deCaires Taylor had submerged four exhibits including "The Silent Evolution," featuring 400

Yalku Lagoon is a great spot for beginner snorkelers.   Gary Walten/logogringo.com

life-size sculptures of human figures. Visits to the site are offered by local tour operators.

One of the top snorkeling spots in the area, ★ Yalku Lagoon (north end of Akumal Bay) has a mix of fresh and salt water, which provides a habitat for a wide variety of fish, including triggerfish, wrasse, parrot fish, needlefish, and sometimes sea turtles. The shoreline has several metal sculptures imported from Mexico City, plus a few picnic tables and stairways to the water. The bottom and sides are more rocky than sandy, so walking can be treacherous, but a pair of water shoes and a careful eye make it worth the effort. Float along in the cool water, watch the colorful fish, and listen to the tropical birds singing from the trees.

Horseback Riding

The huge Rancho Loma Bonita (along Highway 307, at km 315, 988-887-1708) houses more than 150 horses and is a popular spot for tour groups and cruise-ship passengers. Typical packages include two hours of horseback riding, two hours of ATV riding and a buffet. Horseback rides go through the ranch to the beach, where you can even take the horse in the water for a swim in the waves. Events such as donkey polo and soccer matches can be custom designed.

Once part of one of the largest and most prosperous commercial ranches along the Yucatán coast, Rancho Punta Venado (along Highway 307 in Paamul, 10 minutes south of Playa del Carmen, 998-898-1331, www.puntavenado.com) is now open to visitors. Occupied by Mayan natives 1,500 years ago, the ranch still exhibits evidence of their existence through stone fences, small dwellings, and other minor structures. In the 1950s, cattle baron Miguel Joaquin Ibarra purchased nearly 10,000 acres of land at this site and ran more than 600 head of cattle, in addition to farming coconuts, watermelons, limes, and cucumbers. In the 1970s, blight struck the coconut crop, and Ibarra sold all but 2,000 acres. In 1988, Hurricane Gilbert hit, thinning the herd down to only 40 head. Some 10 years later, the ranch opened as a tourist destination, turning the working cowboys into riding instructors and expedition guides. Better care was taken during Hurricane Emily in 2005, and the only losses were to the structure and were quickly repaired.

The ranch has 30 *cenotes*, caves, pristine beaches, and unexplored jungle, and offers horseback riding, snorkeling, and ATV adventure excursions through the property. With any paid expedition, guests can stay at the ranch all day and enjoy the other facilities, including the beach club, hiking trails, and snack bar.

Bike Riding

Bike rental is available in all urban areas. Many all-inclusive resorts also provide complimentary bikes for guest use, so double check with your hotel before you rent from a third party.

In Playa, Playa del Carmen Bikes (Eighth Street at 10th Avenue, 984-879-4992, www.playadelcarmenbikes.com) offers some attractive cycling options and EuroBike Rentals (30th Avenue at 26th Street, Playa del Carmen, 984-803-4733) does a variety of motorbike rentals, from Vespa and Piaggio scooters to Gilera, KTM, and Ducati motorcycles. Akumal Travel Services (Akumal Marina, 984-875-903, www.akumaltravel.com) offers a 5-mile bike ride on a beautiful private ranch just west of Akumal.

Parasailing, Skydiving & Plane Tours

Certified by the U.S. Parachute Association, Sky Dive Playa (Plaza Marina, Playa del Carmen, 984-873-0192, www.skydive.com.mx) offers tandem and solo jumps. Its rectangular parachutes have ram-air canopies, allowing for a very stable and controlled descent. Dives include instruction and have about 45 seconds of freefall, plus a six- to seven-minute parachute descent. Landings are on Playa's main beach.

At Ultralight Flights—Alas Sky Tour (984-871-4020), small lightweight airplanes take off from an open field near Xcaret for a 20-minute trip, heading north along the coast to Playa del Carmen, circling out over the water, and then back to the landing strip.

Offering sightseeing tours, private transportation, and air taxi service, Aerosaab (www.aerosaab.com) services Playa del Carmen, Cozumel, Holbox, and Chichén Itzá.

Well-respected Riviera Maya Parasail Adventures (Oasis Hotel, Puerto Aventuras, 984-873-5683) offers tandem and solo rides around the Puerto Aventuras bay and beachfront.

Organized Tours

Just handful of group tour and travel providers service the Riviera Maya, and they own the vehicles, employ the guides, set the itineraries, negotiate rates, and provide the actual tours. Sometimes they sell directly to the public, but primarily they rely on tour resellers to market their tours and book the majority of reservations. Nearly every hotel has a tour desk, and there are tour offices on nearly every block of Quinta in Playa del Carmen. Some restaurants have tour kiosks at their entrances and tour representatives even walk the beaches carrying a notebook describing the trips they can sell. Authorized agencies and individuals have licenses and ID cards, and it's recommended that you verify tour representatives' credentials before giving them any money. Most sellers have the same catalog of 20 or so tours, though there can be some variation in the selection. Prices are generally fixed and do not vary much from one operator to another.

Most tours require advance reservations so that transportation and meals can be planned accordingly. If you're interested in a spur-of-the-moment trip, your choices may be limited, but there's usually something available. When a tour is reserved, a deposit or even full payment is normally required, and you'll receive a voucher that proves you have paid and tells you when and where to go for the trip. Most major tours include hotel pickup and drop-off, while others begin at a predetermined location. The balance of the fee is paid at the start of the tour if you have only put down a deposit.

Many tours and adventures can be purchased well in advance, through your local travel agent, through the web site where you booked your flight, or directly with the tour operator. This can be a good way to guarantee availability and set your itinerary before your trip even begins, but prices are generally the same whether you book in advance or not.

TOUR OPERATORS

Aldebaran Tours (10th Street between Quinta and the beach; and Quinta between 14th Street and Constituyentes Avenue, 984-803-3880, www.aldebaran tours.com) takes small groups in vans to many of the key attractions around the region, including Tulum, Coba, Xel-Ha, Sian Ka'an, Xcaret, Chichén Itzá, Ek Balam, and Rio Lagartos. They also run a trimaran tour to Isla Mujeres.

Alltournative Expeditions (various locations along Quinta, Playa del Carmen, 984-873-2036, www.alltournative.com) specializes in natural and cultural tours, eco-adventure, and alternative adrenaline-rush activities, and trips can be custom-designed for large groups. Many tours stop at the company's crafts shop, where profits are shared with the indigenous communities who offer their land to be used for the adventure trip. Tours are adventurous, educational, and a great way to meet other travelers. Most of the activities require participants to be in relatively good physical shape. Many of tour locations are on private land and cannot be visited any other way.

CancúnVista Tours (avenida Cobá, no. 31, Cancún, 998-898-4312 or 1-800-860-5917 from the U.S., www.cancunvista.com) offers some great combination tours for travelers who want to see and do a bit of everything during their stay. It

A Mayan Legend

Following the great flood, the world was dark and full of chaos. Nothing moved and nothing existed. The sea and the sky were empty. On the second day, the gods became tired of dancing over cold waters, so they created a thin layer of solid land where they could rest while they finished their work. "Let there be land," they said, and a beautiful layer of earth rose from the ocean. On the third day, the gods called upon Chaac, the god of rain, who poured rich water into the cracks of the land, giving life to the plants, flowers, and trees.

As the rain continued on the fourth day, water filled all the cracks and basins, producing amazing lagoons and *cenotes*. On the fifth day, Kukulcán, the god of wind, flapped his wings, blowing warm breezes over the land, giving all living things a gentle dance. On the sixth day, Kukulcán turned his winds toward the sea, creating waves and forming Ixchel, the goddess of the moon and woman-hood. Ixchel rose to heaven and gave birth to Itzámna, the lord of the skies, who created the day and the night and then painted the night with thousands of stars. "Let the trees have their own guardians," the gods ordered on the eighth day, and birds were created in astonishing varieties, including Mo, the scarlet macaw, who became the guardian angel of the skies. On the ninth day, Hunab-Ku buried a white knife in the land, and from it flowed all sorts of animals, including reptiles, jaguars, monkeys, and Huh, the iguana and guardian of the land.

Like a falling star, Ixchel descended from the night sky on the tenth day. She dove naked into a *cenote,* and the waters came alive with millions of fish, of all colors and sizes. The gods then picked the parrotfish, or Kay-Op, as the guardian of the waters. The gods rested on the eleventh day, but they were feeling cold, so they asked the sun god to help them. He came from the skies with his magic fire and heated the waters of the sea, the lagoons, and the *cenotes,* thus creating a warm and gentle climate.

On the twelfth day the gods created humans, the most perfect of living crea-tures. With their intelligence, speech, sight, smell, taste, hearing, and touch, they were the ones gifted with the right to enjoy all the magic the gods had made for them. The gods danced and sang, full of joy for what they had created, and then they returned to the heavens. Pleased with what they saw and the world they had created, they decided to name it Xel-Ha, or "the place where the water is born."

also represents many of the standard water sports, adventure, and Mayan ruins tours offered by other agencies.

↬ EcoColors (www.ecotravelmexico.com) appeals to environmentally con-scious travelers who want to experience the Riviera Maya but don't want to alter it. Adventures include boat trips through Sian Ka'an, bird-watching, biking, kayaking, *cenote* swimming, and jaguar discovery trips. The company also offers guided trips to Chichén Itzá, Cobá, and the lesser-known ruins of Muyil.

Budget tour company SeaMonkey Business Tours (984-876-3306 or 954-323-8227 from the U.S., www.seamonkeybusiness.com) offers many of the same tours as other agencies, but often at a discounted rate. The company's Web site has destination information, travel resources, and photos and descriptions of dozens of tours and activities.

Yucatán Explorer (south of Playacar, 984-873-1626, www.Yucatánexplorer.com .mx) offers expeditions by land, sea, and air that tend to be a bit more extreme than those of other operators—in a good way. The ATV tours take about two hours and take participants deep into the Mayan jungle to swim and snorkel in a hidden *cenote*. They offer 12-man powerboat tours along the Riviera Maya coastline to secret snorkeling spots and ultralight plane tours that afford amazing views of the beachfront and jungle.

Boasting a catalog of "tours for people who don't take tours," YucaTreks Far Out Adventures (984-106-3686, www.yucatreks.com) features intensive excursions to some of the area's top historical Mayan sites, *cenote* and zip-line experiences, and some lesser-known alternatives that most people have never even heard of.

POPULAR TOURS & EXPERIENCES

Unless otherwise specified, these tours can be reserved through the above tour operators or through local agencies. Availability, times, and prices can vary.

An active adventure experience, ATV Tours (Highway 307, between Playacar and Xcaret, Playa del Carmen, 984-873-1606, www.atvexplorer.com) offer a two-hour ATV ride through the jungle, stopping at a freshwater lagoon, caves, Mayan ruins, and other attractions.

Although there's no pillaging and plundering on the ★ Captain Hook Dinner Cruise (Cancún), there is plenty of eating, drinking, and laughing on this swash-buckling adventure. Board a 93-foot replica Spanish galleon and sail the waters of Cancún while enjoying a pirate-themed show and dinner.

Catamaran Sailing Adventures (Puerto Aventuras, 984-876-3316, www.fatcat sail.com) offers you the chance to sail through the Caribbean aboard a 41-foot catamaran: the Fat Cat. Launching at 9 AM, the first stop is the hidden beach of Xaac, where you can go snorkeling, climb the Mayan ruins, play on the beach, and grab a bite to eat before undertaking some more open-water sailing.

Catamaran cruising in Puerto Aventuras   Philip Gamon

✐ 25 Kid-Friendly Spots for Families

1. 100% Natural restaurant (Cancún & Playa del Carmen)

2. Akumal Beach Resort (Akumal)

3. Arena Blanca condos (Playa del Carmen)

4. Barcelo Maya Resort Complex (Xpu-Ha)

5. Cancún Palace resort (Cancún)

6. Cozumel Mini-Golf (Cozumel)

7. Cozumel Palace hotel (Cozumel)

8. Crococun Crocodile Farm & Zoo (Puerto Morelos)

9. Dolphin Discovery swim park (Puerto Aventuras, Cozumel & Isla Mujeres)

10. Gran Bahia Principe resort (Akumal)

11. Grand Palladium Kantenah Resort & Spa (Kantenah)

12. Gran Porto Real resort (Playa del Carmen)

13. Iberostar Resorts (Playa Paraíso & Playacar)

14. La Buena Vida restaurant (Akumal)

15. La Cueva del Chango restaurant (Playa del Carmen)

16. Las Palapas hotel (Playa del Carmen)

17. Mayan Palace Riviera Maya (Playa Paraíso)

18. Mini Golf El Palomar (Xcaret)

19. Pericos restaurant (downtown Cancún)

20. Playa San Francisco beach (Cozumel)

21. Señor Frog's restaurant (before 10 PM; Cancún, Cozumel & Playa del Carmen)

22. Turtle Bay Café (Akumal)

23. Wyndham Cozumel resort (Cozumel)

24. Xaman-Ha Aviary (Playa del Carmen/Playacar)

25. Xcaret park (Xcaret)

A family that plays together stays together. Riviera Maya Destination Marketing Office

Chichén Itzá Deluxe (departs from Playa del Carmen and hotels along the Riviera Maya) is a good bet for a first-class visit to the legendary ruins. The trip includes a pass through the colonial city of Vallodolid, entrance to Ik-Kil nature park, entrance to the Chichén Itzá ruins, and a traditional folkloric show.

Mixing Mayan history and modern adventure, the ✧ Cobá & Chimuch trip includes a two-hour visit to the Cobá ruins, an authentic Mayan lunch buffet, and a trip to two different eco-parks for kayaking, rappelling, and zip-lining.

Unique, educational, and entertaining, ★ Dos Palmas Mayan Ceremony Night (984-803-2462, www.dospalmas.info) includes Mayan cultural lessons, a Mayan jungle ritual with bonfire and torches, a temazcal steam bath ceremony, and *cenote* swimming. This activity must be reserved for a group of 10 or more.

↬ Eco-Tour Nohoch escorts guests on a snorkeling and hiking expedition through Rancho San Felipe and the Nohoch Nah Chich *cenote* system.

You don't have to spend the night in a sweaty, un-air-conditioned lodge to experience incredible ★ Fly-Fishing or Light-Tackle Fishing in Ascension Bay. This all-day trip starts with a pick-up from your hotel at 5 AM for the

This traditional Mayan ceremony is performed at special events. Mike Stone

adventurous drive through the Sian Ka'an biosphere. Spend the day fishing for bonefish, permit, tarpon, snook, barracuda, and other game fish, plus have lunch on the boat. You'll be back at your hotel by 8 PM.

Marina Maroma Paradise (www.maromaparadise.com) offers a variety of exciting tours for adventure seekers, including combinations of ATV/speedboat trips, snorkeling at Paradise Reef, deep-sea fishing, and horseback riding.

Mayan Canopy Expedition, an all-day trip combining water fun and jungle adventure, includes a bike ride through a Mayan farm, zip-lining, a visit to the Xtabay *cenote,* snorkeling in Chikin-Ha *cenote,* and a visit to Aluxes *cenote* for a purification ritual.

An eco-friendly trip deep into the jungle offered by Alltournative tours, the ★ ↬ Pac-Chen Tour (www.alltournative.com) visits Cobá, where you will have a guided tour of one of the most dramatic Mayan ruins, and the traditional village of Pac Chen, a lagoon-side town of 100 residents living much as their ancestors did centuries ago.

The ★ Rio Lagarto and Ek Balam Tour lasts a full day, taking travelers to the traditional town of Tizimin and to the Ek Balam ruins in the northern part of Yucatán State. The highlight is the visit to Rio Lagarto, a remote river where hundreds of flamingos make their home.

If you want to see a couple of Mayan sites but don't have much time, Tulum & Cobá is a good option taking you to two of the best-known sites of the Mayan world.

The combo trip ★ Tulum & Xel-Ha offer something for travelers who want to see the ruins but also want to do something active. First stop is Tulum, where visitors will have a chance to see the cliffside ruins and the ocean below. Next is

Xel-Ha water park, where you can play in the water, snorkel, or lie on the beach.

The seasonal ★ Whale Shark Tour (Holbox Adventures tour office at 10th Street between First and 10th avenues, Playa del Carmen) offers the chance to swim and snorkel with the docile 50-foot-long whale sharks at Isla Holbox, north of Cancún. Tours include transportation to a dock north of Cancún and then the boat ride to Holbox. Not available year-round, this tour must be scheduled in advance, based on availability and presence of the sharks.

Other Activities

★ Bullfights at the Plaza de Toros (Bonampak Avenue, downtown Cancún) are held every Wednesday at 3:30 PM and sometimes on Sunday. Depending on the day, there will either be a tourist-oriented show with folkloric dancing, Mexican rodeo, and a single bullfight, or a full bullfighting competition with two matadors and six bulls.

South of Playa del Carmen and before Xcaret, ◈ Mini Golf El Palomar (Highway 307, km 285.5, 984-803-2606, www.minigolfelpalomar.com) offers a Mayan-themed mini golf course with 18 holes surrounded by fruit trees, water fountains, bridges, and tropical flowers.

If you just need a complete escape from your holiday, a three-screen, air-conditioned Movie Theater (Plaza Pelicano, 10th Avenue between Eight and 10th streets) shows fairly new releases that are usually in English with Spanish subtitles. Some older films and kids' movies are dubbed in Spanish.

Ek Balam is much less frequented than other sites.   Dr. John Anderson

6

Mayan Ruins

IF YOU COULD TRAVEL BACK IN TIME and see the Riviera Maya as it was centuries ago, you'd see a thriving civilization with a complex social, political, and religious community. From the Cancún hotel zone to the Playa del Carmen shoreline to the beaches and jungles of the Riviera Maya, there were hundreds of structures, religious temples, dwellings, stone roads, and even recreational facilities. When the Maya abandoned their cities, the jungle reclaimed their buildings and many deteriorated. Some sites retained their spiritual significance and were occasionally used as ceremonial sites by the local population until not long ago.

Archaeologists began uncovering these sites in the early 1900s, and little by little, more sites were rediscovered, studied, and, in some cases, restored to their original splendor. Many have been declared federal property by the Mexican archaeological institution and turned into public parks where locals and tourists can visit, learning about Mayan culture and history and experiencing firsthand the places where the ancient Maya lived, worked, prayed, and played. Many other sites remain buried, shrouded by jungle, sometimes just out of view. Some are too remote to be easily discovered, but new sites continue to be uncovered.

If you're investing the time to visit these sites, it's also worth reading up on the Maya. Many tour guides seem to want to stimulate the crowd with tales of human sacrifice (which did indeed occur) at the expense of broader aspects of Mayan culture.

If you can't make time to visit any of the area's major sites, you can always peek through the fence on the east side of avenida Quinta at 14th Street in Playa del Carmen to see an authentic, though quite unassuming, bit of Mayan history. Surrounded by a chain-link fence and official-looking signs declaring it a federal archaeological site is a small temple built at the base of a tree. It's not labeled, but it's rumored to be a small ceremonial site or even an ancient dwelling.

Make sure you bring some water and a hat when you visit any of the other ruins. The humidity and the sun will get to you faster than you think.

LEFT: Families can enjoy the Mayan ruins together.   The Wilkerson Family

Mexico's best-known Mayan ruin site is 128 miles southwest of Cancún, a two-and-a-half- to three-hour drive from either Cancún or Tulum. Visitors can take the toll road, Highway 180D (cost is about $40 each way), out of Cancún or take the road from Tulum and head inland past Cobá and through Valladolid. The drive through the jungle is interesting, with many picturesque places to stop along the way. The beautiful town square of the colonial city of Valladolid is worth a few minutes' diversion.

Chichén Itzá is the jewel of the Mayan sites easily reachable from the Caribbean coast, and its grandeur makes it the obvious choice if you have time to visit only one of the ancient cities. The site is amazing, and for first-time visitors can be a bit overwhelming. The structures are awe inspiring, and the restoration work makes it easy to picture what the city must have been like at the height of its splendor.

Chichén Itzá

To Mérida

Sacred Cenote

Path to
Sacred Cenote

Temple of the
Bearded Man

Ball
Court

Temple of
the Jaguars

Platform
of Skulls

Main Entrance ★

Platform
of Venus

Platform
of Eagles
& Jaguars

Temple of the Warriors

Pyramid of Kukulkán

N

Cafeteria ★

0   110   220
Yards

Plaza of a
Thousand
Columns

Ossuary

Market

Xtoloc
Cenote

Hotel
Mayaland ★

180

Observatory

Hotel
Hacienda
Chichén ★

Church

Nunnery

© The Countryman Press

To Cancún

The awesome size of Chichén Itzá has made the site famous around the world. Dr. John Anderson

The area covers more than 6 square miles and is divided into two very distinct parts, and you can see classic Mayan as well as later Toltec-influenced structures. Be sure to check out a map and see both—many tours cover only the later structures like the Pyramid of Kukulcán and the *pok-ta-pok* ball court that are typically seen on postcards. These structures are the largest here, particularly the ball court (270 feet long and one of 22 on the entire site), which is the largest in Mesoamerica. However, the large size of the newer city means you could easily miss the old city if you were unaware of it. These older structures also include examples of the softer *pu'uc* architecture (the church and its annex in particular) and display beautiful carvings not seen on later structures—they are not to be missed. A good plan is to head over to the older area and work your way back to where you started.

The Pyramid of Kukulcán and the Nunnery (where an explosion was used in the 19th century to access one side of the structure) are the two places where you can really see that the Maya built these structures in successive additions in their religious time cycle. The temple interior is interesting as long as you're not claustrophobic, but don't spend your time standing in line for it if you haven't seen the rest of the site. The exterior features are more impressive.

Not mentioned on many tours, a museum on the grounds displays some of the small artifacts that weren't taken to other museums around the world. If you're visiting on your own, it's worth seeing, but if you're on an organized tour, your limited time is likely better spent outdoors.

There are night shows here with light and sound, but these are impractical for the traveler from the coast, given the long drive back after dark.

The entrance fee is $10 per person, and tours (including transportation, snacks, and drinks) can be arranged through any local travel agency or tour desk.

A large iguana catches some rays at Tulum.   Dr. John Anderson

TULUM

Given its proximity to the hotels of the Riviera Maya, Tulum (2 miles east of Highway 307, 40 miles south of Playa del Carmen) is one of the most frequently visited Mayan sites.

Tulum is unlike any of the other major Mayan ruins in Mexico in that it is right on the coast. Originally called Zama, meaning "sunrise" in Mayan, it faces due east. The beauty of the Caribbean Sea enhances the structures, and many people say this is what makes Tulum so appealing. The site, known as the Walled City, rose to prominence during the post-Classic period (A.D. 1000–1500), and it is the polar opposite of Chichén Itzá in terms of what makes it beautiful.

While Chichén Itzá has a sense of isolation about it given its distance and the thick jungle surrounding it, Tulum has a sense of openness and airiness brought on by the ocean itself, and the ocean views are amazing. At the same time, being next to the ocean leads to a great deal of erosion, and between this and the many hurricanes that hit the Caribbean, most of the detail of Tulum's structures has been lost. Some restoration work has been done, but the structures do not at all bear the crisp lines of those at Chichén Itzá. Instead, they are well-rounded, bleached limestone, and the few remaining detailed carvings are protected by woven structures to keep the rain off. As such, you won't get an accurate picture of the Maya if it's the only ruin you see.

Since it is so close to the population centers, there are many more tourists for the size of the area than you would see elsewhere (this is also in part because it's a small area, and more difficult to find a place to retreat from large groups). The convenient access also means that many of the tourists are not particularly interested in the Maya and come because it's close and "worth seeing." This can make for a somewhat less sacred atmosphere than one finds at the other sites.

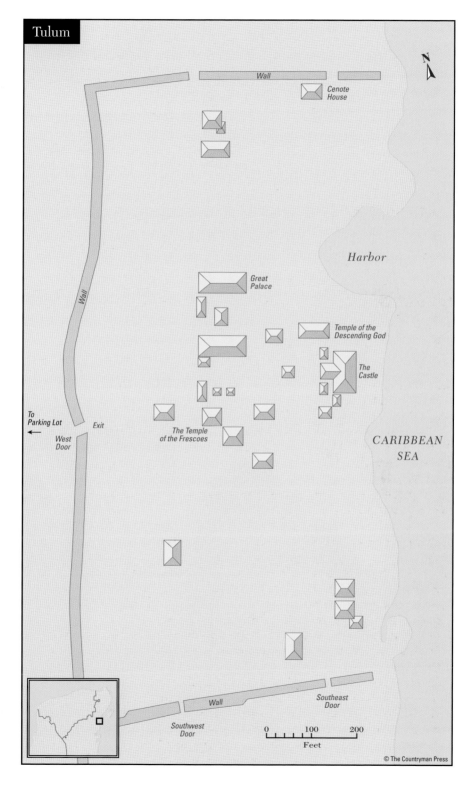

Tulum

Wall

Cenote House

Harbor

Great Palace

Temple of the Descending God

The Castle

To Parking Lot

Exit

West Door

The Temple of the Frescoes

CARIBBEAN SEA

Wall

Southeast Door

Southwest Door

0   100   200

Feet

© The Countryman Press

But as a relatively small site, there is no problem finding time to see all the major elements of the Tulum ruins. This makes it a good first stop if you're visiting several ruins, and a choice to consider if you are traveling with small children or anyone with limited mobility. If you have your own vehicle, you can easily start off at Tulum early and go to Cobá the same day. In fact, most commercial tours combine visits with other activities in the area.

Free parking is available at Tulum's back gate. To get there, head south of the main highway entrance to the ruins and turn east at the Tulum crossroads, by the San Francisco de Asis grocery store. After 2 miles, the road will dead-end at the Tulum beach road. Turn left and the ruins are straight ahead, 2 miles down the road, past a wonderful public beach at Playa Maya. This gate is used for bicycle and walking access by travelers staying at hotels along Tulum beach. Park along the side of the road and walk the half mile to the entrance booth.

Entrance is $5, and bilingual guide service is available.

COBÁ

In its heyday, Cobá city had 44 miles of urban sprawl, making it one of the largest cities in the Mayan civilization. It is located an hour inland from Tulum, on the road that starts at Tulum pueblo and passes several popular *cenotes*, such as Grand Cenote and the Carwash (see chapter 5), before yielding to the jungle.

Ride bikes between the major sites of Cobá.　Dr. John Anderson

Off the Beaten Path

The ancient Mayan city of Ek Balam is one of the Yucatán's most extraordinary sites, but amazingly, it's also one of the least visited. Excavation began in 1987 and has uncovered a long stretch of perfectly preserved sculpturework on part of the main temple, which shows how elaborate the exterior of these ruins once was. The enormous toothed mouth of the Witz Monster, symbolizing the entry to the underworld, is surrounded by elaborate Mayan figures. Ek Balam makes a great side trip during a visit to Chichén Itzá.

The city of Cobá flourished during the Classic period (A.D. 300–1000) and was once home to more than 50,000 inhabitants. It's the least excavated of the region's major ruins. Thick jungle encroaches onto the site and near the structures themselves, creating an atmosphere of discovery (Chichén Itzá is also surrounded by jungle, but the area around the structures themselves has been largely cleared). A number of the ruins at Cobá are partially reconstructed, but not in the finished way that one sees at Chichén Itzá, so unlike at other sites the ruins look like ancient, unrestored buildings. Because of this, things appear much as they would have looked when European explorers first arrived.

The city of Cobá was very large, and the excavated ruins are in groups spread across the jungle. Bicycles come included with many commercial tours (or can be rented for $2.50; tricycle taxis for two go for $7.50) and are advisable. If you're on an organized tour you'll have limited time here, and more of it can be spent exploring the ruins if you can move between the groups more quickly. However, if you have the time, the jungle walk is pleasant and relaxing.

The highlight of Cobá is Nohoc Mul, the largest pyramid in southern Mexico (138 feet tall), and it's considerably larger than the Pyramid of Kukulcán at Chichén Itzá. The fact it's surrounded by jungle rather than open space further magnifies the size difference. Like the Pyramid of Kukulcán, this structure can be climbed, but take great care: While the stone steps are stable, they are very irregular compared to the climb at Chichén Itzá. The view from the temple atop Nohoc Mul is beautiful, and you can see the tops of many other structures, the lake (rare in the Yucatán) on which Cobá sits, and also a vast canopy of surrounding jungle. The ball court here, one of the smallest in the Mayan world, is also an interesting counter to Chichén Itzá's massive court.

There are several other significant structures, including Xaibe (the Crossroads Pyramid), a rounded, tiered structure very different from any other structures on this side of the Yucatán and more reminiscent of Uxmal. There are also many stelae (standing stone markers) here noting important events in the Mayan history, and many are still detailed enough to see the forms carved onto them.

Tours to Cobá are still less common than to the other ruins, and so the area can be less crowded than the others. If you are looking for a place with fewer tourists, this is likely your best choice. A number of commercial tours combine a visit to Cobá with a tour of a local Mayan village, intending to both show the ancient architecture and expose the visitor to the Maya in their modern lifestyle.

Entrance is $5, and guide service is available. Open 9–5 daily.

Beware the Bewitching Call of X'tabai

According to Mayan legend, X'tabai (Ish-TAH-buy) was a beautiful woman and ensnarer of men known to live in the Yucatán jungle. Much like Greece's mythological sirens, she reportedly drew unsuspecting males to her with her beauty. After which, they were never seen again.

But rather than entrancing men through song, she is said to have possessed them as soon as they first spied her great physical beauty and flowing black hair.

Modern accounts contradict themselves as to whether she was a singular spirit or a race of females, but most stories claim X'tabai is connected to the beautiful *ceiba* tree found throughout tropical Latin America.

Known for its winding, tall, and wall-like roots, the *ceiba* tree has often been used in Mayan ceremonial art. From the roots, which depict the underworld, the tree connects it to the terrestrial world via its trunk and ultimately reaches up in every direction to the heavens through its branches.

Stories suggest that X'tabai removed men from the terrestrial world, though some speculate that she provided passage to the heavens, rather than to the underworld.

Today in the Riviera Maya, warnings of X'tabai still persist, though often with a knowing wink. Given that some reports question whether it was her deep eyes, her lustrous hair, or simply her willingness to expose her breasts that stunned the men, it seems like she might easily conceal herself in plain sight on the beaches of Playa del Carmen.

CHUNYAXCHE/MUYIL

Fifteen miles south of Tulum on Highway 307 and 7 miles from the coastline, the ruins of Chunyaxche/Muyil are located within the Sian Ka'an biosphere and are significantly less visited than the better-known temples of the Caribbean coast. Some researchers believe, however, that the site will someday rival Tulum in its scale and importance to the historical record. Inhabited from 300 B.C. until the Spanish conquest, the site has some 75 individual structures believed still hidden beneath the jungle vegetation. The University of the Yucatán is leading the excavation, though scarce funds have significantly delayed the project. Archaeological evidence indicates the site was built to honor Ixchel, the Mayan goddess of fertility.

Built on La Laguna freshwater lake, the site has narrow canals that lead to the ocean and once served as passageways for seafaring adventurers and traders.

Entrance fee is $5, and guide service is available.

SAN GERVASIO

The center of Cozumel's Mayan World, San Gervasio was inhabited from A.D. 200 until the arrival of the Spaniards. It was of great spiritual importance and many Maya women traveled to the island to make offerings and pay homage to the fertility goddess Ixchel.

Although there are no grand pyramids, the site features about 40 structures, including smaller temples, pyramids, and dwellings. Structures are congregated around a central plaza, much like a traditional Roman forum. Experts theorize that the structures were once larger due to additions and extensions made from wood and thatched leaves. Tiny red handprints still visible on an interior wall of one home named Manitas have prompted jokes that it was probably a village day care for visiting mothers.

Set in relative isolation, amid the Cozumel rainforest, the ruins remain overgrown today and are home to many tropical birds and large iguanas. Visitors can easily walk around the 2-square-mile site.

The entrance is located on Cross-Island Road at km 7.5.

Entrance is $5.50 (free for children under eight) and guide service is available. Open 7–4 daily.

7

Diving & Snorkeling

THE RIVIERA MAYA is home to some of the most unequaled dive sites in the world. It's one of the few places where you can swim with a green moray eel on a 100-foot wall dive in the morning, go free-diving and snorkeling with dolphins after lunch, explore virgin caverns on a freshwater cave dive in the afternoon, and then pet sleeping sharks on a shallow-water dive that same night.

The Great Mayan Reef is the second longest living barrier reef in the world, and only Australia's Great Barrier Reef is larger. It starts in Cancún and extends just offshore along the eastern tip of the Yucatán Peninsula and all the way down to Honduras. From many towns the reef is only a short swim from the beach, making for excellent snorkeling without the need for a boat or special equipment. You can usually see the water breaking over the reef, which helps to pinpoint its location. The reef itself is razor sharp and extremely delicate, so touching it, bumping it with your equipment, or even kicking sand onto it can cause serious damage from which it takes years to recover. It is home to hundreds of species of live corals, fish, anemones, eels, rays, and other life forms, small and large.

A unique snorkeling opportunity at Playa Mia in Cozumel Playa Mia Cozumel

The water itself is gin-clear, with horizontal visibility up to 150 feet in some areas. The prevailing current is north to south, though it varies widely depending on the weather and local geographic conditions. Water temperature ranges from a low of 75 in the

LEFT: Small boats called *pangas* can be chartered for $200 for four hours.

winter months up to the mid-80s in the height of the summer. Many divers choose to dive without a wet suit, which lessens the amount of weights they are required to carry, making for a less-encumbered dive and more bottom time. Other divers opt for a spring suit, shortie, or Farmer John–style wet suit, which provides a good layer of warmth while still allowing for freedom of movement.

There are a variety of open-water dives available. Divers in Cozumel and Akumal frequently go on shore dives, either in small independent groups or with a dive master. In these locations the reef comes within 100 yards of the shore, enabling divers to reach excellent dive spots with a short underwater or surface swim. Cozumel is also known for its wall dives and drift dives, where the dive boat will stop at one end of a reef and let the divers out, follow their bubbles as they drift along with the current, and then be waiting to pick them up when they surface at the end of the dive. This type of diving can be very relaxing for the divers, who hardly need to swim as they're swiftly drawn along with the current, which travels up to 5 mph.

On other dives, where there isn't as much current, such as off the coast of Puerto Aventuras, Isla Mujeres, or Playa del Carmen, the boat will anchor, the dive master will lead the group on a dive, and then all divers will return to the entry point. Diving this way requires all divers to stay in sight of the others, ensuring that nobody gets lost underwater. If you don't have a dive buddy, you'll be assigned one on the boat before the dive begins.

Gear up and plan an outing at one of the scuba shops around town.

Open-Water Dives

Experienced divers can go on self-guided dives right from the shore at many hotels, particularly in Cozumel and Akumal. You can bring your own gear or rent it at the hotel dive shop. Most shops have tanks available for less than $10, allowing you to custom-create the dive profile that you want and then go for it. On these dives, the maximum depth is usually around 50 feet, but divers can see just as much variety and just as much beautiful underwater scenery as on boat dives.

Organized boat trips are another way to go. These trips are normally booked at least one day in advance so that the boat captain can prepare all gear and ensure there will be enough assistants on the boat to handle the group. These trips offer either one or two dives and can be in the morning, afternoon, or even night. Most boat rides will be 30 minutes to an hour long, giving you plenty of time to prepare your gear, document the trip in your log book, socialize with other divers, and even do some sight-seeing along the way. The boats range from 14-foot, open-hull *pangas* carrying just a couple of divers all the way up to 40-foot yachts that can accommodate more than a dozen divers and have air-conditioning, a galley, a shower, and other luxuries. Divers can choose to go on a private trip or can join a group trip with other divers. Nondivers can accompany divers on the boat trip for a nominal fee, though this must be arranged in advance so the captain can plan for the extra space and refreshments.

There are several types of open-water dives common in the area. One of the most common is a reef dive, where divers swim or drift along the top of the reef. Off many beaches there is a steep wall within a few miles of shore, where the depth drops from around 80 to 100 feet to more than 1,000 feet, almost straight down, and on these dives either the divers swim along right at the edge of the drop-off, with the reef below them and the vast depths of the blue ocean just beyond, or they swim along the wall itself, with the reef to the side and the depths straight below. When wall diving this way, it is important for divers to watch their depth gauges closely since it's deceptively easy to go deeper and deeper without even noticing it. For recreational scuba diving the maximum depth is usually considered to be 120 feet. Plus, the deeper you go, the shorter amount of time you can stay, so most divers prefer to keep their maximum depth to around 80 feet, which gives them 30 to 40 minutes of underwater time.

Most dive boats carry sodas, water, and juice, and many stop for lunch between dives. Lunch can be taken on the boat, or the boat will pull up to the beach, where buffet meals are served. This is most common in Cozumel, though it's done in other areas as well.

Diving at night is a completely different experience than diving during the day, and is a real thrill. All divers carry their own lights and backup lights and also wear glow sticks to make them visible, even if their lights should fail. Octopuses, sharks, rays, squid, and other marine life are more prevalent at night since this is the time they normally feed. The same dive site will look totally different at night, with different colors on the coral, different types of fish swimming around, and a different sense of depth for divers since they can see only where they point their lights. On a clear night with a big moon, the divers can also see light from above and can sometimes see large fish or the dive boat silhouetted against the moonlight.

Cenotes & Freshwater Dives

A surprise to many first-time Riviera Maya divers is the presence of many freshwater dive spots, just as close and accessible as the saltwater ones. Throughout the Yucatán Peninsula, there are caverns and spring-fed lagoons called *cenotes* that offer unique dive opportunities for both amateur and experienced divers. The word *cenote* comes from the Mayan word *dzonot*, which was used to describe the sinkholes that formed after the collapse of the thin limestone earth revealed a cave underneath, which then filled with freshwater from the water table (quite near the ground in the porous crust of the Riviera Maya). Once a major source of drinking water for the ancient Mayan villagers, these *cenotes* range from the size of a kiddie pool up to that of a large lagoon covering several acres of land. Some are on private ranches and have been recently opened to visitors, and others are commercially operated as recreational parks and have resident dive operations, on-site instructors and tour guides (see chapter 5).

The water in the *cenotes* is crystal clear and remains a fairly constant temperature of around 72 degrees. Most cenotes are fairly shallow, making even snorkeling and free-diving quite rewarding. Others have deeper holes, up to 50 feet deep, and are best explored with scuba gear. Since they are relatively small and the water does not circulate, it is important that all swimmers and divers rinse off any mosquito repellent or sunscreen before entering the water. The fish are colorful but fairly small, giving snorkelers and divers the feeling that they are diving inside an aquarium. The bottom is rocky and sometimes covered in algae, and the sides are craggy, making entry and exit a bit tricky, especially in areas that are less frequented by visitors. The major sites, though, have wooden docks and ladders and can be easily entered, even by divers in full gear. With their shallow depth, clear water, and easy accessibility, *cenotes* make for great dives for beginner divers. They are sometimes even used for training classes since there is no wave action and no current, and it's easy to keep track of where all the divers are.

Caves and caverns, on the other hand, offer a completely different scenario. Diving in these situations should be done only by experienced and certified cave divers since they often require the use of specialized equipment, including redundant air systems, lighting systems, and navigation aids. Cave and cavern diving requires the diver to leave the open-water realm and enter restricted areas where there is no easy escape and no way to surface without retracing your path to the entry point. Without the proper precautions, this type of diving can be extremely dangerous, though it can also be rewarding for divers who know how to do it properly.

In these dives, divers carry extra air tanks and lights because they do not have the luxury of surfacing at any time should something go wrong. They also run lines of rope from their entry point so that they can always retrace their paths and will never get lost. Some caverns are quite narrow, requiring divers to actually remove their tanks from their backs and carry them in front of them so they can fit through. Others are wide enough to allow several divers through at a time and can even be enjoyed by relative newcomers to cave diving, as long as an expert guide is close at hand.

The Riviera Maya and the Yucatán are home to some of the world's best spots for this type of diving, and it's an amazing feeling to be surrounded by water as clear as air and to see the incredible cave formations, the underwater stalactites and stalagmites, and the fish that call this realm their home. Some of the dives involve entering the cave at ground level and swimming through a series of caverns prior to entering the more enclosed caves, which twist and turn their way for several hundred yards, sometimes opening up into wide rooms where divers can congregate and rest before continuing the adventure. With the proper preparation, equipment, training, and guide, it's easy to see why this can be one of the most incomparable diving experiences you will ever have.

Outfitters, Instruction & Certification

Each town has its own local dive shops, located around the town square, on the touristy streets, on the beach, or on-site at the larger hotels. Depending on the location, they offer NAUI and PADI training and certification, boat dives, shore dives, drift dives, reef dives, wall dives, night dives, *cenote* dives, and cavern/cave dives, as well as name-brand equipment and gear for sale or rent. All reputable dive shops and tour operators require divers to have a current certification, commonly called a C-card, prior to renting equipment or going on any guided trip.

Instruction and certification are offered at most shops, and many of the larger hotels offer free scuba introduction classes at their on-site pools. In this confined and safe environment, people new to the sport can practice using a mask and fins, snorkeling, and even breathing underwater from the scuba tank through the regulator. This can be a great way to experience the thrill of scuba diving for the first time, and it just may convince you to take a class and do it in the ocean.

Most dive operators offer a "resort course," which includes a bit of instruction on scuba theory and techniques, some time to practice in the pool, and then an actual scuba dive in open water with a certified dive master right by your side. Although the diver will not receive certification with this type of training, it is the best way to go from having no experience to going on an actual dive in only half a day. For safety reasons, the dive master will keep the dive above a depth of 30 feet and will monitor the diver throughout the adventure.

Many dive shops in the area offer full certification classes and even private certification classes. Although normal dive classes are spread out over a few weeks, a private instructor can take the student through a legal certification program in just a matter of days, including classroom lessons, pool practice sessions, and the open-water checkout dive. Some student divers take the classroom and swimming pool portions of the class at home and then just do their open-water certification

Divers Alert Network

Divers wanting to be extra cautious should investigate the Divers Alert Network (DAN) (www.diversalert network.com) before their visit. For a yearly fee, DAN provides diving safety information and offers air-evacuation insurance should a diver need to be airlifted back home for treatment of a diving-related injury.

dives while on vacation. If you plan on doing this, your home instructor will need to fill out a training referral form, and then your instructor in the Riviera Maya will complete the course with you and issue your C-card.

On group tours the depth and bottom time will be recorded by the dive master, and there will be time after each dive for participants to note the details in their log books. Dive operators use the recreational dive tables to plan the dives, the maximum depth, the required surface interval, and the available bottom time. Divers using their own dive computers may plan alternate dive profiles as long as they communicate with the dive master and boat captain so they know what to expect. The crew performs a head count at the start and end of each dive to ensure the safe return of everyone in the group.

While ascending from a dive more than 30 feet in depth, it is customary to perform a safety stop at 15 feet for three minutes. This is a precaution to help eliminate any cases of decompression sickness. If anyone does experience symptoms of "the bends," the crew will take quick action to get the diver to a medical facility and even to a hyperbaric chamber, if necessary. There are several chambers in the Riviera Maya, usually within a 30-minute drive from shore. Most dive operators charge a $1 insurance fee for every dive, which ensures that divers will be covered if they need to enter the chamber. Divers should remember not to dive within 24 hours of flying on an airplane, since doctors say the risk of decompression sickness and other diving ailments increases if you do so.

For most dives, except for extensive cave and cavern diving, no special training or licenses are required beyond the basic open-water scuba diving certification. However you decide to dive, remember what you learned in dive training class: plan your dive, then dive your plan.

CANCÚN

Known across the world as a mecca for water sports, Cancún is at the far northern tip of the Great Mayan Reef and doesn't have as much coral growth as the areas farther south. The water is as clear as a shot of tequila blanco, though, and some 500 species have been documented. Most of the dives, including La Bandera, Punta Cancún, and Punta Nizúc, are fairly shallow and can be enjoyed by both snorkelers and scuba divers.

ISLA MUJERES

With an average underwater visibility of up to 100 feet and nearly 50 different dive sites within range of a 30-minute boat ride, Isla Mujeres, whose name translates to "island of the women," is also the island of the snorkelers and divers. Popular dives include Camaronero, a shrimp boat that sank in the late 1990s; the Cave of the Sleeping Sharks where a brisk current allows sharks to temporarily halt their perpetual swimming and park themselves in an apparent stupor; Los Marinos, a sunken Mexican navy vessel lying at only 70 feet; and MUSA (www.musacancun.com), a stunning manmade site featuring striking submerged sculptures (see chapter 5).

ISLA CONTOY

With white-sand beaches, shallow bays, and open-water drop-offs, this tiny island offers big variety for snorkelers and divers. Contoy isn't sheltered by the mainland, so the water can be rougher than elsewhere along the Yucatán coast. Ixlache, a very shallow reef popular with snorkeling tours and beginners, and the virtually untouched Las Calderas are the primary dives.

COZUMEL

One of the most popular dive destinations anywhere, Cozumel has enough world-class dive sites that you could stay there for a week, diving every day, and never go to the same spot twice. From shallow-water snorkeling spots to sheer walls that drop thousands of feet, Cozumel has superb dives for every skill level. The most popular type of diving is drift diving, which can take some getting used to but brings a whole new dimension to the diving experience. Most dive sites are on the island's southwest coast, facing the Riviera Maya mainland, where the reef runs parallel to the beach and the water is relatively calm since it is sheltered from the open ocean. It's home to Palancar Reef, regularly ranked as one of the top five dive sites in the world.

Other popular dives include the Santa Rosa Wall with an average depth of 90 to 100 feet, and the shallower Tormentos with a resident green moray eel, more than 6 feet long, sometimes known to eat fish right from the dive master's hand.

PLAYA DEL CARMEN & PLAYACAR

The unofficial capital of the Riviera Maya is also home to the greatest concentration of diving and dive-related activities and services. There are more than a dozen dive shops along paseo del Carmen and in the water-sports centers of the larger hotels, particularly those in Playacar. Dive sites accessible by boat from Playa range from shallow reefs good for snorkeling to deep-water drop-offs best reserved for advanced divers. The Buceo Mexico Hyperbaric Chamber (10th Avenue and 28th Street, 987-873-1365), the leading facility in the treatment of diving accidents, including cases of "the bends," is open every day and is well known by all major dive operators.

Popular dives in this area include Las Barracudas offshore from the Xcaret ecological park, whose shallow water is known for the presence of its namesake fish; Chen Zubul, frequently visited by novice divers and for night dives; and the more advanced Moche Deep.

Dive Shops
The Abyss (Blue Parrot Hotel, 12th Street and the beach, 984-873-2164, www .abyssdiveshop.com) offers PADI and NAUI instruction, open-water dives, and *cenote* trips.

Open since 1983, Cyan Ha Divers (north of town, between Hotel Las Palapas and Mahékal Beach Resort, 987-873-0978, www.cyanha.com) has several boats, an on-site training pool, and PADI instruction, and specializes in small groups, *cenote* dives, and reef dives.

Explora Divers (Tukan Beach, 28th Street at the beach) specializes in *cenote* and cave dives, but also offers windsurfing instruction and area tours.

Go Cenotes (First Avenue between 24th and 25th streets) offers *cenote* trips, open-water dives in Playa and Cozumel, snorkeling tours, and trips to Holbox Island.

Scuba Playa Dive Shop (Second Street between Quinta and the beach; and 10th Street between First Avenue and Quinta, 984-803-3123, www.scubaplaya .com) offers a variety of open-water and *cenote* dives.

On the north side of the town square, Studio Blue (First Street between the beach and Quinta, 984-873-1088) is a full-fledged dive shop with retail showroom, dive school, and snorkel and dive tours.

Tank-Ha Dive Shop (Quinta between Eighth and 10th streets, 984-873-0302, www.tankha.com) has PADI and NAUI instruction, an on-site training pool, and cenote dives, open-water dives, and reef dives.

Yucatek Divers (15th Avenue between Second and Fourth streets, 984-803-2836, www.yucatek-divers.com) offers one- and two-tank dives, night dives, cavern and cave dives, and scuba instruction.

PAAMUL

This relaxing beach is home to some of the best diving in the area. With little in the way of tourism development, the reefs are still in pristine condition, and the sea life is prolific. The shallow bay offers excellent snorkeling since the reef is healthy and full of life, even in just a few feet of water.

Good for all certified divers, the 45-foot-deep Horst's Reef offers some small swim-throughs. Large coral heads, sea sponges and abundant marine life can be spotted at the intermediate Paraíso Shallow. The beautiful Xel-Ha Reef, offshore from the park, is open for exploration, provided divers follow Xel-Ha's preservation rules.

PUERTO AVENTURAS

Boats depart from the Puerto Aventuras Marina several times per day, shuttling divers to the nearby reefs. Although it's always best to book ahead, dives can sometimes be planned at the last minute if a boat has extra space available. Local dives include the deep, 75-foot Los Caniones with steep canyons, groove formations, and plenty of fish; the easy-to-access Brisa Caribe, between the public marina and the Oasis beach; and the colorful Mook-Che reef near Playa Xcalacoco.

Dive Shop

This full-service Dive Aventuras (in the Omni Puerto Aventuras, 984-873-5031, www.diveaventuras.com) offers all levels of instruction in multiple languages, including a 45-minute tune-up course for certified divers who haven't been in the water for a while.

AKUMAL

Akumal is a shallow bay with calm water, slow currents, and coral beaches. There are many good spots to dive in the 20- to 40-foot range, making it a good spot for beginning and intermediate divers who want the thrill of an ocean dive but aren't quite ready for deep walls and cave systems. More advanced divers will appreciate the deeper sites such as Gonzalo's Reef, famous for frequent close encounters with a sea turtle, which reaches 85 feet in some spots.

Other favorites include Dick's Reef, named for the retired owner of the original Akumal Dive Shop; Motorcycle Reef, named for the sunken motorcycle lying 60 feet below; and the appropriately named Shark Cave.

Dive Shops

Akumal Dive Adventures (on the beach next to Buena Vista Restaurant, 984-875-9157 or 1-888-4AKUMAL from the U.S., www.akumaldiveadventures.com) offers snorkeling, cave dives, cavern dives, *cenote* trips, and dives in Akumal and other open-water sites.

Open since 1980, the Texan-owned ⚓ Akumal Dive Shop (near the main gate to the Akumal development, 984-875-9032, www.akumal.com) offers dives in and around the Akumal area, plus certification classes, "bubblemaker" classes for kids, and sailing and fishing trips.

TULUM

Known for its Mayan ruins and relaxed atmosphere, the Tulum area also has some great snorkeling and diving sites, particularly Tulum Reef, within sight of the ruins.

Dive Shop

Tulum's first dive shop, Acuatic Tulum (on Highway 307 at the Tulum crossroads; and at Cabañas Don Armando hotel, ½-mile north of the crossroads, 984-100-7122, www.acuatictulum.com.mx) offers snorkeling, ocean diving, and *cenote* diving trips.

COSTA MAYA

The Costa Maya starts an hour south of Playa del Carmen and extends nearly to Mexico's border with Belize. The reef is especially healthy in this section because it sees fewer divers and cruise ships. The coral is healthier, the colors are brighter, and the fish are larger. It's also harder to reach, so expect longer boat trips.

Banco Chinchorro offers diving opportunities along it thriving and expansive coral reef. There are also dozens of viable, remote and rarely visited dive sites at the protected biosphere reserve Sian Ka'an, a UNESCO World Heritage Site.

8

Golf

ALTHOUGH THE MAYA NEVER USED THE WHEEL, they did have the ball, and it is believed that they took great pleasure in playing various games. Their most famous ball game was called *pok-ta-pok,* and it was serious business. The ball was about the size of a kickball, and the game was played on a large field about the size of a basketball court. Similar to basketball, the game's object was to shoot the ball through a hoop mounted above the playing surface. Considering that players weren't allowed to use their hands, though, scoring was quite rare and was considered a tremendous feat. Large numbers of villagers turned out to watch the games, which had great religious and ceremonial importance. Fans sang songs, acted boisterously, and even bet on who would win. The winners of the game were given a hero's welcome, and a celebration was held in their honor. As legend has it, the losers were put to death.

Today, the open fields, beachfronts, and carved-away jungles of the Riviera Maya make a perfect backdrop for the more "civilized" ball game of golf. There are 15 courses within the Riviera Maya, including courses in Cancún, Cozumel, and the town of Bacalar (south of the Riviera Maya). Some of the courses are par-3, but others are par-72 championship courses designed by some of the best golf architects in the business, including Jack Nicklaus, Robert Trent Jones Jr., and Robert von Hagge.

Most of the courses have beautiful views of the ocean and the tropical jungle. Iguanas, colorful birds, and other animals are commonly sighted. Most have multiple water and sand features, and several even have actual Mayan ruins next to the fairways.

Most courses have clubs for rent, and unless you're a real pro or planning on playing multiple rounds, the loaners are normally sufficient. Balls can be expensive (and the loss ratio can be high), so it's usually best to bring some of your own, as they're cheap back home and fairly easy to pack. The larger courses have full-service pro shops with name-brand equipment and apparel, club repair, and instruction.

LEFT: The Iberostar complex is one of the area's largest—and nicest—resorts.   Iberostar Resorts

Some of the courses operate with an all-inclusive concept, where the greens fee includes a cart, range balls, and all the food and drink you care to consume during your round. To keep the costs down, consider playing in the afternoon to take advantage of discounted twilight rates. Just make sure to bring a hat, sunscreen, and plenty of water.

The Riviera Maya is becoming more of a golf destination each year. Although many of the planned courses in the region were delayed or halted due to the global economic recession, it is expected that several will follow through on their plans in the coming years. For information on all area golf courses, check with the Mexican Caribbean Golf Association (www.cancungolf.org).

Golf Courses

RIVIERA MAYA

Managed by Fairmont Hotels, El Cameleón Golf Club at Mayakoba (Highway 307, km 297, north of Playa del Carmen, 1-800-540-6088 from the U.S., www.fairmont.com) is the first course in Mexico to be designed by Greg Norman. It curls around the Fairmont Mayakoba hotel and along the beach of the 1,600-acre tourism development. Players enjoy unusual hazards such as *cenotes*, mangrove swamps, and other tropical features. The course spans more than 7,000 yards and has five sets of tees. Two of the holes are right along the beach, while 15 holes have some sort of water hazard. There is a driving range and putting green, plus well-stocked pro shop and steakhouse overlooking the 18th hole. A novelty in Mexico, all carts have GPS navigation and yardage systems, allowing players to keep score, monitor other players' scores, and order refreshments while on the course. This course is the site of the yearly PGA Mayakoba Golf Classic pro tournament, first played in 2007 marking the first PGA event in Mexico.

The 27-hole Bahia Principe Golf Club (Highway 307, km 250, 984-875-5085 or 1-866-347-1667, www.bahiaprincipegolf.com), designed by Robert Trent Jones Jr., is part of a massive real estate development with condos, private residences, and resorts. It's about an hour from the Cancún airport and 30 minutes south of Playa del Carmen.

Designed by P. B. Dye and opened in 2005, Iberostar Playa Paraíso Golf Club (Highway 307, km 309, Playa Paraíso, 984-877-2847 www.iberostar.com) is convenient for players throughout the Riviera Maya. It features 18 holes stretched across 6,800 yards, with wide fairways, deep sand traps, and undulating greens. Rental equipment from brands such as Titleist, Nike, and Mizuno is available.

Opened in 1994, Playacar Club de Golf (paseo Xaman-Há, 26 Fraccionamiento Playacar, Playa del Carmen, 984-873-0624 or 1-800-635-1856 from the U.S., www.palaceresorts.com) was designed by Robert von Hagge and acquired by Palace Resorts in 2005. The course runs 7,202 yards and has many jungle, sand, and water features to keep golfers challenged and entertained. There are even a few actual Mayan ruins along the fairways and greens.

Grand Coral Golf Club (Playa del Carmen, www.grandcoralmexico.com) introduced the region's first Nick Price–designed course in early 2011.

Part of the Puerto Aventuras development, the nine-hole, 3,236-yard, par-36

World-Class Names in Golf Define the Mexican Caribbean

By Greg Bond

Things in the Mexican Caribbean are changing faster than Nick Price's backswing. In fact, the former number one golfer in the world saw the debut of his first Riviera Maya design in early 2011. With his creation, Grand Coral Golf Club, Price is just the latest to join the ranks the game's best designers, whose work dots the peninsula from Cancún to Tulum.

Greg Norman. Now with two tracks, both great tests of golf, on either end of Cancún, Norman has teed up the region's golf scene. El Cameleón is consistently ranked one of the best courses in Mexico and is host to the PGA Tour's Mayakoba Golf Classic. North of Cancún, his challenging and recently opened Playa Mujeres is notable for its spectacular views of Isla Mujeres and Caribbean Sea.

P. B. Dye. Just up the street from El Cameleón is Dye's amazing Iberostar Playa Paraíso Golf Club. The course boosts the best conditions you'll find anywhere and has hosted the Iberostar Riviera Maya Open, an event on the Canadian Tour.

Robert Trent Jones Jr. When he opened the first course in the region back in 1976, Jones got golf started in the Riviera Maya. He returned to create a spectacular layout at the Riviera Maya Golf Club just north of Tulum.

Jack Nicklaus. When his design at the Moon Palace Golf Club opened in 2003, and hosted the Mexican Open that same year, Nicklaus set the new standard for world-class golf facilities in the region.

Nicklaus Design Group. If you want to get away from the mainland and have a relaxing and truly unique golf experience, then just hop the ferry to Cozumel. You'll find a great Nicklaus Design Group course, designed by Steve Nicklaus, at the Cozumel Country Club. Just keep an eye out for crocodiles and boa constrictors.

As you can see, the area offers a plethora of golf options with great designers, great courses, great conditions, and very reasonable prices. See you on the first tee.

Greg Bond is vice president of the Mexican Caribbean Golf Association (www.cancungolf.org) and the director of golf at one of his favorite courses, the Iberostar Playa Paraíso Golf Club.

Puerto Aventuras Club de Golf (Highway 307, km 269.5, Puerto Aventuras, 984-873-5109, www.puertoaventuras.com.mx) was designed by Thomas Lehman and built in 1990. No credit cards.

The Jack Nicklaus–designed par 3 Riviera Maya Golf & Tennis Club—Mayan Palace Golf Club (Highway 307, km 310, Playa Paraiso, 984-206-4043. www.mayanresortsgolf.com) opened in 2003. It spans 2,823 yards and has lots of water and sand features. The signature 17th hole skirts a large lagoon and has an island sand trap, making your approach shot a crucial factor.

Inaugurated in 2008 in a large-scale development just north of Cancún, the 808-acre, 18-hole, par-72 Puerto Cancún Golf Course (east of Bonampak Avenue, near where Kukulcán Avenue meets downtown Cancún, 998-884-7608, www .puertocancun.com), designed by Tom Weiskopf, features 185 acres of water features, sand traps, and manicured greens. An additional course, designed by Tom Fazio and Nick Price, is being contemplated.

Designed by Greg Norman, the 18-hole, 7,250-yard, par-72 Playa Mujeres Golf Club (Bonampak Avenue, Punta Sam, 998-887-7322, www.playamujeres .com.mx) snakes through tropical mangroves, the beachfront, and a saltwater lagoon.

The Jack Nicklaus Signature Course, Moon Palace Spa & Golf Club (Highway 307, km 340, Cancún, 984-881-6000 or 1-800-525-5025 from the U.S., www .palaceresorts.com) includes three separate courses, each with distinct environments (jungle, lake and dune), totaling 27 holes and a par of 108. Its total length is 10,798 yards. The layout requires golfers to navigate through native vegetation, wetlands, and a plethora of sandtraps.

Designed by Robert Trent Jones Jr., 6,636-yard-long Cancún Country Club—Pok-Ta-Pok (boulevard Kukulcán, km 7.5, Cancún hotel zone, 998-883-1230, www.Cancúngolfclub.com) is the destination's first course, opening in 1976. With 18 holes and a par of 72, it has several holes along the beach and a few Mayan ruins scattered about.

Near Cancún's southern end and designed by Isao Aoki, Hilton Cancún Beach & Golf Resort (boulevard Kukulcán, km 17.5, Cancún hotel zone, 998-881-8016, www.hiltonCancún.com) has 18 holes, par-72, and 6,767 yards of play. Opened in 1994, it features holes along Nichupté Lagoon, with peacocks, an occasional crocodile, and lots of iguanas. From the 15th and 16th holes, players have a great view of the Ruinas El Rey, Cancún's most important Mayan ruins site.

Two simple Cancún courses are options for inexperienced golfers or those who may just want to swing at a ball and be outdoors without spending all day. The Melia Cancún Golf Club (boulevard Kukulcán, km 16, Cancún hotel zone, 998-883-1230, www.solmelia.com), next to the Gran Melia Cancún hotel, has 18 par-3 holes and a nicely manicured putting green. The nine-hole par-3 Cancún Oasis Golf Club (boulevard Kukulcán, km 16.5, Cancún hotel zone, 998-885-0867, www .oasishotels.com) is between the Oasis Cancún hotel and the main road through the Cancún hotel zone.

COZUMEL

Designed by Nicklaus Design in 2001, Cozumel Country Club (carretera Costera Norte, km 6.5 Interior, Cozumel, 987-872-9570, www.cozumelcountryclub.com .mx) has four sets of tees, with the longest being 6,734 yards. There are many sand and water features to contend with as the course skirts native mangroves and tropical swamps.

9

Fishing

FISHING HAS BEEN A WAY OF LIFE in the Riviera Maya since the indigenous inhabitants paddled their dugout canoes through the shallows, plunging their wooden spears into the water to snare their catch. They also fished with reed baskets or nets, woven with the same techniques used to make hammocks. In some areas, fish were caught with bows and arrows or even poisons. These were thrown into the water, killing the fish, which floated to the surface for harvest. Later, the Maya even used a pole and line, possibly even making a sport out of it.

With its variety of good fishing locations in such a relatively small geographic area, the Riviera Maya is one of the world's top spots for sportfishing and deep-sea fishing. The waters off the northeastern coast of the Yucatán are prime for finding numerous species and a wide variety of fishing conditions. From deep channels to wide flats and shallow reefs to rocky points, there's always a spot that's producing, no matter the time of year and the weather conditions, unless a major storm keeps the boats in port.

Fishing options range from a do-it-yourself wade-fishing expedition to a full-day excursion trolling on a luxury yacht, complete with meals, drinks, guides, gear, and a video recording of all the action. From your hotel in the Riviera Maya, several distinct fishing spots are within easy reach. From the deep waters off Cancún to the north, through the reefs of Puerto Morelos, to the shallows of Cozumel, to the drop-offs near Playa, to the bays of Akumal and Puerto Aventuras, and all the way down to the flats of Sian Ka'an, each area holds something unique and exciting for fishing. And whether you're a novice who just enjoys being out on the water and reeling one in, a regular enthusiast in search of your first marlin, or an old pro going for a coveted grand slam, you can find what you're looking for in the Riviera Maya.

Fishing is great year-round, but if you're looking for a specific type of fish, then you'll need to take note of the seasons to make sure your target is around when you plan to visit. Many visitors come to Playa seeking the majestic billfish,

Arrange a fishing trip directly with the boat captains at this booth in front of the Gran Porto Real in Playa del Carmen.

which produces a thrill like no other when it takes the bait and then jumps in the air for all to see. These beautiful creatures, weighing up to 500 pounds, are seen throughout the year, though the prime time is from March to July, when they ply the deep waters between Cozumel and the Yucatán mainland in abundant numbers. Each year, there are several billfish grand slams recorded, when a single group manages to boat a blue marlin, a white marlin, and a sailfish on the same trip. When fishing for these beauties, a strict catch-and-release policy is followed, so make sure to bring your video camera to capture the moments for bragging rights.

Tuna, mahi-mahi, bonito, bonefish, and wahoo prefer the warmer waters and generally are more active from March to August or September, though catches of each have been recorded in every month of the year. Due to the varied underwater terrain and year-round temperate climate, however, many fish species can be caught throughout the year, including barracuda, grouper, kingfish, shark, skipjack, snapper, and other reef and bottom fish. They're so abundant, in fact, that many chartered boats promise to prepare a meal on the boat or on a hidden beach, and they rely exclusively on the day's catch to supply the main course. Although certainly it has happened that bad luck strikes and the group is left to dine on crackers, salsa, and sides, the trips almost always end with a bounteous feast of ultrafresh ceviche or fried fish.

A Mexican fishing license is required for boat fishing, and the fees go toward worthwhile conservation and regulation programs. Reputable tour operators, such as those listed in this guide, include all required licensing in the prices of their tours.

Often seen while snorkeling, hovering nearly motionless next to the reef, seemingly watching every move you make, the barracuda is one of the most feared of all ocean creatures. Given its muscle-packed body, large eyes, gaping mouth, and razor-sharp teeth, it's easy to see why. Their fearless nature makes them great fighters, and they're commonly caught while drift fishing or bottom fishing, all across the Riviera Maya's shallows and deepwater cuts. Caught year-round.

The largest of the billfish, the blue marlin can reach up to 1,800 pounds in the deeper Atlantic waters, though they seldom grow to more than 500 pounds in the local region. Average catches are in the range of 80 to 120 pounds. Caught while trolling using artificial baits, the blue marlin will be landed only if the angler is strapped in tightly to the fighting chair and ready for an exhaustive struggle. Keeping tension on the line is the only way to keep the blues from spitting the hook while jumping into the air. Best months: May to September.

White and blue, with a beautiful pointed "horn," the white marlin (50–80 pounds on average) is famous for long fights and high jumps, often twisting its body when it's out of the water. Found in the highest numbers in the Cozumel channel, between the island and the mainland. Best months: April to August.

One of the most exciting sport fish around, the sailfish is known for its long, protruding dorsal fin, which looks like a sail. It is also known to fly through the air once it's hooked, offering up superb photo opportunities. Mostly 30 to 50 pounds, they're caught by trolling through the drop-offs and deeper channels, and can be

Fishing boats along the Isla Mujeres waterfront

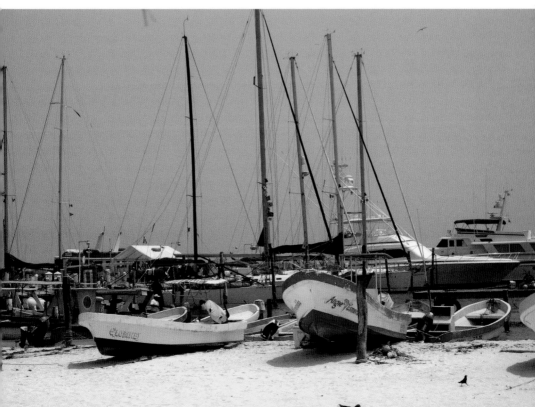

Fishing Seasons in Playa

FISH	JAN	FEB	MAR	APR	MAY
Amber jack	high season	high season	high season	high season	high season
Barracuda	high season	high season	high season	high season	high season
Blue marlin	off season	off season	some catches	some catches	high season
Bonefish	some catches	some catches	high season	high season	high season
Bonito	off season	high season	high season	high season	high season
Bottom fish	high season	high season	high season	high season	high season
Grouper	high season	high season	high season	high season	high season
Kingfish	high season	high season	high season	high season	high season
Mackerel	high season	high season	high season	high season	high season
Mahi-mahi	off season	some catches	high season	high season	high season
Permit	high season	high season	high season	high season	high season
Sailfish	off season	some catches	high season	high season	high season
Shark	high season	high season	high season	high season	high season
Snapper	high season	high season	high season	high season	high season
Tuna	off season	off season	some catches	high season	high season
Wahoo	off season	off season	high season	high season	high season
White marlin	off season	off season	some catches	high season	high season

very hard to land since they twist and turn a lot while jumping and fighting. Best months: March to August.

Noted for their exceptional fighting strength given their relatively small size, bonefish are taken with light tackle, generally fly-fishing, though spinning tackle can also be used. The angler normally casts when the fish breaks the surface or is swimming just below. The strike is hard and fast, requiring a high level of skill and

JUN	JUL	AUG	SEPT	OCT	NOV	DEC
high season	high season	high season	some catches	some catches	some catches	some catches
high season	high season	high season	high season	high season	high season	high season
high season	high season	high season	high season	some catches	off season	off season
high season	high season	high season	some catches	some catches	some catches	some catches
high season	high season	high season	some catches	some catches	off season	off season
high season	high season	high season	high season	high season	high season	high season
high season	high season	high season	high season	high season	high season	high season
high season	high season	high season	high season	high season	high season	high season
high season	some catches	some catches	some catches	some catches	high season	high season
high season	high season	high season	high season	off season	off season	off season
high season	high season	high season	high season	high season	high season	high season
high season	high season	high season	off season	off season	off season	off season
high season	high season	high season	high season	high season	high season	high season
high season	high season	high season	high season	high season	high season	high season
high season	high season	some catches	off season	off season	off season	off season
high season	high season	high season	high season	off season	off season	off season
high season	high season	high season	off season	off season	off season	off season

making for a thoroughly entertaining day of fishing. One of the best spots in the world for finding bonefish is in Ascension Bay, at the southern end of the Sian Ka'an biosphere. Best months: March to August.

A member of the sea bass family, groupers are strong fighting fish and quite abundant in the warm Caribbean waters. They come in various colors, from dark gray to bright orange. Scuba divers are fond of watching groupers eat, a process that involves a slow circling around the prey, followed by a quick kick of the tail fin and a hard swallow, which lets them suck in large pieces of food at one time. They are generally caught while bottom fishing. Caught year-round.

One of the best-tasting fish in the Caribbean, the mahi-mahi (sometimes called dorado or dolphin fish) has a big face with a high, protruding forehead and beautiful blue dorsal fin running the length of its back. The body is thick and strong and seems to glow with every color of the rainbow. Can be caught trolling or bottom fishing, depending on the water depth. Best months: March to September.

Members of the jack family, permit are broad fish with a silvery blue body that range in size from 3 to 30 pounds. Great fighters with fierce striking power, they can be taken with flies and light tackle. They're common in the shallow flats of Ascension Bay and near Isla Holbox. Since they stay in the warm, shallow water, fishing is good year-round.

Long prized by natives for their liver oil, sharks are still commercially fished for their meat, teeth, and jaws. The English word *shark* is said to come from the Mayan *xoc*. A year-round catch, they can be caught while trolling, bottom fishing, or even wade fishing. Though attacks are very infrequent, sightings are somewhat common, especially by local fishermen and others who spend a lot of time on the water.

The Riviera Maya is home to yellowfin, blackfin, and skipjack tuna. Each is quick, strong, and can put up a great fight. Most often caught while trolling, tuna can be served grilled, in lime-marinated ceviche, or even raw. Can't beat that for fresh sushi! Best months: April to July.

Wahoo are long and thin, with a barracuda-like face and sleek body that can cut through the water at an incredible 45 mph. When a wahoo hits the bait, you better make sure the pole is fastened in the rod holder or securely in someone's arms, or you'll end up losing your whole rig to the depths. Most often caught while trolling, wahoo can be cut into large steaks and are great for frying. Best months: March to September.

TOP FISHING DESTINATIONS

Akumal has been a sportfishing town for more than 30 years. One of the top guides in the area and 25-year resident, Pillo offers two-hour trips for up to four anglers (sometimes four more). Reservations can be made in person at Lot 40, near the Nah Kin Condos.

Recognized as the best place in the world for a permit, tarpon, and bonefish grand slam, Ascension Bay and Boca Pila are also prime spots for snook, barracuda, Spanish mackerel, and permit. The bay has various inlets, ensuring that your boat captain can find fishing no matter the wind direction. Anglers can visit on a day trip from the Riviera Maya or stay overnight at one of the many lodges found between Boca Paila and Punta Allen.

Excursions from Cancún promise day- and night-fishing expeditions to the reefs not far from shore, between the coastline and Isla Mujeres. Common catches include grouper, hogfish, mackerel, and snapper.

The lagoons, jagged shorelines, and flats of Cozumel Island offer up excellent bonefishing, which is most often done using fly-fishing tackle or a lightweight spin-

10 Hotspots for Manly Men

1. Bahia Principe Golf Club at Gran Bahia Principe resort (Akumal)

2. Bonefish Bum Lodge (Punta Allen)

3. Bullfights (downtown Cancún)

4. El Cameleón Golf Club at Mayakoba (Punta Bete)

5. El Rey Polo Country Club (Puerto Morelos)

6. Iberostar Playa Paraíso Golf Club (Playa Paraíso)

7. Pesca Maya fishing lodge (Punta Allen)

8. Playa Mujeres Golf Club (Playa Mujeres)

9. Puerto Cancún Golf Club (Cancún)

10. Tequila Barrel sports betting lounge (Playa del Carmen

ning reel. There's good bottom fishing along the northern coast near Passion Island and on the island's east coast, where the coral reef is not part of the federal reserve. Farther from shore, in the Cozumel channel, anglers troll for marlin, sailfish, and other large game.

The fishing mecca of Puerto Aventuras is the southernmost deep-water marina in the Riviera Maya, with many sportfishing and deep-sea fishing charters available. A walk around the marina reveals the dozens of well-equipped boats awaiting their next expedition.

10

Local Knowledge

ONCE YOU'RE ON THE GROUND, and sometimes even before you get arrive, it's handy to know a little bit more about the practices and social norms of your destination. Think of this chapter as a handy reference to things you might need to know on the fly or may just require some additional cultural insight.

CALLING HOME

Don't dial direct from your hotel room! Even a quick call home from your hotel can carry a charge of $25 or more, due to high connection fees and even higher per-minute tolls. Most hotels offer local calls for around $1 each, about the same as in the States, but long-distance calls—especially international—are a completely different story. If you don't have Internet access and a Skype or VOIP account, your best option is to buy a prepaid phone card (called LADA cards, or *tarjetas LADA*) and make all calls with it. Even then, it's best to make the calls from a public phone to ensure you won't be billed a connection fee, which is common even for "toll-free" calls.

Official Tourism Office
Stop in the state-run Tourism Office (avenida Juárez at 15th Avenue, Playa del Carmen) for free area maps, promotional information, tour recommendations, safety tips, and lists of approved vendors.

Post Office
Playa's main post office (avenida Juárez between 15th and 20th avenues, 984-873-0300) is open 8–5 Monday–Friday and 9–noon Saturday. Postcards are cheap and always appreciated by the folks you left back home. It can take weeks for mail to arrive, however, so don't mail any critical messages. Stamps can be purchased at many convenience stores or hotel gift shops. To send anything quickly or of any

LEFT: The author and his wife on a scouting trip near Playa del Carmen   Jessica Loera value, use private courier Estafeta (on Fourth Street between 30th and 35th avenues, www.estafeta.com), Mexico's largest document and package delivery company.

Beach Etiquette

All Mexican beaches are federal property. No hotel can restrict access to the beach (from the water) or make their own regulations about what you can and can't do. That said, hotels don't have to allow you to cross their private property to access the beach, and they can prevent access to the hotel from their beach-front. Many hotels set up a cordoned-off section, supplying beach chairs or shade umbrellas for the exclusive use of their guests, which is legal.

Going nude, or even topless, isn't permitted by Mexican decency laws. Topless sunbathing is tolerated (and sometimes appreciated) by the local police in many areas, though, and many visitors to Playa del Carmen and the Riviera Maya—particularly Europeans—enjoy this freedom. To avoid any trouble with the law, it's best to restrict such European-style sunbathing to times and places when there are other people doing the same. In Playa, for instance, the beaches adjacent to the ferry dock are popular with local families and children, and tourists should be respectful of the local customs and refrain from going topless in these areas. Farther south of the dock, closer to the Gran Porto Real hotel, topless tanning becomes more of the norm, and visitors should not have any problem, except for an occasional passing gawker. To the north, most beaches are topless-friendly, though it is uncommon in front of the family-oriented hotels.

Elsewhere in the Mayan Riviera, local attitudes will dictate whether or not topless sunbathing is acceptable. On most beaches it's no problem, though in some areas it's frowned upon. The general rule is that the more locals or families, the less appropriate it is to go topless. Full nudity is generally frowned upon in all but a few specific areas, namely in front of the nude resorts, such as Hidden Beach, Desire Resort, and Playa Secreto.

The Mayan Riviera still has some relatively deserted beaches, accessible only by a four-wheel-drive vehicle and a bit of courage. Although these beaches do see occasional patrols from the Mexican army or local police, discreet travelers can generally enjoy the freedom of being one with nature, however they choose to define it.

YEARLY EVENTS CALENDAR

January 1, New Year's Day.

January 6, Day of the Three Kings. A traditional day of Christmas gift giving, marking the Christian holiday of Epiphany, when the three wise men arrived to give gifts to the baby Jesus.

January 10, Quintana Roo's Constitution Day. Banks are closed, but not much else happens.

January 11, anniversary of Quintana Roo's restatement as a territory.

February 5, Constitution Day. A federal holiday, but there's not much social celebration.

Giving Back

The Playa del Carmen Children and Family Services Department accepts donations for its health and literacy programs, so if you can save a bit of space in your luggage to bring donations, Playa's residents would greatly appreciate it. For medical items, please do not bring outdated medicines or equipment.

Requested items include:

Kindergarten and primary-school workbooks (in Spanish)

Number 2 pencils, colored pencils, crayons

Coloring books

Children's books (in Spanish)

Educational toys (no batteries required)

Glucometers and glucose test strips

Stethoscopes

First-aid kits

Lumbar-sacral body supports

Neck collars

Tension wraps/bandages

Fiberglass cast kits

Arm slings

Infant and children's clothing

Blankets/children's blankets

Children's toothpaste

Eyeglasses (children's and adults', including prescription lenses)

Vitamins (children's and prenatal)

Items can be dropped off at the Ajua Maya restaurant on Fourth Street between Quinta and 10th avenues. For more information call 984-803-1118 (Playa del Carmen) or 804-201-4142 (in the United States), or log on to www.americamaya.org.

February 14, Day of Lovers and Friends. Similar to Valentine's Day in the United States. Street vendors sell flowers and balloons; restaurants offer special romantic meals for couples.

February 24, Flag Day. A ceremony is held in Cancún and Cozumel at the sites of their giant flags.

February, Mayakoba Golf Classic (date varies). The PGA descends on the Mayakoba resort for its only tour event in Mexico. Spectator tickets start at $10.

February–March, Carnaval. Fluctuates with the Christian calendar. It's mostly celebrated in Cozumel and Playa del Carmen, where school children dress in colorful costumes and parade through the streets. In Playa, there's a week of festivities and impromptu parades, capped by a long procession down Quinta and up 12th Street to the municipal park, where a live music stage, food vendors, midway games and revelers keep the party going late into the night. Mostly locals, but tourists are welcomed.

March 20 or 21, vernal equinox. This marks the first official day of spring, when daylight and night are the same length. It's celebrated at Chichén Itzá, where the shadow of the serpent Kukulkán snakes down the side of the temple when the sunlight hits it just right.

March 21, birthday of Benito Juárez. Former president and reform movement leader, Juárez pops up frequently in the Riviera Maya, in street names, building names, and statues. All banks and government offices are closed, but most tourist businesses stay open.

March or April, Easter and Holy Week. This is a very popular travel time for Mexican families since schoolchildren get two weeks' vacation. The holiday, which celebrates Christ's resurrection, is traditionally celebrated even more than Christmas.

April 21–May 2, Sol a Sol Regatta. Annual sailboat race from St. Petersburg, Florida, to Isla Mujeres (www.regatadelsolalsol.org). Live music, street festival, and celebrations.

May 1, Labor Day. National holiday.

May 5, Cinco de Mayo. Celebration of Mexican independence from France during the 1862 Battle of Puebla. Not as widely celebrated as the September 16 holiday marking independence from Spain.

May, Cancún Jazz Festival (date varies). Annual music festival sponsored by the Cancún Hotel Association.

June 1, Navy Day. Honors sailors lost at sea. Celebrations vary by municipality.

Last weekend of June, Playa del Carmen Sportfishing Tournament. This major fishing tournament helps fill hotels and restaurants, but the town doesn't get too involved.

July, Reggae Fest (date varies). Reggae bands from Mexico and around the world meet in Playa for a weeklong beach party, with concerts, food, and drink.

August, Día de la Asuncion Festival, Oxkutzcab, Yucatán (date varies). Week-long Assumption Day celebration near Loltún Cave, about three hours from Playa.

Second weekend of August, Ferragosto Italian food festival (date varies). Restaurant specials and a yearly "largest pizza in the world" exhibition, where Quinta restaurants pitch in to create (and then serve) a pizza spanning some six blocks through town. Coincides with a similar celebration in Italy, so Playa's Italian population celebrates all weekend at the many Italian-owned restaurants and bars.

August 17, Isla Mujeres Founding Day. Locals celebrate the date of their town's founding with parades, parties, live music, and street dancing. Underwater ceremony at Los Manchones Reef, where a large bronze cross is attached to the coral.

September 1, Presidential State of the Union Address. Mexicans love politics, and many stay riveted to their TVs to watch the speech. Bars and stores are not allowed to serve alcohol until it's over, but it usually turns into a party afterward.

September 16, national holiday marking Mexico's independence from Spain in 1821. Widely celebrated with parades, fireworks, and street parties. Much more important to locals than Cinco de Mayo.

September 22 or 23, autumnal equinox. Marks the first day of fall. Date varies according to the year.

September 27–October 13, Fiesta de Cristo de las Ampollas in Mérida. Religious festival honoring a sacred relic housed in the main cathedral.

October 12, Día de la Raza (Columbus Day). Celebrated throughout Mexico as a day to honor the many types of people that make up its population.

October 31, All Souls' Day. Festivities inspired by the American Halloween celebration.

November, Latin Jazz Fest (date varies). This three-day festival brings together jazz musicians from around the world for concerts, dancing, and all-night parties.

November 1–2, Day of the Dead. Mexico's predominant Halloween-time holiday honors the dead. Friends and relatives gather at the graves of loved ones to celebrate their lives and honor their deaths.

November 20, Mexican Revolution Day. Marks Mexico's 1910 Revolution. It's mostly a federal holiday, with little local observance.

December 8, Feast of the Immaculate Conception. Religious holiday celebrated throughout the Riviera Maya.

December 24, Nochebuena, or Christmas Eve. A religious and social holiday with parades and street parties.

December 25–January 2, Christmas week. Weeklong festival with candlelight processions, Catholic mass, nightly parties, and religious ceremonies.

December 31, New Year's Eve. Many bars offer drink specials and all-you-can-eat specials. At the stroke of midnight, it's good luck to eat 12 grapes, one for each month of the new year. Nightclubs stay open until dawn.

BOOKS FOR RIVIERA MAYA TRAVELERS

Try these great reads in preparation for your trip, while you're lying on the beach, or to ease your transition back to the real world.

A Salty Piece of Land by Jimmy Buffett. A cowboy moves to Sian Ka'an to become a fishing guide. Many Riviera Maya and Buffett-song-inspired references.

A Tourist in the Yucatán by James McNay Brumfield. An action-adventure mystery set among the Mayan ruins.

Captains Outrageous by Joe R. Lansdale. A comedic and bumbling tale of intrigue, with travels from east Texas to the land of the Mayans.

Chaos in Cancún by Susan Murray. This detective novel for teens takes its main characters on a whirlwind tour through the Riviera Maya. Includes some fun references to local spots that kids will find entertaining.

Cinnamon Skin by John D. MacDonald. A boat-bum detective travels to Cancún and the Riviera Maya to solve a crime for a friend.

Don't Stop the Carnival by Herman Wouk. This meandering tale may change your mind about wanting to open a hotel in the Caribbean.

Incidents of Travel in Yucatán by John Lloyd Stephens and Frederick Catherwood. Originally published in the 1840s, it's an amazing account of the life and times of the Mayans.

The Ruins by Scott Smith. A group of friends on holiday to Cancún and the Riviera

Maya stumble across a mysterious secret in the Mayan jungle and struggle to get away. It may make you think twice about hiking in the jungle!

The World Is Blue: How Our Fate and the Ocean's Are One by Dr. Sylvia A. Earle. A fascinating, simple and clear explanation of our impact on the seas, including the Great Mayan Reef, and what must be done to counter it.

Where the Sky Is Born: Living in the Land of the Maya by Jeanine Lee Kitchel. Thinking of moving to the Riviera Maya or curious what it would be like? Learn from someone who's done it.

Wicked Spanish by Howard Tomb. This tongue-in-cheek language guide will teach you some naughty phrases and fun sayings to try out on bartenders and fellow bus riders.

Top Five Places to Pop the Question

1. The cliffs at the Mayan ruins of Tulum

2. On a private sailboat in Soliman Bay

3. On the beach at Playa Maroma

4. On top of the rocks at the Xaman-Ha Beach in Playacar

5. In the canals of the Sian Ka'an Biosphere

From Brenda Alfaro, owner of Ajua Weddings (www.ajuaweddings.com)

SPANISH CLASSES

As a sign on the wall of the Señor Frog's bar says, WE DON'T SPEAK ENGLISH, BUT WE PROMISE NOT TO LAUGH AT YOUR SPANISH. Not only is learning a bit of the local language a good way to win the favor of the locals you meet, but it can also be a lot of fun.

Programs in Playa del Carmen include Playalingua (984-873-3876. www.playa lingua.com), Solexico Spanish School (984-873-0755 or 1-877-266-8988 from the U.S., www.solexico.com) and International House (14th Street between Quinta and 10th avenues, 984-803-3388, www.ihrivieramaya.com).

WEDDINGS IN PARADISE

If your idea of the perfect wedding is exchanging vows during a beachside ceremony with the sun going down, tropical flowers forming the aisle, a Mexican trio providing romantic music, and your guests dancing the salsa while they sip tequila, then getting married in the Riviera Maya may suit you.

Although most weddings in the region are fairly casual outdoor affairs, the facilities and services exist to put on a spectacular formal ceremony for hundreds of guests, complete with all the traditions and comforts of a wedding in your own hometown. Both civil and religious ceremonies can be planned, depending on the couple's preference.

There are several independent wedding planners in town, in addition to the onstaff planners at the larger hotels. They can assist with all of the details, from cakes to flowers, from hotels to photography, and from rehearsals to receptions. Due to the legal requirements for foreigners getting married in Mexico, it is recommended that the couple arrive in Playa del Carmen at least three business days prior to their wedding day, to file the necessary paperwork.

LEGAL REQUIREMENTS FOR GETTING MARRIED

At least two days before the ceremony, the couple must go to the local courthouse and present:

• A valid tourist card (your temporary visa, issued at the airport),

• A notarized copy of each person's birth certificate (must have a raised seal)

• An official Spanish translation of the birth certificate (should be done locally by a court-approved translator)

• A health certificate certifying blood type and AIDS/STD status. (The tests must be performed and certified by a court-approved facility.)

• The proper court documents if either person is divorced or widowed

• Two witnesses, with valid passports showing name, age, address, and nationality

• Basic fees, which total about $475

MEDICAL CARE

The vast majority of Riviera Maya visitors never need to think about medical care during their stay, but accidents do happen—even while on vacation.

Medical facilities in Cancún, Cozumel, Isla Mujeres, and Playa del Carmen are modern and more than sufficient for most moderate emergencies and standard medical care. Most are operated by the Red Cross (La Cruz Roja) and truly are first-class facilities, by any standard. Many of the doctors are U.S. trained and can provide care equivalent to what can be received at an average facility of a similar size in first-world countries. A fairly large modern hospital called Hospiten opened in 2007, just south of Playacar on Highway 307 in Playa del Carmen. The

---

♂ Top Five Places to Host a Wedding Reception or Other Special Event

1. Ajua Maya Lobster & Steak House (Playa del Carmen): Great food, playful waiters, live music

2. Hotel Básico (Playa del Carmen): Choose the patio seafood restaurant or the exclusive rooftop terrace

3. Kartabar (Playa del Carmen): A trendy spot for food and drinks in the middle of Playa's party zone

4. Maroma Resort & Spa (Punta Maroma): Hosts upscale events that your guests will be proud to attend

5. Rancho Punta Venado: A private beachfront ranch with all the necessary facilities (www.puntavenado.com)

emergency medical first responders in the region are especially well trained and equipped, and they are well versed on procedures related to scuba-diving accidents, falls, car wrecks, animal bites, broken bones, and other common incidents. There are also many private clinics with English-speaking doctors who can treat nonemergency cases and make house calls to hotels or other locations.

The farther you travel from the main cities, the fewer medical facilities you will find available. In Akumal, Puerto Aventuras, and Tulum, there are small clinics, though emergency services lag behind those of the larger cities in terms of quality and reliability.

Common sense and common precautions will prevent most accidents, and taking good care of yourself, including drinking plenty of water and moderating your alcohol intake, will reduce your chances of getting sick. After all, even though the medical facilities are generally quite good, they're not as nice as the beach.

EMERGENCY NUMBERS

Police, Fire, or Ambulance: 066 (free call from any phone)

Red Cross: 984-873-1233 or 065

Cancún Hyperbaric Chamber: 998-888-6872, www.sssnetwork.com

Hospiten Hospital: 984-803-1002, www.hospiten.es

Playa del Carmen Hyperbaric Chamber: 984-873-1365, www.sss network.com

Playa del Carmen Fire Department: 984-879-3669, www.bomberosriviera maya.org

Medica de Carmen Hospital: 984-873-0885

American Hospital in Playa del Carmen: 984-884-6133

Ameri-Med Ambulance Service: 984-881-3400

Playa del Carmen Police: 984-877-3340

Highway Police: 998-884-1107

LOCAL TRANSPORATION AND RESOURCES

Directory Assistance: 020

Cancún Airport: 984-873-0804, www.cancun-airport.com

Bus Station: 984-873-0109

Cozumel Ferry Office (Ultramar): 998-881-5890, www.granpuerto.com.mx

Cozumel Ferry Office (Mexico Water Jet): 984-879-3112, www.mexicowater jets.com.mx

Taxi Office, Playa del Carmen: 984-873-0032

LOST CREDIT CARDS

American Express, 1-800-333-3211 (U.S.)

MasterCard, 1-800-307-7309

Visa, 1-800-847-2911 (U.S.)

Numbers Game

Country code for the United States: 01

Country code for Mexico: 52

Area code for Cancún: 998

Area code for Playa del Carmen: 987

Prefix for dialing Mexican mobile phones: 044

5 Spots to Show (or See) Some Skin

It's generally accepted for women to be topless on many beaches across the Riviera Maya, but there are several places in the region where both men and women are encouraged to reduce their tanlines a bit more.

1. Azulik hotel (Tulum): Even though it's adults-only, there's no funny business at this rustic clothing-optional beachfront hotel.

2. Cabañas Copal hotel (Tulum): Truly a naturists' destination, this clothing-optional hippie resort is very low-key about nudity, and the setting is entirely non-sexual—families with children are welcomed as warmly as adults.

3. Desire Resort & Spa (Puerto Morelos): Pretty much anything goes at this fairly wild, couples-only swingers resort for the "lifestyle" set.

4. Hidden Beach Resort (Kantenah): Singles and couples are welcome at this upscale clothing-optional resort, known for its more traditional (and definitely non-swinging) position on PDA.

5. Temptation Resort Cancún (Cancún): A topless pool, sexy shows and heavily flirtatious undertones tease travelers at this stylish adults-only resort.

LONG-DISTANCE SERVICE

AT&T, 1-800-288-4472 (U.S.)

MCI, 1-800-021-8000 (U.S.)

Sprint, 1-800-877-8000 (U.S.)

AIRLINES

AeroMexico, 1-800-021-4000 (U.S.) or 998-287-1860

Aerosaab (charter), 984-873-0804

AirCanada, 1-888-247-2262 (Canada & U.S.) or 01-800-719-2827

Allegro (charter), 998-887-3459

American, 1-800-904-6000 (U.S.) or 998-886-0086

British Airways, 998-866-0554

Continental, 1-800-523-3273 (U.S.) or 01-800-900-5000

JetBlue, 1-800-538-2583 (U.S.) or 001-800-861-3372

Magnicharters (charter), 998-884-0600

United, 1-800-538-2929 (U.S.) or 01-800-003-0777

CONSULATES

Consulate offices are open weekday mornings and by appointment.

United States
(www.usembassy.gov)
Playa del Carmen, 984-873-0303,
202-370-6708 from the U.S, or
984-807-8355 (Emergency)
Cancún, 998-883-0272
Cozumel, 987-872-4574

Canada
(www.canadainternational.gc.ca)
Playa del Carmen, 984-803-2411
Cancún, 998-883-3360 or
998-883-3361

United Kingdom
(www.ukinmexico.fco.gov.uk)
Cancún, 998-881-0100

Index

A

Abyss Dive Shop (Playa del Carmen), 223
Aca Los Tacos (Playa del Carmen), 58, 78
accommodations. *See* all-inclusive resorts; lodging; *and specific accommodations*
activities, 191–205; 7 active ideas, 147. *See also* fishing; golf; scuba diving; snorkeling
Acuatic Tulum, 225
Adelia Maria Suites (Playa del Carmen), 64
adults-only resorts, top 15, 123. *See also specific resorts*
adventurous travelers, 7 active ideas for, 148
Aerosaab, 32, 185, 199, 247
Ah Cacao (Playa del Carmen), 91, 113
airports, 15, 29; customs and immigration, 29, 108; duty-free shopping, 19–20; in Playa del Carmen, 32; sample transport fares, 31; transportation to/from, 29–34. *See also* Cancún International Airport
air travel (airlines): charter flights, 32, 199, 247; contact information, 247; plane tours, 199
Ajua Maya Lobster & Steak House (Playa del Carmen), 56, 79, 241, 245
Aktun Chen, 192
Aktún-Ha, 196
Akumal, 135–36; beaches, 135; biking, 199; cenotes, 196; dining, 136; fishing, 236; golf, 135, 228; lodging, 135; nature park, 192; scuba diving/snorkeling, 225
Akumal Beach Resort, 135
Akumal Dive Adventures, 225
Akumal Dive Shop, 225
Akumal Travel Services, 199
Akumal Villas, 133
Al Cielo Hotel (Xpu-Ha), 132, 134
Aldea Thai Resort (Playa del Carmen), 75
Aldebaran Tours, 200
Alfaro, Brenda Long, 114–15
All Souls' Day, 243
all-inclusive (AI) resorts, 15; about, 120–21; Akumal, 135; Cancún, 170, 172–73; Cozumel, 165, 166; Kantenah, 134–35; Kohunlich, 169; Playa Paraíso, 153–54; Playacar, 122–23; Puerto Aventuras, 129–30; Puerto Morelos, 159; Xpu-Ha, 133
Alltournative Expeditions (Playa del Carmen), 200, 204
Alux (Playa del Carmen), 85
aluxo'ob, 42
Amaris (Playa del Carmen), 86
ambulance service, 246
American Express, 246
American Hospital (Playa del Carmen), 246
Ameri-Med Ambulance Service, 246
Ana y José Charming-Hotel & Spa (Tulum), 143
Antigua Posada Barrio Latino (Playa del Carmen), 60
Aqua Cancún Unlimited, 154, 170, 172
archaeological sites. *See* Mayan ruins; *and specific sites*
area codes, 246
Arena Blanca's (Playa del Carmen), 75

arrival by air. *See* airports; Cancún International Airport
Ascension Bay: fishing, 147, 149, 204, 236; lodging, 149
Ascension Bay Bonefish Club, 149
Asian cuisine, in Playa del Carmen, 89–90
Atlantis Submarines (Cozumel), 197
AT&T, 247
attractions: Cozumel, 169–70; Isla Mujeres, 184; Playa del Carmen, 51, 53–58; Puerto Aventuras, 130–31; Xcaret, 126. *See also specific attractions*
ATV tours, 161, 192, 198–99, 202
Aura Resort (Cozumel), 166
autumnal equinox, 242
avenida Quinta (Playa del Carmen), 24–25, 46; dining, 76–90; map, 52; nightlife, 93, 96–102, 112; shopping, 106–7; walking tour, 53, 55, 57–58
Aventura Mexicana (Playa del Carmen), 71–72, 74
Aventura Spa Palace (Puerto Aventuras), 129–30
Aviario Xaman Ha (Playacar), 193–94
Azul Beach Hotel by Karisma (Puerto Morelos), 159
Azul Cenote, 196
Azulik (Tulum), 141–42, 247

B

Ba Ba Club & Lounge (Playa del Carmen), 100
Babe's Noodle House (Playa del Carmen), 89
Baby's Hot (Playa del Carmen), 94
Bacalar. *See* Laguna Bacalar
Bahia Petempich: lodging, 158–59
Bahia Principe Golf Club (Akumal), 135, 228
Balamku Inn (Mahahual), 189
Banana Hotel (Playa del Carmen), 60
Banco Chinchorro, 189, 225
Banyan Tree Mayakoba (Punta Bete), 151–52
Barbachano, Fernando, 42
Barcelo Maya Resort Complex (Xpu-Ha), 132–33
barracuda, fishing for, 147, 233, 234–35
bars, 23; 15 party spots, 160; bar lingo, 69; Cancún, 175; Cozumel, 167–68; Isla Holbox, 187; Isla Mujeres, 183; Playa del Carmen, 93–97, 100–106
Básico Terrace Bar (Playa del Carmen), 100
beach clubs: Cozumel, 168; Playa del Carmen, 104–6
beaches, 15, 66–67, 99; etiquette, 240; ocean safety, 62; Akumal, 135; Cancún, 170; Chemuyil, 137; Cozumel, 168, 169; Isla Mujeres, 181; Kantenah, 134; nude, 24, 159, 247; Playa del Carmen, 24, 57, 67, 111, 240; Playa del Secreto, 153; Playa Mujeres, 178; Playa Paraíso, 153; Playa Xcalacoco, 153; Playacar, 119, 122; Puerto Aventuras, 126, 129; Puerto Morelos, 156–57; Punta Maroma, 155; Punta Solimán, 138; Tankah, 139; Tulum, 142–43; Xcacel, 138; Xpu-Ha, 131–32. *See also* nudist beaches; *and specific beaches*
Beer Bucket (Playa del Carmen), 101–2
beers of the Riviera Maya, 105. *See also* bars
Big Lobster (Playa del Carmen), 91
biking (bike rentals), 15, 199; Cobá, 213
Bikram Yoga Riviera Maya (Playa del Carmen), 110